Welcome to Atkins Holiday Recipes

What better time to celebrate the pleasure and ease of th lifestyle than at the holiday season?

For those of you who are trying to lose excess pounds or simply maintain your weigh of year may be your undoing. In the past, if you tried to stick to a low-fat/low-calorie program, you were forced to content yourselves with small portions of inherently unsatisfying foods. Forget about indulgences like duck with crispy skin, creamy lobster bisque, and pumpkin cheesecake. They're simply off limits on other eating plans.

Not so with the Atkins Nutritional Approach™ (ANA™): You can eat such delectable holiday foods until you feel satisfied—and still lose or maintain your weight. When you eat natural fats—think nuts, butter, olive oil—and fish, meat, and poultry, you don't finish your meal yearning for something else, as you do when you eat paltry portions of low-fat foods. The natural fats you consume on Atkins actually help you lose weight (and decrease your risk factors for heart disease) so long as you control the amount of carbohydrates you take in.

There's a never-ending array of luscious-tasting foods to eat—fish and seafood like elegant Roast Salmon with Fennel and Herbs, satisfying vegetable dishes such as Fried Okra and Rosemary-Roasted Sweet Potatoes, and of course, plenty of glorious, sweet, and gooey desserts, including our pick for chocoholics: Fudge Nut Swirl Pie. Each recipe has been tested in home kitchens to ensure that you can easily replicate

it in your own kitchen. Whether you're just beginning the program or you're maintaining your weight, there are recipes for all four phases of Atkins.

Most important, you can host sumptuous feasts, traditional holiday meals, and casual gatherings for groups of friends—and never stray from the controlled-carb lifestyle that is working for you and likely many of your guests. And visitors who are not yet in the know will be amazed at how tasty and varied low-carb meals can be.

This book contains all the recipes you'll need to dine and entertain lavishly—while staying in control of your weight. Before you dig into the 150-plus recipes, you will find:

- A brief explanation of why and how the ANA™ works and the foods that will help you reach your weight-control and health goals.

- Menus for Thanksgiving, Hanukkah, Christmas, and New Year's.

- Advice about the ingredients that make the Atkins lifestyle so manageable.

We've also provided complete nutrition information for each recipe, including grams of Net Carbs and the Atkins phases for which it is suitable. Finally, Atkins Tips tell you where to find less common ingredients and help you master techniques to simplify preparation and serving.

We hope that this book will help make your holiday season a time of joy, good memories, and plenty of fun, as you cook and eat your way to a healthy weight.

From all of us in the Atkins Kitchen,
Happy Holidays!

Allison Fishman

Allison Fishman
Senior Food Editor

Time Inc. HOME ENTERTAINMENT

President: Rob Gursha
Vice President, New Product Development: Richard Fraiman
Executive Director, Marketing Services: Carol Pittard
Director, Retail & Special Sales: Tom Mifsud
Director of Finance: Tricia Griffin
Prepress Manager: Emily Rabin
Book Production Manager: Jonathan Polsky
Product Manager: Victoria Alfonso

Special thanks: Bozena Bannett, Alex Bliss, Bernadette Corbie, Robert Dente, Gina Di Meglio, Anne-Michelle Gallero, Peter Harper, Suzanne Janso, Robert Marasco, Natalie McCrea, Margarita Quiogue, Mary Jane Rigoroso, Steven Sandonato, Grace Sullivan

Published by Time Inc. Home Entertainment
Time Inc. Home Entertainment is a subsidiary of Time Inc.
Time Inc.
1271 Avenue of the Americas
New York, New York 10020

A ROUNDTABLE PRESS BOOK
For Roundtable Press, Inc.:
Directors: Marsha Melnick, Julie Merberg
Editor: Sara Newberry
Production Editor: John Glenn
Design: Barbara Scott-Goodman

ATKINS NUTRITIONALS, INC.
Paul D. Wolff: Chairman & CEO
Scott Kabak: President & COO

Atkins Health & Medical Information Services
Senior Vice President: Michael Bernstein
Vice President, Editorial Director: Olivia Bell Buehl
Executive Editor: Christine M. Senft, M.S.
Senior Food Editor: Allison Fishman
Managing Editor: Jennifer L. Moles
Assistant Food Editor: Amanda Dorato
Vice President, Director of Education & Research: Colette Heimowitz, M.S.
Coordinator, Education & Research: Eva Katz, M.P.H., R.D.

Project Editor: Marge Perry
Consulting Food Editor/Recipe Development: David Bonom
Additional Recipe Developers: Julie Grimes Bottcher and Alice Thompson
Recipe Testers: Wendy Kalen, Trudy Solin, and Sabra Waxman
Photography © 2004 by Mark Ferri, with the exception of photographs © 2004 by Judd Pilossof on pages 53 and 70.
Food Stylist: A.J. Battifarano
Prop Stylist: Francine Matalon-Degni

For more information on Atkins, go to www.atkins.com.

CONTENTS

Page 5 Holiday Menus

Treat your guests to these holiday recipes for Thanksgiving, Christmas, Hanukkah, and the New Year.

CELEBRATE THE HOLIDAYS WITH ATKINS

Page 12
The Party Pantry for Quick and Easy Entertaining

Page 13
Today's Ingredients

Page 15
Atkins in a Nutshell

RECIPES

Page 18 Soups

Our selection of seasonal soups, stews, and bisques are the perfect festive starters.

Page 28 Salads

Delight your guests with a variety of nutritious and tasty greens, indulgently dressed for your holiday table.

Page 40 Appetizers & Hors d'Oeuvres

From the simple to the sumptuous, these first courses and small bites set the tone for every occasion—from casual cocktails to a sit-down meal.

Page 62 Entrées

Treat your friends and family to something truly special. You need not be a gourmet chef to create these impressive entrées.

page 155

Page 90 Vegetables & Side Dishes

We've retooled the traditional holiday side dishes and added a few that are sure to become new favorites.

Page 118 Brunch

Serving classic brunch fare, like pancakes, waffles, and crêpes, makes daytime entertaining effortless. Our versions have carb counts that are equally agreeable.

Page 132
Desserts & Sweets

Wonderful desserts and baked goods are some of the season's many pleasures. Our satisfying sweets let you do it without the guilt.

Page 158 Index

HOLIDAY RECIPE CARB GRAM COUNTER

page 51

page 72

A TRADITIONAL THANKSGIVING

Cheddar and Scallion Pie Squares
Walnut Meatballs

Cumin-Lemon Butternut Squash Soup

Turkey with Spinach Cornbread Stuffing*
Candied Ginger Sweet Potatoes*
Green Beans Amandine*
Cauliflower–Sour Cream Purée*

Apple Crisp
Pumpkin Pie with Pecan Crust

A GLOBAL THANKSGIVING

Vietnamese Stir-Fried Shrimp
Tandoori Chicken Wings

Coconut Curried Pumpkin Soup

Roast Salmon with Fennel and Herbs
Roasted Spiced Delicata Squash
Sautéed Brussels Sprouts

Almond Mousse Soufflé
Pumpkin Cheesecake

A SOUTHWESTERN THANKSGIVING

Pepper Jack Quesadillas
Verdemole

Spinach and Pomegranate Salad

Southwestern Turkey
Kale with Bacon and Garlic
Southwestern Cornbread
Sweet Potato–Pumpkin Purée

Pumpkin Flan
Maple Pecan Pie

(*recipes shown in photo)

A CHRISTMAS EVE SEAFOOD DINNER

Bagna Cauda
Sweet and Spicy Nuts
Cheddar and Scallion Pie Squares

Roasted Pepper and Escarole Salad

Roast Snapper Provençal
Roasted Fennel with Red Peppers
Broccolini with Shallot-Lemon Butter

Espresso Panna Cotta
Chocolate Macaroons

AN ELEGANT CHRISTMAS EVE

Smoked Trout Mousse in Cucumber Cups
Roast Beef with Horseradish Cream

Field Greens, Pears, Pecans, and Gouda

Tricolor Peppercorn Roasted Goose*, or
Beef Tenderloin with Dijon Herb Crust, or
Crown Roast of Lamb Florentine
Creamed Spinach*
Butter-Braised Turnips*
Glazed Carrots*

Bûche de Noël
Coconut-Cashew Chocolate Truffles

A LIVELY CHRISTMAS DAY GATHERING

Stuffed Prosciutto Pillows
Spicy Lamb and Mushroom Brochettes

Maple-Mustard Glazed Baked Ham
Broccoli Florets with Lemon Butter Sauce
Collard Greens with Ham and Onions
Rosemary Roasted Sweet Potatoes

Holiday Gingerbread
Maple Walnut Bread Pudding
Double-Chocolate Brownies

(*recipes shown in photo)

A HEARTY HANUKKAH CELEBRATION
(KOSHER STYLE–MEAT)

Latkes*
Cauliflower-Pea Pancakes

Classic Brisket*
Roasted Fennel with Red Peppers
Roast Carrots with Cinnamon and Cumin*
Kale with Pears and Onions*

Apple Fritters
Hanukkah Jelly Doughnuts

A DO-AHEAD HANUKKAH BUFFET
(KOSHER STYLE–DAIRY)

Jalapeño-Cream Cheese Stuffed Celery
Sesame-Tofu Dip
Lemon Fennel Biscotti

Asparagus and Romaine Salad

Roast Salmon with Fennel and Herbs
Roasted Asparagus
Cauliflower-Pea Pancakes

Fudge Nut Swirl Pie
Chocolate-Dipped Almond Cookies
Apple Fritters

A SIT-DOWN HANUKKAH DINNER

Endive, Arugula, and Radish Salad

Spice-Roasted Cornish Game Hens
Warm Cauliflower and Broccoli Salad
Latkes

Spiced Bundt Cake
Sabayon with Berries

(*recipes shown in photo)

NEW YEAR'S DINNER AT EIGHT

Scallops Wrapped in Bacon
Citrus and Basil Marinated Goat Cheese
Baked Stuffed Mushrooms

Lobster Bisque

Standing Rib Roast with Caramelized Onion
Bacon-Cheddar Biscuits
Asparagus with Brown Butter

Chocolate Mini Cheesecakes

LAVISH HORS D'OEUVRES PARTY

Shrimp and Scallop Ceviche
Prosciutto-Wrapped Asparagus
Red Pepper Pancakes with Smoked Salmon
Short-Cut Pigs in a Blanket
Sesame-Tofu Dip
Lemon-Fennel Biscotti
Smoked Turkey and Cheddar Spread
Walnut Meatballs

INDULGENT DESSERT PARTY

Lemon-Berry Trifle*
Coconut-Cashew Chocolate Truffles*
Chocolate-Drizzled Vanilla Biscotti*
Lemon Meringue Squares*
Double-Chocolate Brownies*
Nutty Chocolate Swirl Cheesecake*

(*recipes shown in photo)

Once you understand
the four phases of Atkins,
you'll want to know how
they mesh with the
fabulous recipes on the
following pages. To select
appropriate recipes at a
glance as you move
through the phases, look
for our colorful icons to
tell you whether that
recipe is suitable for the
phase you are in.

Phase 1 Recipes:
* Main dishes generally
contain no more than
7 grams of Net Carbs
per serving.
* Side dishes, appetizers,
soups, and desserts
generally contain no
more than 3 grams of
Net Carbs per serving.
* Excluded are fruits,
fresh cheeses, pasta,
starchy vegetables,
grains, nuts and seeds,
nut and seed butters,
and legumes.

Celebrate the Holidays with Atkins!

The winter holiday season is full of celebrations, and—let's be honest—most of them
involve fabulous-tasting, tempting foods, many of which we have a chance to experience
only a few times a year. We all look forward to another season of elegant crown roasts
and racks of lamb, plate after plate of tempting hors d'oeuvres, latkes, pies, mile-high
layer cakes with clouds of fluffy frosting, and the occasional golden-brown goose.

Sounds like a tough time to lose or maintain weight, doesn't it? Of course it does,
if you choose to limit your portions or stick to low-fat, low-flavor foods. But what if
satisfying portions of all those wonderful holiday delicacies could be part of your
weight-loss program?

That's just one of the countless reasons the Atkins Nutritional Approach™ is an eating
plan you can stick with for life. You'll never feel deprived, even at the time of year when most
people fall prey to the barrage of culinary enticements around them. And when you don't
feel like you're missing out on the special treats of the season just because you're losing
weight and improving your health…well, let's just call that the perfect holiday gift!

The Party Pantry for Quick and Easy Entertaining

Because you'll probably be entertaining more, during the holiday season it's especially
important to keep a well-equipped pantry. Start by stocking your kitchen with the just-
right combination of dry goods, freezer foods, and more stable refrigerated items (those
that keep for at least a couple of weeks).

Following is a roundup of must-have foods to keep handy for all of your entertaining,
from a planned fête to an impromptu get-together. Simple culinary suggestions describe
how to transform these kitchen staples into speedy, tasty dishes and are sure to spark your
own culinary creativity.

From the cupboard:
- Dried porcini mushrooms: Soaked in warm water for a few minutes, these mushrooms
  rehydrate and contribute sweet, earthy flavor and aroma to an array of dishes. They
  pair especially well with meat and poultry. Reduce the amount of soaking liquid and
  cook them with cream or butter for an ethereal sauce!

- Chipotles en adobo: These canned, smoked jalapeños in tomato sauce are so fiery
  hot, a little goes a long way. Combine with mayonnaise and cheddar cheese for an
  instant dip to serve with crudités or low-carb chips.

- Olive paste (tapenade): This flavorful paste can turn boring grilled poultry or vegetables
  into an exciting meal. Try thinning it with a little olive oil, or mix in with goat cheese.
  Spread on a chicken breast near the end of the cooking time.

- Curry paste: Check out the Asian foods section of your supermarket for red or green
  Thai curry paste. Stir-fry vegetables with less than a teaspoon of either paste for lots
  of kick. Blended with coconut milk, it's a soup base—just add cooked leftover turkey
  or chicken, tofu, or fast-cooking seafood like scallops and shrimp.

From the freezer:
- Berries: Thaw and purée frozen, unsweetened berries for a quick sauce. Add reduced-
  carb whole-milk dairy beverage or half-and-half for an instant smoothie! Drop a few
  frozen berries in a glass of iced Champagne for an extra-special holiday toast.

- Shrimp, scallops, and crab: Frozen peeled shrimp, scallops, and crabmeat thaw in less
  than 20 minutes in a bowl of cold water. Season with a pre-blended spice blend (such
  as Cajun seasoning), sear two minutes per side, and serve as an hors d'oeuvre.

- Artichoke hearts and spinach: Chop and combine either one with mayonnaise, sour cream, and Worcestershire sauce for a hearty vegetarian appetizer. Serve alongside low-carb toast points and fresh vegetables.

- Precooked frozen sausage (check ingredients to be sure there are no added sugars or high-carb fillers): Thaw, wrapped, in a bowl of cold water or overnight in the refrigerator. Cut into one-inch pieces and cook with greens (such as kale, collards, and spinach)

From the refrigerator:
- Crumbled and shredded cheeses: Buy blue cheese and feta already crumbled; cheddar, Monterey Jack, and mozzarella are available shredded. These cheeses keep for up to two weeks in the refrigerator. They are integral to many recipes, and add panache to mixed greens. Convenience can make up for the higher cost.

- Deli meats: Sliced fresh roasted turkey and roast beef not only make great sandwiches; they make fun casual hors d'oeuvres, too. Roll them up in a low-carb tortilla with any combination of sliced cheeses and a large lettuce leaf. Refrigerate for at least 30 minutes, then slice crosswise. Serve pinwheels fastened with a toothpick, if needed.

- Bottled chopped ginger and garlic: These three conveniently packaged embellishments add immediate flavor to food. Cook ginger or garlic 30 seconds before searing meats, fish, poultry, or vegetables.

Today's Ingredients

Some of the ingredients in this book may be new to you. All of our recipes are designed to deliver maximum taste for minimum carbs. In some cases, we have discovered that certain products and ingredients help contribute to good health and weight loss—while delivering great flavor and texture—better than others.

Sugar Substitutes

Sucralose, which is sold under the brand name Splenda®, is a sweetener that is made from sugar but, unlike sugar, does not raise blood sugar levels. One of its advantages over other sugar substitutes is that you can cook and bake with it in the same way you would use sugar. Packets of Splenda® (similar to sugar packets) contain a finer grain than the Splenda® sold in boxes, which is similar in texture to kosher salt. All baking and cooking recipes, unless otherwise specified, use the granular sugar substitute (Splenda®) sold in boxes, which is formulated so that is can be used measure for measure in place of sugar. However, you may find, as the Atkins Kitchen staff did, that you prefer the taste of items when you use a little less Splenda®.

Flours

Whole-wheat flour (including whole-wheat pastry flour), vital wheat gluten (the protein part of wheat, ground into powder), soy flour, nut flours, and Atkins Quick Quisine™ Bake Mix can be used, in one way or another, to perform some of the duties once assigned to bleached white flour. These flours can be purchased at natural foods stores, gourmet stores, and some supermarkets. Bake mix is also available online at www.atkins.com. In a pinch, you can grind nuts such as almonds in a food processor to stand in for the nut flour. (Just be sure you don't over-process the nuts—they should form a powder, not clump into a ball.) While all of these flours and flour substitutes still contain carbohydrates, their Net Carb values are lower than refined flour—plus, they offer more nutrition. Use them in moderation. Only the bake mix and soy flour are acceptable in Induction.

Phase 2 Recipes:
* Main dishes generally contain no more than 12 grams of Net Carbs per serving.
* Side dishes, appetizers, soups, and desserts generally contain no more than 9 grams of Net Carbs per serving.
* Ingredients can include low-carb pasta, all cheeses, and nuts and seeds and their butters.

Phase 3 and Phase 4 Recipes:
* May include ingredients restricted in earlier phases.

Note: Depending upon your metabolism and tolerance for certain carbohydrate foods, you may not be able to eat all dishes coded for the phase you are in. If you have a high metabolism, you may be able to eat meals coded for Phases 3 and 4 while you are still in OWL. Remember that you still must count your daily intake of Net Carbs.

What Are Net Carbs?

When you do Atkins, you actually count only Net Carbs—the total carbohydrate content of the food minus the fiber content (along with glycerine and sugar alcohols found in some low-carb foods). Net Carbs reflect the grams of carbohydrate that significantly impact your blood sugar level. The Net Carb number is almost always lower than the total carbohydrate number. The exception is a food such as cream that has virtually no fiber content. In such cases, the total carbs and Net Carbs are identical.

Oils

Fruit oils, nut oils, seed oils—one of the many pleasures of the Atkins lifestyle is being able to include a variety of wonderful oils in your eating plan! Fruit oils, such as olive and avocado, bear some flavor of the fruit, and tend to be round and rich; they can be used with meats, fish, and vegetables. Nut and seed oils—macadamia, hazelnut, and walnut—contribute deep, warm, nutty flavor and aroma; they can be used in baking and to whip up simple but tasty salad dressings. Nut oils are less stable than many other oils (they should be refrigerated after opening) and tend to be expensive. But they deliver incredible flavor and can transform a dish from the ordinary to the extraordinary. Canola and grapeseed oils, on the other hand, have subtle flavors and are good cooking oils, so they're perfect for sautéing. It's a good idea to keep several oils in your pantry.

Thickeners

Certain products allow you to thicken sauces and custards the way cornstarch and flour might, but with fewer carbs. Using cream, butter, and eggs to thicken sauces and custards is one way to get results. You can also turn to ThickenThin™ not/Starch or Thick It Up™ (both available at www.atkins.com) for flavorless thickening. In addition, many sauces can be thickened—and intensified—by simmering or "reducing" until they are sauce-like and syrupy.

Breads

Where would we be without the new class of low-carb breads and tortillas? Use them with discretion and they will expand your meal options without expanding your waistline. The tortillas can be cut in any shape you need and fried, baked, brushed with butter and sprinkled with Splenda® and cinnamon, rolled like a wrap sandwich, and much more. Low-carb breads can be toasted, dried and pulverized into crumbs, used as a crust…they are simply indispensable. And low-carb bagels let you once again enjoy those chewy, crusty treats. Look in your grocery store, natural foods store, or shop online at www.atkins.com. You will also find a variety of low-carb pancake, waffle, muffin, and cake mixes.

THE ALTERNATIVES

The ways we have become accustomed to serving and eating foods are difficult to abandon, and there are times when those traditions don't fit into your Atkins lifestyle. Fortunately, there are always simple, satisfying alternatives:

Instead of cheese and crackers, serve
- Cheese and toast points (made from low-carb rye or white bread)
- Cheese and "crackers" (made from baked or fried low-carb tortillas cut into squares)
- Cheese and low-carb flatbread and/or crispbread
- Cheese spread on vegetables and lettuces (see our serving suggestion for Citrus and Basil Marinated Goat Cheese)

Instead of mashed or whipped potatoes, serve
- Puréed cauliflower with butter and cream

Instead of roasted potatoes, serve
- Roasted Sweet Potato Spears (page 92) or Butter-Braised Turnips (page 99)

Instead of bread, serve
- A mixed breadbasket with Lemon-Fennel Biscotti (see page 57), Southwestern Cornbread (see page 93), herb toasts made with low-carb white and rye breads brushed with oil, garlic powder, and herbs.

Once you begin to think beyond the usual and sample the sumptuous foods that are available with Atkins recipes, you'll never again feel like you're missing out on any of your favorite edibles. Instead, you'll always look forward to the vast number of food and menu options available to you.

Atkins in a Nutshell

Perhaps a friend's impressive weight loss was the driving force behind your decision to do Atkins. Or maybe you were motivated by the positive media reports on the many health benefits of a controlled-carb lifestyle. Perhaps this publication is serving as your inspiration. Whatever the reason, and whether you're just beginning or you're an old hand at Lifetime Maintenance, we're thrilled that you're experiencing a better life doing Atkins.

There's no doubt that Atkins is the most effective and most enjoyable way to lose weight. You can eat satisfying foods, like salmon, poultry, eggs, lamb chops, and lobster, in quantities that never leave you feeling hungry or deprived—and that means you can stick with Atkins for the rest of your life.

Here's how it works. Your body runs on two fuels: carbohydrates and fats. It first turns to carbohydrates as an energy source. If carbs aren't available, your body primarily burns fat, including your body fat, instead. Picture it: just to power the activities of sitting in a chair and reading, your body is burning fat! It's a nice thought, isn't it? But let's take it one step—or one phase—at a time.

PHASE 1: INDUCTION

The first phase of the Atkins Nutritional Approach™ is called Induction. This is the most restrictive phase, but it's also when you'll experience the fastest, most efficient weight loss. During Induction, you'll eat primarily protein and fats and your total intake of carbohydrates per day will be 20 grams of Net Carbs, most of which will come from salad and other vegetables. (See What Are Net Carbs? on page 14).

During Induction, your body turns primarily to fat rather than carbohydrates for fuel as you stabilize your blood sugar and eradicate your cravings for sweet and starchy foods. Sound good? It gets better. While your body is becoming a fat-burning machine and you lose weight, you get to eat as much of that juicy steak, cheddar omelet, turkey with cream gravy, or shrimp scampi as it takes to help you feel satisfied. Enjoy crisp romaine with real blue cheese dressing. Tuck into a hearty plate of roasted chicken with creamy mashed cauliflower. You can eat all of these things, lower your triglycerides, raise your HDL ("good") cholesterol, stabilize your blood sugar—and lose weight.

During Induction, you can enjoy:

- Any meat, poultry, fish, tofu (soy), or shellfish—but limit oysters, clams, and mussels to 4 ounces per day

- Eggs

- Full-fat cheeses (4 ounces a day), except fresh cheeses, such as cottage, ricotta, and farmer's

- Butter, cream (3 ounces a day), mayonnaise, sour cream (1 ounce a day in lieu of cream)

- Oils: nut, seed, fruit, vegetable

- Salad vegetables (4 cups per day)

- Non-starchy vegetables, including asparagus, artichokes, broccoli, cauliflower, Brussels sprouts, green beans, leeks, okra, pumpkin, and many more (1 cup per day, in lieu of the fourth cup of salad vegetables). (For a complete listing, see *Dr. Atkins' New Diet Revolution* or *The Atkins Essentials*, or visit www.atkins.com.)

- Half of a Haas avocado, 10 to 20 olives, and 3 tablespoons of lemon or lime juice (per day).

How to Calculate Net Carbs

You can guesstimate the grams of Net Carbs for a particular packaged food by using the information provided by the Nutrition Facts panel on the label. Simply subtract the grams of fiber (as well as sugar alcohols and glycerine, when applicable) from the grams of total carbs per serving and you've got a pretty good sense of the Net Carb number. For fresh foods and other unpackaged foods, you'll need to refer to a carb gram counter. For a complete carb gram counter, see *Dr. Atkins' New Carbohydrate Gram Counter* or www.atkins.com.

Our nutritional analysis is based on the nutrient content of our own products, which do not contain added sugars, bleached white flour, or hydrogenated oils. If you use another low-carb brand, we cannot guarantee the accuracy of the nutrition information or the recipe's successful outcome. To help you choose a low-carb product that does not exceed the Net Carb count in a recipe, use the following key:

- Low-carb bread:
  3 g of Net Carbs or less per slice
- Low-carb tortilla:
  5 g of Net Carbs or less per tortilla
- Low-carb pasta:
  5 g of Net Carbs or less per 2-ounce serving
- Low-carb ice cream:
  3–4 g of Net Carbs or less per ½ cup
- Low-carb pancake syrup:
  0 g of Net Carbs per 2-ounce serving
- Low-carb soy chips:
  4 g of Net Carbs or less per ounce

PHASE 2: ONGOING WEIGHT LOSS

After Induction, which lasts at least two weeks and up to six months, depending on how much weight you have to lose, you'll begin Phase 2, Ongoing Weight Loss (OWL). In Phase 2, you'll gradually and deliberately add back some carbohydrates to your meals, experimenting until your weight loss slows too much or stops. This way, you'll figure out how your body handles more carbohydrates. You'll add back the "powerhouse" carbs at first—the ones that have the most valuable nutrients and fiber, such as additional vegetables, berries, nuts, and fresh cheeses. This is the phase where you'll accomplish most of the remainder of your weight loss. You will also learn your Critical Carbohydrate Level for Losing (CCLL), the number of grams of Net Carbs you can eat each day while continuing to lose weight slowly but steadily.

During OWL, you can add:
- Nuts, seeds, and nut butters
- Fresh cheeses, including mascarpone, cottage, and farmer's
- Berries

Note: Some people can also add back some or all of the following: legumes, other fruits, starchy vegetables, and even whole grains. Others find they must wait until Pre-Maintenance to introduce any or all of these foods.

PHASE 3: PRE-MAINTENANCE

Once you are nearing your goal weight, you'll switch to Phase 3, Pre-Maintenance, to deliberately slow the rate of weight loss. Again, you'll slowly add more carbs to your diet, experimenting to find which foods work for you and still allow you to lose those last five or 10 pounds even more slowly than you shed pounds in OWL. During Phase 3, most people can add back legumes, starchy vegetables, more fruit choices, and whole grains to their eating plans. In this phase, you will find your more liberalized CCLL. Once you reach your goal weight and maintain it for at least a month, you will have found your Atkins Carbohydrate Equilibrium (ACE), the number of grams of carbs you can consume each day while neither gaining nor losing weight.

In Pre-Maintenance, you may slowly add back:
- Whole milk and plain whole-milk yogurt
- Legumes
- Fruits in addition to berries
- Starchy vegetables, including carrots, corn, potatoes, sweet potatoes, parsnips, and beets
- Whole grains, such as barley, whole-grain bread, brown rice, bulgur, whole-grain cereals, cornmeal, and oatmeal

PHASE 4: LIFETIME MAINTENANCE

When you have maintained your goal weight for a month, you have likely also achieved an incredible sense of well-being. Congratulations! In Phase 4: Lifetime Maintenance, you'll establish a permanent controlled-carb lifestyle that will allow you to continue your current weight and fitness level. You'll be able to adjust readily to changes in your lifestyle—whether you're taking up a new sport (which might raise your ACE), or dealing with sudden forced inactivity (which would likely lower it)—while you maintain a healthy weight. Now, you have the knowledge to choose the right foods in any situation.

A WORD ABOUT THE ATKINS LIFESTYLE FOOD GUIDE PYRAMID

In 2004, an alternative food guide pyramid was introduced by Atkins Health & Medical Informational Services. This pyramid emphasizes the importance of healthy protein sources, with vegetables as the primary source of carbohydrates. It also incorporates exercise as a key component of a healthy lifestyle.

THE **ATKINS LIFESTYLE** FOOD GUIDE PYRAMID™

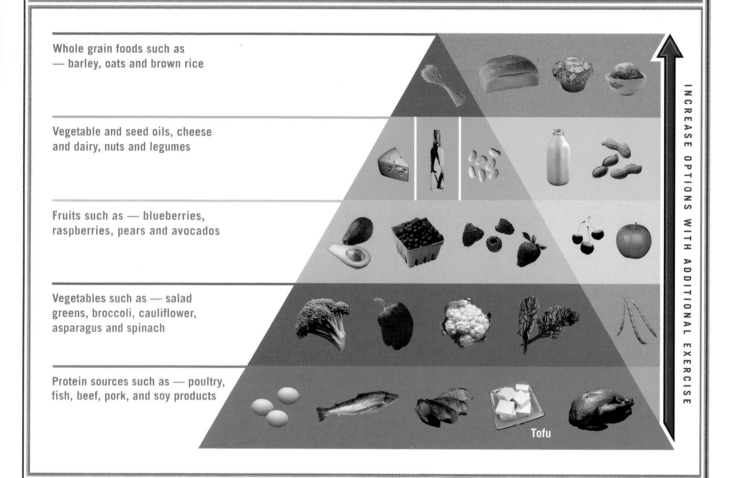

Whole grain foods such as
— barley, oats and brown rice

Vegetable and seed oils, cheese
and dairy, nuts and legumes

Fruits such as — blueberries,
raspberries, pears and avocados

Vegetables such as — salad
greens, broccoli, cauliflower,
asparagus and spinach

Protein sources such as — poultry,
fish, beef, pork, and soy products

Tofu

INCREASE OPTIONS WITH ADDITIONAL EXERCISE

HERE'S WHAT YOU DO:

NO ADDED SUGARS & HYDROGENATED OILS

1. Limit and control certain carbohydrates to achieve and maintain a healthy weight.
2. Choose carbohydrates wisely (vegetables, fruits, legumes, whole grains), avoiding refined carbohydrates and foods with added sugars.
3. Eat until you are satisfied:
   – *to maintain weight, eat in proportion to the pyramid.*
   – *to lose weight, focus on protein, leafy vegetables and healthy oils.*
4. Everyone's metabolism and lifestyle are different. Discover your individual carb level to achieve and maintain a healthy weight. Raise this level with additional exercise.

Coconut Curried Pumpkin Soup, page 20

SOUPS

From traditional holiday choices to exciting ethnic flavors, soups set the tone for the meal to come. Many of these soups can be prepared in advance and kept warm on the stove until your guests are seated.

COCONUT CURRIED PUMPKIN SOUP

 PER SERVING **Net Carbs: 7 grams;** Carbohydrates: 9 grams; Fiber: 2 grams; Protein: 3 grams; Fat: 11 grams; Calories: 140
Makes 6 (1-cup) servings; Prep time: 15 minutes; Cook time: 30 minutes

Mild curry flavor marries beautifully with pumpkin and coconut milk, giving this traditional pumpkin soup (shown on page 18) a whole new outlook. Be sure to buy unsweetened coconut milk—not cream of coconut, which is loaded with added sugar.

2 tablespoons butter

1 small onion, chopped (½ cup)

1 clove garlic, minced (½ teaspoon)

2 teaspoons curry powder

½ teaspoon salt

¼ teaspoon pepper

1 (14½-ounce) can lower sodium chicken broth, plus
   1 can water

1 (15-ounce) can pumpkin purée

¾ cup unsweetened coconut milk

1 Melt butter in a large saucepan over medium heat. Cook onion 5 minutes, until softened. Add garlic, curry powder, salt, and pepper; cook 1 minute more.

2 Add broth, water, and purée; mix well. Reduce heat to low. Cook 20 minutes, stirring occasionally. Stir in coconut milk.

3 Purée soup in a blender in several batches until smooth. Return to saucepan. Heat through before serving.

CREAM OF CAULIFLOWER SOUP

 PER SERVING **Net Carbs: 4.5 grams;** Carbohydrates: 6.5 grams; Fiber: 2 grams; Protein: 4.5 grams; Fat: 15.5 grams; Calories: 176
Makes 8 (1-cup) servings; Prep time: 25 minutes; Cook time: 45 minutes

This velvety soup gets a kick from homemade curry oil, but you could use a store-bought infused oil, such as basil oil, garlic oil, or white-truffle oil.

2 tablespoons butter

1 large onion, diced (1 cup)

1 head cauliflower, cut into florets (about 4 cups)

6½ cups lower sodium chicken broth

¼ cup canola oil

1 tablespoon curry powder

½ cup heavy cream

Pinch cayenne

Salt

¼ cup chopped chives

1 Melt butter in a large pot over medium heat. Add onion; cook, stirring, until onion is softened, 4 to 5 minutes. Add cauliflower florets and broth; cook until florets begin to fall apart, 20 to 30 minutes.

2 Meanwhile, cook oil and curry in a small saucepan over medium heat until mixture begins to simmer. Remove from heat. Strain through a fine sieve and discard the solids.

3 Let soup cool slightly, then purée in a blender in several batches. Return to the pot. Stir in cream and cayenne; reheat. Season with salt to taste. Serve hot, drizzled with curry oil and garnish with chives.

CREAM OF CELERY SOUP

PER SERVING **Net Carbs: 8 grams;** Carbohydrates: 10 grams; Fiber: 2 grams; Protein: 3 grams; Fat: 40 grams; Calories: 427

3 4 Makes 8 (¾-cup) servings; Prep time: 30 minutes; Cook time: 40 minutes

This rich soup is a lovely first course. Prepare the soup (and keep refrigerated) up to two days ahead; heat just before serving. Don't skip the garnish—it makes the soup look as special as it tastes.

3 tablespoons unsalted butter

1 medium celery root, peeled and chopped (2 cups)

1 bunch celery hearts, chopped (2 cups), plus celery leaves for garnish

2 medium onions, chopped (1½ cups)

1 cup dry white wine

2 cups lower sodium chicken broth

1 teaspoon salt

½ teaspoon pepper, divided

6 ounces salt pork

3 cups heavy cream

1 Melt butter in a large saucepan over medium high heat. Add celery root, celery, and onions; sauté 5 minutes. Add wine, broth, salt, ¼ teaspoon of the pepper, and salt pork. Cook until half the liquid evaporates, about 8 minutes, stirring occasionally.

2 Reduce heat to medium. Stir in cream; cook until vegetables are tender, 10 to 12 minutes. Remove salt pork; discard.

3 Let soup cool slightly, then purée in a blender in several batches until smooth. Serve warm, garnished with celery leaves and remaining ¼ teaspoon pepper.

ALE-INFUSED ONION SOUP

 PER SERVING **Net Carbs: 8 grams;** Carbohydrates: 10 grams; Fiber: 2 grams; Protein: 11 grams; Fat: 14 grams; Calories: 200
Makes 8 (1¼-cup) servings; Prep time: 25 minutes Cook time: 1 hour 30 minutes

The best part of onion soup is always the cheese-topped bread that soaks up all the earthy flavor. This version won't disappoint—it's everything onion soup should be and more—thanks to the flavor bonus provided by the ale.

3 tablespoons unsalted butter

3 Spanish onions, thinly sliced

1 teaspoon fresh thyme leaves

1 teaspoon granular sugar substitute

5 (14½-ounce) cans lower sodium chicken broth

1 cup low-carb ale or beer

2 teaspoons Dijon mustard

Salt and pepper

8 slices low-carb white bread, crusts trimmed, toasted

8 ounces Jarlsberg cheese, (8 slices)

1 Melt butter in a large pot over medium heat. Add onions, thyme, and sugar substitute; cook, stirring occasionally, until onions are soft and golden, 50 to 55 minutes.

2 Add chicken broth, ale, and mustard; bring to a boil. Reduce heat to medium-low and simmer 30 minutes. Season with salt and pepper.

3 Heat the broiler. Arrange toasted bread slices on a baking sheet. Top with cheese slices folded to fit. Broil croutons 8 inches from the heat until cheese is melted and bubbling, about 1 minute.

4 Ladle soup into bowls. Float a crouton in each.

SLAVIC-STYLE HOT BORSCHT

PER SERVING **Net Carbs: 8 grams;** Carbohydrates: 10 grams; Fiber: 2 grams; Protein: 27 grams; Fat: 21 grams; Calories: 330
Makes 8 (1¼-cup) servings; Prep time: 15 minutes; Cook time: 2 hours 30 minutes

A deep ruby hue makes this soup stunning to look at; the rich, meaty, earthy flavor appeals even to avowed beet haters.

3 medium beets

2 tablespoons unsalted butter

4 garlic cloves, minced (2 teaspoons)

1 large onion, chopped into ½-inch pieces (1 cup)

1 carrot, chopped into ½-inch pieces

1 medium white turnip, cut into ½-inch pieces (1 cup)

2 pounds boneless beef short ribs

3 (14½-ounce) cans lower sodium beef broth

2 tablespoons tomato paste

Salt and pepper

1 cup sour cream

4 teaspoons chopped fresh dill

1 Heat oven to 400°F. Wrap beets in a foil packet and roast until tender, 1 to 1½ hours. Cool 15 minutes; peel beets, then shred using a box grater.

2 Meanwhile, melt butter in a large pot over medium-high heat. Add garlic, onion, carrot, and turnip; cook, stirring often, until the vegetables begin to soften, 5 to 6 minutes. Transfer to a bowl.

3 Return pot to stove and heat over medium-high heat. Add short ribs; cook on all sides, turning often, until browned, 5 to 6 minutes. Add broth and tomato paste; bring to a boil. Reduce heat to medium-low; cover and simmer, until tender, about 2 hours. Transfer ribs to a cutting board and let cool 5 minutes. Cut into ½-inch cubes.

4 Skim any fat from the surface of the broth and add the reserved vegetables (but not the beets). Bring to a simmer over medium heat, cover and cook until the vegetables are tender, about 10 minutes. Add beets and shredded beef; cook until hot, about 5 minutes. Season to taste with salt and pepper.

5 To serve, divide the borscht among 8 bowls. Top each with 2 tablespoons sour cream and ½ teaspoon dill.

CUMIN-LEMON BUTTERNUT SQUASH SOUP

PER SERVING **Net Carbs: 22 grams;** Carbohydrates: 30 grams; Fiber: 8 grams; Protein: 3 grams; Fat: 8 grams; Calories: 190

3 4

Makes 12 (1-cup) servings; Prep time: 30 minutes; Cook time: 35 minutes, plus 1 hour cooling

This luscious soup is infused with the bright flavors of cumin and lemon. Use caution when puréeing hot liquids in the blender; work in very small batches, and start processing on a low speed.

2 tablespoons unsalted butter

1 large onion, chopped (1 cup)

3 cloves garlic, minced (1½ teaspoons)

4 teaspoons ground cumin

2 medium butternut squash, peeled, seeded, and cut into 1-inch cubes (14 cups)

4 (14½-ounce) cans lower sodium chicken broth

3 tablespoons lemon zest, divided

¾ cup heavy cream

2 tablespoons fresh lemon juice

Salt

1 Melt butter in a large pot over medium heat. Add onion and garlic, cook, stirring often, until very soft but not browned, about 4 minutes. Add cumin; cook 1 minute. Add squash, broth, and 1 tablespoon of the zest; simmer until squash is very tender, about 30 minutes. Remove from heat and cool.

2 Purée cooled soup in a blender in several batches. Return to pot. Stir in cream and reheat. Season with lemon juice and salt to taste. Ladle soup into bowls. Top each serving with a pinch of the remaining zest.

Slavic-Style Hot Borscht

ROASTED VEGETABLE SOUP WITH PESTO

PER SERVING **Net Carbs: 8 grams;** Carbohydrates: 11 grams; Fiber: 3 grams; Protein: 8 grams; Fat: 19 grams; Calories: 260
Makes 8 (1¼-cup) servings; Prep time: 15 minutes; Cook time: 2 hours 40 minutes

3 4

*Roasting brings out vegetables' natural sweet rich flavors. Swirl the basil pesto into
each bowl before serving.*

8 celery stalks, cut into ¾-inch pieces, divided

5 large carrots, peeled and cut into ¾-inch pieces,
  divided

4 large onions, peeled and cut into 1-inch chunks
  (4 cups), divided

½ cup extra virgin olive oil, divided

2¼ teaspoons salt, divided

2 tablespoons tomato paste

1 cup red wine

4 cups lower sodium beef or vegetable broth

1 bunch broccolini, cut into 1½-inch pieces

PESTO:
3 garlic cloves, minced and divided (1½ teaspoons)

2 cups fresh basil leaves

2 ounces freshly grated Parmesan cheese (½ cup)

¼ cup pine nuts, toasted

1 Heat oven to 500°F. Combine half of the celery, carrots,
and onions, 2 tablespoons of the oil, and 1 teaspoon of
the salt; toss and place in a single layer on a baking
sheet. Bake until vegetables begin to blister, about
20 minutes.

2 Heat 1 tablespoon of the oil in a Dutch oven over
medium-high heat. Add remaining celery, carrots, and
onions; sauté 1 minute. Stir in tomato paste; cook 1
minute, stirring constantly. Add wine; cook until liquid
almost evaporates, 5 to 8 minutes. Add broth and bring
to a boil. Reduce heat and simmer until vegetables are
tender, 28 to 30 minutes. Strain mixture through a
colander, reserving broth and discarding solids.

3 Add 2 tablespoons oil to pan and return to medium-
high heat. Add broccolini, ½ teaspoon garlic, and
1 teaspoon salt; sauté 3 minutes. Add broth; bring to
a boil. Reduce heat and simmer until broccolini is
crisp-tender, about 2 minutes. Stir in roasted vegetables;
cook until heated through, about 2 minutes.

4 FOR PESTO: Combine basil, cheese, nuts, ¼ teaspoon
salt, and remaining teaspoon garlic in a food processor.
Process until smooth, scraping sides. Slowly add
remaining 3 tablespoons oil with the motor running;
process until smooth.

Roasted Vegetable Soup with Pesto

ROASTED GARLIC SOUP

PER SERVING **Net Carbs: 11 grams;** Carbohydrates: 13 grams; Fiber: 2 grams; Protein: 9 grams; Fat: 18 grams; Calories: 240

Makes 6 (1-cup) servings; Prep time: 20 minutes; Cook time: 1 hour 40 minutes, plus 10 minutes cooling

Make this soup up to three days ahead. The roasted garlic flavor blooms as it sits.

4 heads garlic

¼ cup extra virgin olive oil, divided

2 celery stalks, chopped

1 large onion, chopped (1 cup)

1 tablespoon chopped fresh marjoram

2 teaspoons chopped fresh sage

1 teaspoon chopped fresh thyme

2 (14½-ounce) cans lower sodium chicken broth

1 tablespoon grated lemon zest

½ teaspoon salt

¼ teaspoon pepper

6 ounces sharp provolone cheese, shredded (¾ cup)

1 Heat oven to 400°F. Use a sharp knife to slice off the bottom quarter of each garlic head. Rub heads of garlic with 2 tablespoons of the olive oil and wrap in a foil packet. Place packet directly on the oven rack; roast until garlic is lightly browned and very soft, 70 to 75 minutes. Remove from oven; cool 10 minutes.

2 Heat remaining 2 tablespoons oil in a large saucepan over medium-high heat. Add celery, onion, marjoram, sage, and thyme; cook, stirring occasionally, until very soft, 8 to 10 minutes. Squeeze roasted garlic out of its peels and add to vegetables; cook, stirring, for 30 seconds. Add the broth and bring to a boil; reduce the heat to medium and simmer 15 minutes.

3 Purée the soup in a blender in several batches. Transfer soup to a large bowl; stir in the zest, salt, and pepper. Ladle soup into 6 bowls. Top each with 2 tablespoons of cheese.

DOUBLE MUSHROOM SOUP

PER SERVING **Net Carbs: 6 grams;** Total Carbs: 8.5 grams; Fiber: 2.5 grams; Protein: 8 grams; Fat: 13.5 grams; Calories: 177

Makes 6 (1½-cup) servings; Prep time: 15 minutes; Cook time: 45 minutes

This soup packs twice the flavor of ordinary mushroom soups, thanks to the combination of button mushrooms and porcinis. Keep dried porcinis on hand to add musky-sweet flavor and aroma to stews, soups, and sauces.

1 ounce dried porcini mushrooms

3 tablespoons butter

1 large onion, chopped (1 cup)

¾ pound fresh button mushrooms, stems chopped, caps sliced

3 garlic cloves, chopped (1½ teaspoons)

2 tablespoons Atkins Quick Quisine™ Bake Mix

2 (14½-ounce) cans lower sodium beef broth, plus 1 can water

½ teaspoon dried thyme

¼ teaspoon ground nutmeg

½ cup heavy cream

Salt and pepper

1 Place porcinis in a bowl, add enough hot water to cover, and let stand 20 minutes. Strain and reserve the soaking liquid. Rinse the soaked mushrooms; chop finely, and set aside.

2 Melt butter in a saucepan over medium-high heat. Add onion, button mushroom stems, and garlic; cook until onion is golden, about 10 minutes. Add bake mix; stir 2 minutes. Gradually stir in broth, water, reserved porcini liquid, thyme, and nutmeg; bring to a boil. Reduce heat, cover and simmer 25 minutes.

3 Add chopped porcini and sliced button mushroom caps to soup; simmer until softened, 5 minutes.

4 Purée half of the soup in a blender or a food processor; return to pot. Add cream; simmer 2 minutes to heat through. Season with salt and pepper.

LOBSTER BISQUE

 PER SERVING **Net Carbs: 9 grams;** Carbohydrates: 11 grams; Fiber: 2 grams; Protein: 46 grams; Fat: 23 grams; Calories: 480
Makes 6 (1-cup) servings; Prep time: 30 minutes; Cook time: 2 hours

Armagnac is closely related to Cognac but more flavorful, which makes it perfect for adding warmth and depth to seafood bisques. Don't add the cooked lobster meat until right before serving, or it will become chewy.

2 (1½-pound) lobsters

¼ cup extra virgin olive oil

8 garlic cloves, peeled

2 celery stalks, chopped (1 cup)

1 medium onion, chopped (1 cup)

1 carrot, chopped

2 teaspoons fennel seeds

¾ cup dry white wine

¼ cup Armagnac or brandy

3 sprigs fresh tarragon

3 sprigs fresh thyme

1 bay leaf

5 (8-ounce) bottles clam juice

3 tablespoons tomato paste

¾ cup heavy cream

1 Bring a large pot of water to a boil over high heat. Add lobsters and boil until bright red and cooked through, 9 to 10 minutes. Use tongs to transfer lobsters to a large metal bowl. Reserve 1 cup cooking liquid. Cool lobsters 15 minutes.

2 Cut off the lobster tails and claws over a large bowl, to catch and reserve all the juices. Remove tail and claw meat, chop coarsely, and refrigerate until ready to use.

3 Place lobster shells and bodies on a large cutting board. Lay a kitchen towel on top. Use a meat mallet or heavy bottomed saucepan to break the lobster into smaller pieces.

4 Wipe out pot, add oil, and heat over medium-high. Add broken shells and bodies; cook, stirring often, until the shells begin to brown, 9 to 10 minutes. Stir in garlic, celery, onion, carrot, and fennel seeds; cook, stirring often, until the vegetables begin to soften, 2 to 3 minutes. Add wine, Armagnac, tarragon, thyme, and bay leaf; bring to a boil. Continue boiling, scraping up any browned bits from the bottom of the pot, until liquid has almost evaporated, 7 to 8 minutes. Stir in reserved cooking liquid, clam juice, and lobster juices; return to a boil. Reduce heat to medium-low and simmer, uncovered, 1 hour.

5 Strain soup through a wire mesh strainer into a clean pot, pushing down on the solids to extract as much liquid as possible. Stir in tomato paste, return soup to a simmer over medium heat, and cook 5 minutes. Add cream, return to a simmer, and cook until slightly reduced, 15 minutes, stirring occasionally. Stir in reserved lobster meat; cook until hot, 1 to 2 minutes. Divide among 6 soup bowls.

Atkins Tip: If you can't find fresh lobster, try substituting shrimp to make a shrimp bisque. Shrimp shells provide a tremendous amount of flavor and can be used just as you would lobster shells. Skip steps 1 and 2; begin by adding the raw shells to the pot in step 3. Shrimp cook quickly; simply simmer until they turn pink and begin to curl, about 3 minutes.

Oyster and Crab Bisque

OYSTER AND CRAB BISQUE

 PER SERVING **Net Carbs: 2 grams;** Carbohydrates: 4.5 grams; Fiber: 2.5 gram; Protein: 14 grams; Fat: 30 grams; Calories: 342
Makes 8 (¾-cup) servings; Prep time: 10 minutes; Cook time: 20 minutes

Shellfish, such as oysters, are higher in carbs than most other seafood, so you
should limit your consumption to four ounces a day during Induction.

3 tablespoons unsalted butter

1 scallion, finely chopped (1 tablespoon)

2 teaspoons ThickenThin™ not/Starch thickener

½ teaspoon onion powder

¼ teaspoon celery seeds

Freshly grated nutmeg

⅛ teaspoon cayenne pepper

2 cups clam juice

2 cups heavy cream

1 pound shucked oysters, divided

8 ounces cooked fresh lump crabmeat, picked over to
remove shells

2 tablespoons chopped fresh parsley

1 Melt butter in a large stockpot over medium heat. Add
scallion and cook 1 minute. Stir in thickener, onion
powder, celery seeds, nutmeg to taste, and cayenne
pepper. Pour clam juice and heavy cream into pot;
stir to combine. Reduce heat to medium-low to hold
a simmer.

2 In a saucepan, cook 8 ounces of the oysters (with their
juices) over medium-low heat just until edges curl,
about 5 minutes. Pour into a blender and purée; add
to stockpot.

3 Simmer oyster mixture 15 minutes, stirring often. Add
remaining 8 ounces oysters; cook 4 minutes. Gently fold
in crabmeat, taking care not to break up the lumps.
Cook until heated through, 1 to 2 minutes. Divide
bisque among 8 serving bowls, garnish with parsley,
and serve.

SALADS

Salads are essential for following the Atkins lifestyle. Vegetables provide nutrients and fiber, while indulgent dressings ensure satisfying flavor. Start off the festivities with one of our vibrant, tasty salads.

SPINACH AND POMEGRANATE SALAD

3 4

PER SERVING **Net Carbs: 5.5 grams;** Carbohydrates: 10 grams; Fiber: 4.5 grams; Protein: 3.5 grams; Fat: 8.5 grams; Calories: 115
Makes 8 servings; Prep time: 15 minutes; Cook time: 15 minutes

The pomegranate seeds glisten like jewels in this unusual salad (shown on page 28). Use the tortilla strips to add crunch to soups and purées, too.

TORTILLA STRIPS:

¾ teaspoon curry powder

⅛ teaspoon salt

1½ cups vegetable oil

2 low-carb tortillas, halved and cut into ⅛-inch-wide strips

SALAD:

1 tablespoon white wine vinegar

1 tablespoon reduced-sodium soy sauce

1 teaspoon peeled, grated fresh ginger

1 teaspoon dark sesame oil

1 packet sugar substitute

2 tablespoons vegetable oil

Salt and pepper

8 cups baby spinach leaves, rinsed

4 ounces white mushrooms, sliced (2 cups)

1 small red onion, thinly sliced (½ cup)

½ cup pomegranate seeds

1 FOR TORTILLA STRIPS: Combine curry powder and salt in a large bowl; set aside. Heat oil in a small saucepan over medium heat until hot enough to crisp a tortilla strip in 30 seconds. Add one-third of the tortilla strips; cook, stirring occasionally, until lightly golden and crisp, 30 to 45 seconds. Transfer to a baking sheet lined with paper towels. Fry the remaining strips in two more batches. Place fried strips in bowl with curry mixture; toss well to coat.

2 FOR SALAD: Combine vinegar, soy sauce, ginger, sesame oil, and sugar substitute in a bowl. Add vegetable oil in a slow steady stream, whisking continuously until well combined. Season with salt and pepper to taste.

3 Combine spinach, mushrooms, and onion in a large bowl. Add vinegar mixture and toss well to coat. Divide the salad among 8 plates; garnish each with tortilla strips and pomegranate seeds.

SPRING GREENS WITH BASIC VINAIGRETTE

PER SERVING **Net Carbs: 1 gram;** Carbohydrates: 2 grams; Fiber:1 gram; Protein: 0.5 gram; Fat: 7 grams; Calories: 67
Makes 8 servings; Prep time: 5 minutes

Double or triple this basic dressing recipe and keep it on hand for a week or so in the refrigerator for all your salads. For a variation, add fresh finely chopped herbs or substitute lemon juice for the vinegar.

1 tablespoon red or white wine vinegar

1 teaspoon Dijon mustard

¼ teaspoon salt

⅛ teaspoon pepper

¼ cup extra virgin olive oil

6 cups mesclun greens

1 Whisk vinegar, mustard, salt, and pepper in a small bowl. Add oil in a slow steady stream, whisking continuously until well combined.

2 Pour dressing over salad greens and toss immediately before serving.

Atkins Tip: Instead of whisking in the oil to emulsify the vinaigrette, put the ingredients in a jar, seal the top, and give it a good shake.

Red and Green Holiday Salad

RED AND GREEN HOLIDAY SALAD

 PER SERVING **Net Carbs: 2 grams;** Carbohydrates: 3 grams; Fiber: 1 gram; Protein: 1 gram; Fat: 7 grams; Calories: 78
Makes 8 servings; Prep time: 25 minutes

An old favorite—Green Goddess Dressing—makes a splashy comeback in this festive salad. Adjust the herb quantities to suit your taste.

DRESSING:

¼ cup mayonnaise

3 tablespoons sour cream

1 scallion, chopped (1 tablespoon)

¼ cup fresh basil leaves

2 tablespoons fresh tarragon leaves

2 teaspoons white wine vinegar

SALAD:

1 medium head radicchio, leaves torn (4 cups)

2 cups watercress

½ medium cucumber, peeled, seeded, and thinly sliced (½ cup)

1 cup grape tomatoes, halved

½ small red onion, thinly sliced (¼ cup)

1 FOR DRESSING: Combine mayonnaise, sour cream, scallion, basil, tarragon, and vinegar in a blender. Process until smooth, stopping the blender to scrape down sides and stir, if necessary.

2 FOR SALAD: Combine radicchio, watercress, cucumber, tomatoes, and onion in a bowl. Add dressing and toss well to coat. Divide among 8 serving plates.

Atkins Tip: Radicchio, a vibrant and slightly bitter lettuce, is worth seeking out. It can be used in salads, as a base for spreads, or in place of crackers with dips.

FIELD GREENS, PEARS, PECANS, AND GOUDA

 PER SERVING **Net Carbs: 5 grams;** Carbohydrates: 8 grams; Fiber: 3 grams; Protein: 6 grams; Fat: 16 grams; Calories: 190
Makes 6 servings; Prep time: 20 minutes; Cook time: 4 minutes

You can use any of the more aromatic and flavorful nut oils in this dressing: walnut, hazelnut, and macadamia nut oils all lend warm, nutty flavor to balance the curry and pears. Store perishable nut oils in the refrigerator for up to three months.

1 tablespoon unsalted butter

½ cup pecans

1½ teaspoons granular sugar substitute, divided

½ teaspoon ground cumin

¾ teaspoon salt, divided

⅛ teaspoon cayenne pepper

1 tablespoon Champagne vinegar

¼ teaspoon pepper

⅛ teaspoon curry powder

3 tablespoons walnut, hazelnut, or macadamia nut oil

10 cups mixed field or mesclun greens

3 ounces Gouda cheese, cut into matchsticks

1 red pear, cored and cut into thin slices

1 Melt butter in a medium nonstick skillet over medium heat. Add pecans, 1 teaspoon of the sugar substitute, cumin, ¼ teaspoon of the salt, and cayenne pepper. Cook, stirring often, until nuts are toasted and well coated with the spices, 3 to 4 minutes. Transfer to a small bowl.

2 Combine remaining ½ teaspoon sugar substitute, remaining ½ teaspoon salt, vinegar, pepper, and curry powder; mix well. Add oil in a slow steady stream, whisking continuously until well combined.

3 Combine greens, Gouda, and pear slices in a large bowl. Add vinegar mixture and toss well to coat. Divide among 6 plates; garnish with spiced pecans.

ASPARAGUS AND ROMAINE SALAD

 PER SERVING **Net Carbs: 4 grams;** Carbohydrates: 5 grams; Fiber: 1 gram; Protein: 3 grams; Fat: 10 grams; Calories: 120
Makes 8 servings; Prep time: 15 minutes; Cook time: 15 minutes

Select firm, crisp asparagus stalks with tightly closed heads. Store them for up to four days wrapped in damp paper towels in an unsealed plastic bag, or cut a half inch from the bottom of the spears and set upright in an inch of water.

1 bunch asparagus, trimmed and cut into 1½-inch pieces (2½ cups)

½ medium head romaine lettuce, torn (6 cups)

1 small red onion, thinly sliced (¼ cup)

2 tablespoons fresh lemon juice

2 teaspoons Dijon mustard

1 anchovy filet, mashed with a fork

½ teaspoon Worcestershire sauce

½ teaspoon salt

¼ teaspoon pepper

⅓ cup extra virgin olive oil

3 tablespoons grated Parmesan cheese

1 Bring a pot of salted water to a boil over high heat. Add asparagus and cook until crisp-tender, 3 minutes. Drain and rinse under cold water. Transfer to a large bowl. Stir in lettuce and onion.

2 Combine lemon juice, mustard, anchovy, Worcestershire sauce, salt, and pepper in a small bowl; mix well. Add oil in a slow steady stream, whisking continuously until well combined. Stir in Parmesan cheese. Pour over the asparagus mixture and toss to combine.

ENDIVE, ARUGULA, AND RADISH SALAD

 PER SERVING **Net Carbs: 4 grams;** Carbohydrates: 6 grams; Fiber: 2 grams; Protein: 2.5 grams; Fat: 16 grams; Calories: 161
Makes 8 servings; Prep time: 35 minutes

The sweetness of macadamia nuts and oil rounds out the flavor of this spicy salad.
You can substitute olive oil for the macadamia nut oil and red wine vinegar for the
sherry vinegar if you can't find these ingredients.

6 cups fresh arugula

4 heads endive, coarsely chopped (3 cups)

1 bunch radishes, cut into matchsticks (1 cup)

½ cup macadamia nuts, coarsely chopped

1 teaspoon salt, divided

2 tablespoons coarse-grain mustard

2 tablespoons sherry vinegar

1 tablespoon fresh lemon juice

⅓ cup macadamia nut oil

1 small shallot, minced (2 tablespoons)

1 garlic clove, minced (½ teaspoon)

1 Combine arugula, endive, radishes, and nuts in a large bowl. Sprinkle with ¾ teaspoon of the salt.

2 Whisk mustard, vinegar, and lemon juice in a small bowl. Add oil in a slow steady stream, whisking continuously until well combined. Stir in shallot, garlic, and remaining ¼ teaspoon salt. Drizzle dressing over salad mixture; toss gently to coat. Serve immediately.

Endive, Arugula, and Radish Salad

WARM GREENS WITH CORNBREAD CROUTONS

 PER SERVING **Net Carbs: 5 grams;** Carbohydrates: 10 grams; Fiber: 5 grams; Protein: 7 grams; Fat: 18 grams; Calories: 264
Makes 8 servings; Prep time: 15 minutes; Cook time: 10 minutes

*Although you'll only need one quarter of a cornbread recipe to make the croutons,
you'll find that the rest of the batch won't last long—try it for breakfast or as a snack.
It also freezes well, if tightly wrapped.*

CROUTONS:

1 box Atkins Quick Quisine™ Deluxe Corn Muffin &
  Bread Mix, made according to package directions

¼ cup olive oil

SALAD:

8 slices bacon, cut into 1-inch pieces

1 bunch chicory, cut into bite-size pieces (12 cups)

3 tablespoons sugar-free pancake syrup

2 tablespoons white wine vinegar

1 tablespoon country-style Dijon mustard

Salt and pepper

1 FOR CROUTONS: Cut three 1-inch slices of cornbread;
set remainder aside for another use. Cut the slices into
½-inch by 1-inch cubes. Heat oil in a medium skillet over
medium-high heat. Add bread cubes and cook, turning
often, until browned on all sides, 3 to 5 minutes. Drain
on paper towels.

2 FOR SALAD: Heat a large nonstick skillet over medium-
high heat. Add bacon and cook, stirring occasionally,
until crisp, 5 to 7 minutes. Add chicory; toss and
cook until it begins to wilt, about 1 minute. Add syrup,
vinegar, and mustard; toss to coat. Remove from heat.
Season with salt and pepper to taste.

3 To serve, divide greens among 8 salad plates. Top each
with a few croutons.

ROASTED PEPPER AND ESCAROLE SALAD

 PER SERVING **Net Carbs: 4 grams;** Carbohydrates: 7 grams; Fiber: 3 grams; Protein: 5 grams; Fat: 13.5 grams; Calories: 161
Makes 6 servings; Prep time: 15 minutes

*Robust blue cheese is the perfect counterpoint to the pungent greens, while the
red pepper adds a sweeter element.*

1 medium head escarole, torn into 1-inch pieces and
  well rinsed, (10 cups)

2 roasted red peppers, drained, patted dry, and cut into
  ¼-inch strips

¾ cup crumbled blue cheese (3 ounces)

1 tablespoon fresh lemon juice

2 teaspoons chopped fresh oregano

2 teaspoons Dijon mustard

1 teaspoon grated lemon zest

1 teaspoon granular sugar substitute

½ teaspoon chopped fresh thyme

¼ cup extra virgin olive oil

Salt and pepper

1 Combine escarole, red peppers, and blue cheese in a
large bowl and toss.

2 Combine lemon juice, oregano, mustard, lemon zest,
sugar substitute, and thyme in a small bowl; mix well.
Add oil in a slow steady stream, whisking continuously
until well combined. Season with salt and pepper to
taste. Pour over escarole mixture and toss well to coat.

Warm Greens with Cornbread Croutons

WARM CAULIFLOWER AND BROCCOLI SALAD

 PER SERVING **Net Carbs: 3 grams;** Carbohydrates: 5.5 grams; Fiber: 2.5 grams; Protein: 2.5 grams; Fat: 13.5 grams; Calories: 150
Makes 12 servings; Prep time: 10 minutes; Cook time: 25 minutes

The warm vegetables seem to soak up the flavors of the Bagna Cauda, making them that much more sumptuous. This salad also makes great leftovers served at room temperature.

1 head broccoli, cut into florets (4 cups)

1 head cauliflower, cut into florets (8 cups)

¾ cup Bagna Cauda (see recipe on page 42)

1 tablespoon fresh lemon juice

1 teaspoon grated lemon zest

1 Bring a large pot of salted water to a boil over high heat. Add broccoli and cook until crisp-tender, about 2 minutes. Remove with a slotted spoon and drain in a colander and transfer to a large bowl. Return water to a boil, add cauliflower, and cook until crisp-tender, 4 to 5 minutes. Drain into the colander and transfer to a large bowl with broccoli.

2 Meanwhile, warm Bagna Cauda in a small saucepan over medium heat. Stir in lemon juice and zest. Pour mixture over the vegetables and toss. Serve warm.

Atkins Tip: When entertaining, bring a pot of water to a boil up to an hour before you need it. Turn off the heat and cover the pot. The water will come back to a boil much more quickly when you need it.

Bacon and Goat Cheese Salad

ROAST SHALLOT, GARLIC, AND ZUCCHINI SALAD

 PER SERVING **Net Carbs: 8.5 grams;** Carbohydrates: 10 grams; Fiber: 1.5 grams; Protein: 5 grams; Fat: 11 grams; Calories: 151
Makes 8 servings; Prep time: 20 minutes; Cook time: 25 minutes

Oven-roasted vegetables transform a simple arugula salad into a special first course.

16 whole garlic cloves, peeled

5 medium shallots, peeled

2 medium zucchini (1 pound), cut in half lengthwise
and sliced into ¾-inch pieces (2 cups)

5 tablespoons extra virgin olive oil, divided, plus more
for baking sheet

1 teaspoon salt, divided

½ teaspoon pepper, divided

2 bunches arugula, stems trimmed (8 cups loosely
packed)

1½ tablespoons red wine vinegar

1 teaspoon dried oregano

1 cup crumbled feta cheese (4 ounces)

1 Heat oven to 450°F. Oil a rimmed baking sheet.

2 Combine garlic, shallots, and zucchini in a bowl. Add
2 tablespoons of the oil and toss well. Sprinkle with
½ teaspoon of the salt and ¼ teaspoon of the pepper.
Arrange on a baking sheet in a single layer. Roast, tossing
occasionally, until vegetables are lightly browned and
crisp-tender, about 25 minutes. Cool 10 minutes. Transfer
shallots to a cutting board and thinly slice. Transfer
shallots, garlic, zucchini, and arugula to a large bowl;
toss to combine.

3 Combine vinegar, oregano, and remaining ½ teaspoon salt
and ¼ teaspoon pepper in a small bowl; mix well. Add
oil in a slow steady stream, whisking continuously until
well combined. Pour over the arugula mixture and toss
to coat. Divide among 8 plates and top with feta cheese.

BACON AND GOAT CHEESE SALAD

 PER SERVING **Net Carbs: 2.5 grams;** Carbohydrates: 4.5 grams; Fiber: 2 grams; Protein: 14.5 grams; Fat: 24.5 grams; Calories: 294
Makes 6 servings; Prep time: 25 minutes; Cook time: 15 minutes

You can do most of the prep ahead of time, making this an ideal dish for the busy
holiday season.

SALAD:

6 slices bacon, cut into 1-inch pieces

4 cups romaine lettuce, torn into bite-size pieces

2 cups frisée or curly endive, torn into bite-size pieces

3 tablespoons snipped fresh chives

1½ slices low-carb white bread, torn into 2-inch chunks

8 ounces goat cheese, cut into 6 slices

1 egg, beaten

DRESSING:

2 tablespoons olive oil

1½ tablespoons red wine vinegar

1 tablespoon Dijon mustard

¼ teaspoon pepper

1 FOR SALAD: Cook bacon in a large nonstick skillet over
medium heat, turning once, until crisp, about 6 to 7

minutes. Transfer with a slotted spoon to paper towels.
Reserve 1 tablespoon of bacon drippings.

2 In a large bowl, combine romaine, frisée, and chives;
set aside.

3 In a food processor or blender, process bread to make
crumbs; spread crumbs on a plate. Place goat cheese
slices cut side down on work surface and press lightly to
flatten. Dip each slice in egg; let excess drip off. Place in
crumbs; press to coat evenly and completely.

4 Wipe out same skillet with a paper towel; add oil and
heat over medium heat. Add goat-cheese patties and
cook until browned, about 2 minutes per side (reduce
heat if browning occurs too fast or cheese is melting).
Transfer to a plate lined with paper towels. Remove
skillet from heat.

5 FOR DRESSING: Add reserved bacon drippings, olive
oil, vinegar, mustard, and pepper to skillet. Whisk to
combine. Add warm dressing and bacon to bowl with
greens. Toss to combine. Arrange salad on individual
serving plates and top with goat cheese.

SEARED SCALLOPS WITH CELERY AND ONION

 PER SERVING **Net Carbs: 6 grams;** Carbohydrates: 7 grams; Fiber: 1 gram; Protein: 14 grams; Fat: 8 grams; Calories: 150
Makes 6 servings; Prep time: 15 minutes; Cook time: 6 minutes

Serve this elegant first course warm or at room temperature. You can sear the scallops a few hours in advance, and combine all the elements just before serving.

3 tablespoons extra virgin olive oil, divided

1 pound bay scallops

1¼ teaspoons salt, divided

½ teaspoon pepper, divided

4 celery stalks, diced (2 cups)

1 cucumber, peeled, seeded, and diced (1¼ cups)

⅓ cup finely chopped red onion

⅓ cup chopped fresh parsley

2 tablespoons fresh lemon juice

3 cups mesclun greens

1 Heat 1 tablespoon of the oil in a large nonstick skillet over medium-high heat. Sprinkle the scallops with ¾ teaspoon of the salt and ¼ teaspoon of the pepper. Add to the skillet and cook, until browned, 2 to 3 minutes per side. Transfer to a large bowl.

2 Add the remaining 2 tablespoons oil, ½ teaspoon salt, and ¼ teaspoon pepper to the scallops. Add the celery, cucumber, onion, parsley, and lemon juice to the scallops and toss well. Top each of 6 plates with ½ cup of the greens. Divide the scallop salad among the plates.

Atkins Tip: If raw onion disagrees with you, try soaking in ice water for 15 minutes before using. You'll find the flavor is intact but the harshness is gone.

MARINATED SHRIMP SALAD

 PER SERVING **Net Carbs: 2.5 grams;** Carbohydrates: 3 grams; Fiber: 0.5 gram; Protein: 23 grams; Fat: 11 grams; Calories: 208
Makes 6 servings; Prep time: 10 minutes; Cook time: 10 minutes, plus 1 to 8 hours chilling

Basil, lemon, and scallions provide a subtle flavor backdrop for the shrimp in this first-course salad.

1½ pounds large shrimp, peeled and deveined

2 celery stalks, thinly sliced (1 cup)

2 scallions, white and light-green portions thinly sliced on the diagonal (2 tablespoons)

2 tablespoons thinly sliced basil leaves

1 teaspoon Dijon mustard

½ teaspoon finely grated lemon zest

½ teaspoon salt

¼ teaspoon pepper

¼ cup fresh lemon juice

¼ cup extra virgin olive oil

1 Fill a medium saucepan with water and bring to a rolling boil. Add shrimp and stir. Remove from heat. Cover and let stand off heat until shrimp turn pink and are beginning to curl, about 7 minutes; drain. Place shrimp in a bowl of ice water and let stand 3 minutes. Drain and pat dry. Using a sharp knife, halve shrimp lengthwise and place in large bowl. Toss with celery, scallions, and basil.

2 Whisk mustard, zest, salt, pepper, and lemon juice in a small bowl until well blended. Add oil in a slow steady stream, whisking continuously until well combined. Pour over shrimp mixture and toss well to combine. Cover and marinate in the refrigerator at least 1 hour or up to 8 hours. Stir occasionally to blend flavors. Serve at room temperature.

Warm Lobster and Avocado Salad

WARM LOBSTER AND AVOCADO SALAD

 PER SERVING **Net Carbs: 3 grams;** Carbohydrates: 6 grams; Fiber: 3 grams; Protein: 9 grams; Fat: 12 grams; Calories: 170
Makes 8 servings; Prep time: 15 minutes; Cook time: 2 minutes

This delightfully indulgent salad is composed of lush and satisfying ingredients that
are also filled with health-promoting nutrients.

1 medium shallot, finely chopped (¼ cup)

2 tablespoons fresh lime juice

2 teaspoons grated lime zest

1 teaspoon Dijon mustard

2 tablespoons chopped fresh cilantro

5 tablespoons macadamia nut oil, divided

Salt and pepper

8 cups mixed baby greens

1 cup grape tomatoes, halved

1 avocado, peeled, pitted, and cut into 24 thin slices

14 ounces cooked lobster meat, or 2 (8-ounce) lobster
  tails, steamed and chopped or sliced into medallions

1 In a small bowl, combine shallot, lime juice, zest,
mustard, and cilantro. Add 4 tablespoons oil in a
slow, steady stream, whisking continuously until well
combined. Season with salt and pepper to taste.

2 In a large bowl, combine greens and tomatoes. Add
¼ cup of the vinaigrette and toss well to coat. Divide
the salad among 8 serving plates; place 3 avocado
slices on the side of each plate.

3 Heat the remaining tablespoon oil in a large nonstick
skillet over medium-high heat. Add lobster and cook,
tossing, until heated through, 1 to 2 minutes. Divide
among plates; drizzle with the remaining vinaigrette.

Tandoori Chicken Wings, page 52
Jalapeño–Cream Cheese Stuffed Celery, page 45
Smoked Trout Mousse in Cucumber Cups, page 54

APPETIZERS & HORS D'OEUVRES

From the familiar to the exotic, these small bites will whet your guests' appetites and excite their palates. For casual gatherings, serve on platters or as passed hors d'oeuvres. On more elegant occasions, serve as a seated first course. Either way, there are a myriad of low-carb choices to suit your style and your every whim.

BAGNA CAUDA

 PER SERVING **Net Carbs: 1 gram;** Carbohydrates: 1 gram; Fiber: 0 grams; Protein: 1.5 grams; Fat: 20 grams; Calories: 183
Makes 8 servings; Prep time: 5 minutes; Cook time: 5 minutes

The earthy flavors of this classic Mediterranean dip are best when warm. Make it
two to three days in advance and reheat gently before serving.

½ cup extra virgin olive oil

4 tablespoons (½ stick) unsalted butter

6 garlic cloves, thinly sliced

8 to 10 anchovy fillets, patted dry and finely chopped

Pepper

Heat olive oil and butter in a small saucepan set over medium heat. Add garlic and anchovies. Cook gently until garlic is fragrant but not browned, about 5 minutes. Season with pepper to taste. Serve warm.

BAKED STUFFED MUSHROOMS

 PER SERVING **Net Carbs: 1 gram;** Carbohydrates: 1 gram; Fiber: 0 grams; Protein: 2 grams; Fat: 2.5 grams; Calories: 90
Makes 24 servings; Prep time: 35 minutes; Cook time: 10 minutes

Stuff these rich, cheesy mushrooms ahead of time and refrigerate or freeze them
uncooked. Before baking, bring the mushrooms to room temperature to ensure
even cooking.

24 large fresh white mushrooms, cleaned (1 pound)

2 tablespoons vegetable oil, divided

1 pound Italian sausage, removed from casings

½ cup sliced scallions

4 cloves garlic, minced (2 teaspoons)

½ teaspoon Italian seasoning

2½ ounces mozzarella cheese, shredded
(½ cup plus 2 tablespoons), divided

2 tablespoons grated Parmesan cheese

1 Heat oven to 400°F. Remove stems from mushrooms; finely chop enough stems to equal ½ cup (reserve the rest for another use). Place mushroom caps in a bowl and toss with 1 tablespoon of the oil. Arrange caps, gills up, on a shallow baking pan.

2 Heat remaining 1 tablespoon oil in a small skillet set over medium heat. Add sausage, scallions, garlic, Italian seasoning, and chopped mushroom stems. Cook, stirring and breaking sausage into smaller pieces until cooked through, about 5 minutes. Remove from heat. Add ½ cup of the mozzarella and Parmesan cheese; stir just until cheeses melt.

3 Stuff mushroom caps with sausage mixture. Sprinkle with remaining 2 tablespoons mozzarella. Bake until cheese has melted and mushrooms are tender, 12 to 15 minutes.

Atkins Tip: Mushrooms that will be used immediately can be cleaned by rinsing gently under cold water. Otherwise, wipe them clean with a damp cloth or vegetable brush.

CITRUS AND BASIL MARINATED GOAT CHEESE

 PER SERVING **Net Carbs: 1 gram;** Carbohyrates: 1 gram; Fiber: 0 grams; Protein: 6 grams; Fat: 12 grams; Calories: 140

Makes 12 servings; Prep time: 15 minutes, plus 12 to 48 hours marinating

Show off the beauty of this sophisticated appetizer by serving it in on an elegant plate. It can be prepared up to two days in advance and kept covered in the refrigerator. Radicchio leaves make a great low-carb substitute for crackers.

¾ cup extra virgin olive oil

1 clove garlic, minced (½ teaspoon)

¼ cup thinly sliced fresh basil leaves

1 tablespoon grated orange zest

1 tablespoon grated lemon zest

1 teaspoon grated lime zest

10 whole black peppercorns

1 (11-ounce) log goat cheese, cut across into
  6 pieces

1 Combine oil, garlic, basil, orange zest, lemon zest, lime zest, and peppercorns in a bowl; mix well.

2 Place goat cheese buttons in a small, shallow pan. Pour oil mixture over cheese. Cover and refrigerate overnight, turning occasionally. Bring to room temperature before serving. Each goat cheese button serves two.

Citrus and Basil Marinated Goat Cheese

SMOKED TURKEY AND CHEDDAR SPREAD

 PER SERVING **Net Carbs: 3 grams;** Carbohydrates: 4 grams; Fiber: 1 gram; Protein: 11 grams; Fat: 17 grams; Calories: 200
Makes 8 servings; Prep time: 10 minutes, plus 2 hours chilling

Smoky, tangy, and zesty all at once, this spread is ideal for entertaining, since it improves in flavor as it sits. Make it up to three days ahead and store in an airtight container in the refrigerator. Serve as a dip with low-carb crackers or crudité.

¼ cup parsley

½ pound smoked turkey breast, diced

6 ounces sharp cheddar cheese, diced

½ cup pecans

¾ cup sour cream

1 teaspoon Dijon mustard

Pulse parsley in a food processor until chopped. Add turkey breast, cheddar, and pecans. Process until ingredients are finely chopped. Add sour cream and mustard; pulse to just combine. Refrigerate at least 2 hours, and up to 3 days, to allow flavors to develop.

Chorizo Cheese Bake

JALAPEÑO–CREAM CHEESE STUFFED CELERY

 PER SERVING Net Carbs: 2.5 grams; Carbohydrates: 3.5 grams; Fiber: 1 gram; Protein: 4 grams; Fat: 14 grams; Calories: 150
Makes 6 (2-piece) servings; Prep time: 15 minutes

Classic appetizers like this one (shown on page 40) endure because of their universal appeal. Cooks love this dish for the ease of preparation. Guests love it for the contrasts in flavor—from rich cheese to mild spice—and texture—from smooth creaminess to snappy crunch.

1 (8-ounce) package cream cheese, softened

2 tablespoons pickled jalapeño peppers, drained and chopped

2 tablespoons sliced pimientos, drained and chopped

1 tablespoon chopped fresh cilantro

2 teaspoons grated Parmesan cheese

¼ teaspoon salt

4 celery stalks, trimmed and cut into thirds (each about 3 inches long)

1 Combine cream cheese, jalapeños, pimientos, cilantro, cheese, and salt in a bowl; mix well. Mixture can be stored, refrigerated, in an airtight container for up to three days.

2 Fill each celery stalk with approximately 1 tablespoon cream cheese mixture. Refrigerate, loosely covered, until ready to serve.

CHORIZO CHEESE BAKE

 PER SERVING Net Carbs: 3 grams; Carbohydrates: 3 grams; Fiber: 0 grams; Protein: 9 grams; Fat: 17 grams; Calories: 200
Makes 12 servings; Prep time: 15 minutes; Cook time: 35 minutes, plus 10 minutes cooling

Chorizo, a smoky, spicy Spanish sausage, is drier and firmer than the Italian-style sausage to which you may be accustomed. To chop chorizo, first quarter it lengthwise, then slice across into bits.

5 ounces chorizo sausage, finely chopped

1 small onion, finely chopped (½ cup)

1 jalapeño pepper, seeded and minced

1 roasted red pepper, drained, patted dry and finely chopped

2 tablespoons chopped fresh cilantro

1 (8-ounce) package cream cheese, softened

8 ounces sharp cheddar cheese, grated (2 cups)

1 teaspoon hot pepper sauce (such as Tabasco®)

1 Heat oven to 325°F. Heat a medium nonstick skillet over medium-high heat. Add chorizo and cook, stirring occasionally, until it begins to brown, 4 to 5 minutes. Add onion and jalapeño; cook until vegetables soften, 2 to 3 minutes. Add the red pepper; cook 2 minutes longer. Transfer mixture to a bowl. Stir in cilantro. Cool 10 minutes.

2 Add cream cheese and cheddar cheese to the chorizo mixture; mix well. Transfer to a 1-quart oven-proof ceramic or glass baking dish. Bake until cheese melts and puffs slightly, about 25 minutes. Serve warm.

CHEDDAR AND SCALLION PIE SQUARES

PER SERVING **Net Carbs: 4 grams;** Carbohydrates: 4 grams; Fiber: 0 grams; Protein: 12 grams; Fat: 15 grams; Calories: 190

3 4 Makes 24 servings; Prep time: 25 minutes, plus 20 minutes chilling; Cook time: 47 minutes

This quiche-like appetizer can be served warm or at room temperature. To make it in advance, freeze it uncooked, then simply defrost in the refrigerator when you're ready to bake. The recipe makes subtly spicy squares. Increase the hot sauce if you prefer more kick.

CRUST:

½ cup whole-wheat pastry flour

½ cup vital wheat gluten, plus 2 teaspoons for rolling

¼ cup soy flour

¼ teaspoon salt

8 tablespoons (1 stick) cold unsalted butter, cut into ½-inch cubes

1 egg yolk

½ teaspoon cold water

FILLING:

8 large eggs, lightly beaten

¾ cup heavy cream

½ teaspoon salt

¼ teaspoon pepper

¼ teaspoon hot pepper sauce (such as Tabasco®)

12 ounces sharp cheddar cheese, grated (3 cups)

4 ounces fontina cheese, grated (1 cup)

6 scallions, thinly sliced

1 FOR CRUST: Combine pastry flour, gluten, soy flour, salt, and butter in a food processor. Pulse until mixture is the texture of coarse meal. Add egg yolk and water; continue pulsing until dough begins to come together. Turn onto a sheet of wide plastic wrap, form into a square and cover with another sheet of plastic. Flatten to a 4- by 8-inch rectangle. Freeze for 10 minutes.

2 Roll dough between the plastic wrap to a 8½- by 12½-inch rectangle (to facilitate rolling, occasionally remove plastic and dust each side with ½ teaspoon of wheat gluten). Remove top sheet of plastic. Invert pastry into a 9- by 13-inch buttered baking pan. Press to fill bottom of pan. Remove the remaining plastic. Freeze dough 10 minutes.

3 Heat oven to 375°F. Line the dough with foil and a layer of dried beans or pie weights. Bake 10 minutes. Remove beans and foil. Bake until golden, an additional 5 to 6 minutes. Cool on a wire rack 10 minutes. (May be made up to 1 day in advance).

4 FOR FILLING: Heat oven to 350°F. Combine eggs, cream, salt, pepper, and hot pepper sauce in a bowl; mix well. Stir in cheddar cheese, fontina cheese, and scallions. Pour mixture into baked crust and smooth with a spatula.

5 Bake until filling is set and lightly browned, about 35 minutes. Remove from oven. Cool 5 minutes, then cut into 24 squares. Serve warm or at room temperature.

Atkins Tip: Vital wheat gluten is the protein component of wheat and can be found in health food stores. It is also known as gluten flour, instant gluten flour, pure gluten flour, and vital wheat gluten flour, depending on the manufacturer. Because it is 75 to 80 percent protein, it's a great additive for low-carb baking—when used in unleavened bread recipes, such as this crust, it improves texture and elasticity; when used in yeast bread recipes, it produces a higher rise.

PEPPER JACK QUESADILLAS

PER SERVING **Net Carbs: 5.5 grams;** Carbohydrates: 13 grams; Fiber: 7.5 grams; Protein: 9 grams; Fat: 12 grams; Calories: 172

Makes 8 (3-wedge) servings; Prep time: 15 minutes; Cook time: 28 minutes

Make more than you think you'll need—these get snatched up quickly! If you can't find Monterey Jack cheese with jalapeños, simply add chopped fresh or canned jalapeños before cooking the quesadillas.

2 tablespoons macadamia nut oil or canola oil

1 large onion, thinly sliced (1 cup)

½ teaspoon salt

6 low-carb tortillas

6 ounces Monterey Jack cheese with jalapeños, shredded (1½ cups), divided

1 tablespoon chopped fresh cilantro, divided

1 Heat oil in a large nonstick skillet over medium-high heat. Add onion and salt; cook, stirring occasionally, until golden, 10 to 12 minutes. Transfer onions to a small bowl and cool. Wipe out skillet.

2 Place tortillas on work surface. Sprinkle the lower half of each with ¼ cup cheese, 1 tablespoon onions, and ½ teaspoon cilantro. Fold each tortilla in half over filling to form a semicircle.

3 Heat skillet over medium heat. Add quesadillas 2 or 3 at a time; cook, turning once, until surface is lightly browned and cheese is melted, 3 to 4 minutes per side. Transfer quesadillas to a cutting board. Repeat with remaining ingredients. Cut quesadillas into 4 wedges.

Atkins Tip: Macadamia nut oil, available in health and specialty food stores, is rich in health-promoting omega-3 fatty acids. Whether cooked or not, it lends foods a wonderful macadamia-nut flavor and aroma.

Pepper Jack Quesadillas

VIETNAMESE STIR-FRIED SHRIMP

 PER SERVING **Net Carbs: 4.5 grams;** Carbohydrates: 5.5 grams; Fiber: 1 gram; Protein: 16.5 grams; Fat: 8.5 grams; Calories: 163
Makes 6 servings; Prep time: 30 minutes; Cook time: 7 minutes

This aromatic dish comes together quickly, so have all of the ingredients prepared before you start cooking. The traditional presentation in lettuce cups is a visually appealing, low-carb method that can be used for other dishes as well.

3 tablespoons vegetable oil

2 serrano chiles or jalapeños, seeded and minced

2 teaspoons grated fresh ginger

6 cloves garlic, minced (1 tablespoon)

1 pound small or medium shrimp, peeled and deveined

¼ teaspoon salt

1 medium tomato, seeded and chopped (1 cup)

2 tablespoons fish sauce

3 tablespoons fresh lime juice

6 scallions, white and light-green parts only, thinly sliced on the bias (6 tablespoons)

½ cup thinly sliced fresh mint leaves

½ cup fresh cilantro leaves

6 Boston lettuce leaves, rinsed and dried

¼ cup peanuts, toasted and coarsely chopped

1 Heat oil in a wok or large skillet over high heat. Add chiles, ginger, and garlic; cook, stirring, 30 seconds. Add shrimp and salt; stir until shrimp are just pink, 2 to 3 minutes. Add tomato; cook until just heated through, about 1 minute. Stir in fish sauce, lime juice, and scallions; cook 1 minute.

2 Remove skillet from heat. Stir in mint and cilantro. Arrange lettuce leaves on a platter or on 6 individual plates. Spoon shrimp mixture over leaves. Sprinkle with peanuts. Serve immediately.

Atkins Tip: Salty, earthy fish sauce (nuoc nam or nam pla), a staple of Vietnamese cooking, adds incomparable depth of flavor. It is now available in most grocery stores in the Asian foods section, but if you can't find it, simply season the finished dish with soy sauce or more salt to taste.

TUNA TARTARE

 PER SERVING **Net Carbs: 1 gram;** Carbohydrates: 1 gram; Fiber: 0 grams; Protein: 27 grams; Fat: 10 grams; Calories: 210
Makes 6 servings; Prep time: 20 minutes

Sushi lovers will adore this luxurious first course. Always buy the freshest tuna from a reputable store the day you plan to use it. Mix it with the other ingredients just before serving.

1½ pounds tuna, cut into ¼-inch dice

¼ cup chopped fresh cilantro

2 tablespoons fresh lime juice

2 tablespoons extra virgin olive oil

1 teaspoon grated fresh lime zest

1 teaspoon grated fresh orange zest

1 teaspoon finely chopped jalapeño

Salt and pepper

1 Combine tuna, cilantro, lime juice, olive oil, lime zest, orange zest, and jalapeño in a bowl; mix well to combine. Season to taste with salt and pepper.

2 Fill a lightly oiled ½-cup dry measure with the tuna mixture. Pack it slightly by tapping the cup on a table. Invert the cup measure over a first course plate. Repeat with the remaining tuna.

Atkins Tip: To help offset the potential risks associated with eating uncooked fish, you can freeze the tuna first—a practice employed by top sushi chefs. Freezing not only inhibits the growth of bacteria, it also makes it easier to cut the tuna into small pieces.

Vietnamese Stir-Fried Shrimp

SCALLOPS WRAPPED IN BACON

PER SERVING **Net Carbs: 3.5 grams;** Carbohydrates: 4.5 grams; Fiber: 1 gram; Protein: 5 grams; Fat: 10 grams; Calories: 140
Makes 12 (2-piece) servings; Prep time: 25 minutes; Cook time: 15 minutes

An updated version of rumaki (chicken livers wrapped in bacon), these scallops get
an Asian accent from the ginger and soy. Assemble these early in the day, but wait
until 10 minutes before cooking to drizzle with the marinade.

24 bay scallops (about 5 ounces)

12 strips bacon, cut across in half

1 (8-ounce) can sliced water chestnuts, drained

¼ cup reduced-sodium soy sauce

½ teaspoon granular sugar substitute

½ teaspoon ground ginger

1 Remove the tough connective strap from the side of
each scallop. Press a water chestnut slice together with
a scallop; bind together by wrapping a piece of bacon
around them and securing with a toothpick. Repeat
with remaining scallops, chestnuts, and bacon.

2 Combine soy sauce, sugar substitute, and ginger. Pour
over the wrapped scallops; marinate 10 minutes.

3 Heat the broiler. Place wrapped scallops on a broiler pan.
Broil, turning once, until bacon is crisp and scallops are
cooked but still moist, 5 to 6 minutes.

Shrimp and Scallop Ceviche

SHRIMP AND SCALLOP CEVICHE

 PER SERVING **Net Carbs: 5.5 grams;** Carbohydrates: 7.5 grams; Fiber: 2 grams; Protein: 22 grams; Fat: 5 grams; Calories: 163
Makes 8 (½-cup) servings; Prep time: 15 minutes; Cook time: 15 minutes, plus 1 hour chilling

Ceviche is a classic Chilean fish dish "cooked" or cured with an acid, such as lemon juice. Here, the shrimp and scallops are briefly poached before they're tossed with the robust citrus dressing. Prepare seafood and dressing a day ahead, but don't toss with the dressing more than an hour or two before serving.

1 pound peeled and deveined large shrimp

1 pound bay scallops

1 small avocado, pitted, peeled, and diced

1 jalapeño, seeded and finely chopped

1 small red onion, diced (¼ cup)

¼ cup diced red bell pepper

3 tablespoons chopped fresh cilantro

½ cup fresh orange juice

¼ cup fresh lime juice

½ teaspoon hot pepper sauce (such as Tabasco®)

1 teaspoon salt

1 Bring a large pot of lightly salted water to a boil. Add shrimp; cook until opaque and just heated through, 1 to 2 minutes. Use a mesh strainer to transfer to a bowl of ice water. Return the cooking water to a boil. Add scallops; cook until opaque and just heated through, 1 to 2 minutes; transfer to the ice water bowl.

2 Combine avocado, jalapeño, onion, bell pepper, cilantro, orange juice, lime juice, hot pepper sauce, and salt in a large bowl. Drain seafood well; toss with avocado mixture.

3 Cover and chill for 1 to 2 hours; stir every 15 minutes.

Atkins Tip: When purchasing scallops, take a sniff: they should smell fresh, with no trace of ammonia. Scallops may be tinged with pink or yellow (from the algae they consume). Avoid snow-white scallops, a telltale sign that they have been soaked to pump up their volume. Before preparing, rinse scallops briefly in cold water and pat dry.

CRAB COCKTAIL

 PER SERVING **Net Carbs: 3.5 grams;** Carbohydrates: 4.5 grams; Fiber: 1 gram; Protein: 24 grams; Fat: 9.5 grams; Calories: 204
Makes 8 servings; Prep time: 15 minutes

This luxurious dish looks spectacular served in individual goblets or glass bowls with one or two frisée (curly endive) leaves as garnish. Prepare ahead, but to preserve the texture of the crab, wait until just before serving to toss with the dressing.

1 cup finely diced yellow bell pepper

1 cup very thinly sliced yellow onion

½ cup fresh lime juice

⅓ cup mayonnaise

1 tablespoon finely chopped fresh parsley

1 teaspoon salt (or more to taste)

2 pounds fresh refrigerated lump crabmeat, picked over

Combine all ingredients except crab in a medium bowl. Just before serving, gently fold in crab to coat, keeping the chunks intact.

Atkins Tip: Although the Net Carbs are too high to make this an Induction appetizer, the ingredients are fine. If you stay within your daily carb limits, you may enjoy this first course.

TANDOORI CHICKEN WINGS

PER SERVING **Net Carbs: 2.5 grams;** Carbohydrates: 3.5 grams; Fiber: 1 gram; Protein: 38 grams; Fat: 22 grams; Calories: 365
Makes 8 servings; Prep time: 10 minutes, plus 4 hours marinating; Cook time: 30 minutes

Bake these aromatic wings (shown on page 40) in the morning, then pop them back in the oven to rewarm when guests arrive. To make cleanup easier, line the baking sheet with foil. While these are not quite as messy to eat as most chicken wings, be sure to have plenty of napkins on hand when you serve them.

¾ cup plain whole-milk yogurt

3 tablespoons fresh lemon juice

1 tablespoon grated, peeled fresh ginger

4 garlic cloves, minced (2 teaspoons)

1 tablespoon paprika

1 teaspoon ground cumin

1 teaspoon ground coriander

½ teaspoon ground cardamom

3 pounds chicken wings, tips removed and split at the joint

1½ teaspoons salt

1 Combine yogurt, lemon juice, ginger, garlic, paprika, cumin, coriander, and cardamom in a large bowl; mix well. Add chicken wings and toss well to coat. Cover with plastic wrap. Refrigerate 4 to 24 hours.

2 Heat oven to 500°F. Lightly oil a wire rack and set it on a rimmed baking sheet. Remove wings from the marinade and shake off excess. Place them at least ½-inch apart on the rack and sprinkle with salt. Roast until wings are browned and cooked through, about 30 minutes.

SPICY LAMB AND MUSHROOM BROCHETTES

PER SERVING **Net Carbs: 1.5 grams;** Carbohydrates: 2.5 grams; Fiber: 1 gram; Protein: 19 grams; Fat: 13.5 grams
Calories: 207 Makes 8 (2-skewer) servings; Prep time: 30 minutes, plus 8 hours marinating; Cook time: 7 minutes

These big-flavored brochettes make for easy eating at cocktail parties because they're served on skewers. If you use bamboo skewers, be sure to soak them in water for 30 minutes so they don't scorch when you cook the meat.

5 tablespoons extra virgin olive oil, divided

¼ cup chopped fresh parsley

6 garlic cloves, minced (1 tablespoon)

2 teaspoons dried oregano

2 teaspoons dried mint

2 teaspoons paprika

½ teaspoon cayenne pepper

¼ teaspoon saffron threads, lightly crushed

¼ teaspoon ground cinnamon

1½ pounds boneless leg of lamb, trimmed and cut into 32 (¾-inch) cubes

16 small white mushrooms

1 teaspoon salt

¼ teaspoon pepper

16 bamboo skewers, soaked in water 30 minutes

1 Combine 4 tablespoons of the oil, parsley, garlic, oregano, mint, paprika, cayenne pepper, saffron, and cinnamon in a large bowl; mix well to combine. Add lamb and stir until well coated. Transfer lamb to a resealable plastic bag. Refrigerate at least 8 and up to 24 hours.

2 Heat the broiler. Toss mushrooms with the remaining 1 tablespoon oil in a bowl. Thread a mushroom between two pieces of lamb on each skewer. Place skewers in a single layer on a broiler pan. Broil 4 inches from heat until lamb and mushrooms are browned and cooked through, 6 to 7 minutes. Serve immediately or at room temperature.

RED PEPPER PANCAKES WITH SMOKED SALMON

PER SERVING **Net Carbs: 3 grams;** Carbohydrates: 3.5 grams; Fiber: 0.5 gram; Protein: 4.5 grams; Fat: 9.5 grams; Calories: 127

3 4   Makes 12 (3-piece) servings; Prep time: 15 minutes; Cook time: 20 minutes

Make these mildly spicy pancakes, seasoned with bell pepper and cilantro, a few hours in advance and rewarm them in the oven on low heat. To make tiny canapés, form each pancake using only one teaspoon of batter.

2 eggs, separated

½ cup Atkins Quick Quisine™ Bake Mix

2 tablespoons cornmeal

¼ teaspoon salt

Pinch of cayenne pepper

⅔ cup heavy cream

½ cup diced red pepper

2 tablespoons chopped fresh cilantro

1 tablespoon unsalted butter, melted

½ cup sour cream

6 ounces smoked salmon, cut into 36 thin strips

1 Whisk egg yolks, bake mix, cornmeal, salt, cayenne, and cream in a medium bowl until smooth. Beat egg whites in a medium mixing bowl with an electric mixer at high speed until stiff peaks form. Gently fold egg whites into batter. Mix in red pepper and cilantro.

2 Heat a large nonstick skillet over medium-high heat; brush with butter. For each pancake, use 1 tablespoon batter and spread with the back of a spoon. Make four pancakes at a time. Cook pancakes until bubbles appear on surface, about 1 minute; flip and cook about 30 seconds more. Transfer to a wire rack. Repeat with remaining batter.

3 Top each pancake with a small dollop of sour cream and a salmon strip.

Red Pepper Pancakes with Smoked Salmon

SMOKED TROUT MOUSSE IN CUCUMBER CUPS

 PER SERVING **Net Carbs: 1.5 grams;** Carbohydrates: 2 grams; Fiber: 0.5 gram; Protein: 6.5 grams; Fat: 6 grams; Calories: 87
Makes 12 (4-piece) servings; Prep time: 40 minutes; Cook time: 7 minutes, plus 50 minutes chilling

You can prepare the mousse and cut the cucumbers for this elegant appetizer (shown on page 40) a day in advance, but wait to assemble it until just before serving. A small measuring spoon, such as ¼ teaspoon, is the perfect utensil for scooping out the cucumbers.

3 slices bacon

1 teaspoon unflavored gelatin

¼ cup cold water

¼ cup boiling water

8 ounces smoked trout, skinned and flaked

3 tablespoons chopped fresh chives, divided

1 tablespoon grated onion

2 teaspoons fresh lemon juice

1 teaspoon Worcestershire sauce

½ teaspoon salt

¼ teaspoon hot pepper sauce (such as Tabasco®)

½ cup heavy cream

3 cucumbers, cut across in 48 ½-inch slices (see Tip)

1 Cook bacon, drain on paper towels, and cool. Crumble into small pieces.

2 Sprinkle gelatin over cold water in a small bowl. Let stand until dissolved, about 2 minutes. Pour boiling water over gelatin; stir to combine. Chill until it begins to set, about 30 minutes.

3 Combine trout, 2 tablespoons chives, onion, lemon juice, Worcestershire sauce, salt, and hot pepper sauce in a bowl; mix well. Stir in gelatin mixture.

4 Beat cream with an electric mixer at high speed until stiff peaks form. Gently fold trout mixture into cream; chill until slightly set, about 20 minutes. Gently stir.

5 Spoon out the middle of each cucumber round, leaving a ⅛-inch border around edges and bottom. Spoon about 2 teaspoons mousse into each round. Garnish with bacon and remaining tablespoon chives.

Atkins Tip: When using cucumbers as a "cup," you can leave them unpeeled, peel them entirely, or make a decorative edging by peeling alternating strips before slicing. For an elegant touch, try garnishing with a 1-inch piece of chive, instead of chopped chives.

WALNUT MEATBALLS

 PER SERVING **Net Carbs: 1 gram;** Carbohydrates: 2 grams; Fiber: 1 gram; Protein: 16 grams; Fat: 18 grams; Calories: 233
Makes 6 (3-piece) servings; Prep time: 10 minutes; Cook time: 15 minutes

These meatballs may be made up to one month in advance. Freeze the uncooked meatballs on a tray and store them in a heavy-duty freezer bag. Thaw overnight in the refrigerator before baking.

1 pound ground beef (85% lean)

3 tablespoons sour cream

1 tablespoon diced onion

½ cup finely chopped walnuts

2 cloves garlic, minced (1 teaspoon)

1½ teaspoons salt

Heat oven to 400°F. Mix beef, sour cream, onion, walnuts, garlic, and salt in a medium bowl. Form into 24 small meatballs; place on a baking sheet. Bake until browned, about 15 minutes.

Prosciutto-Wrapped Asparagus

PROSCIUTTO-WRAPPED ASPARAGUS

PER SERVING **Net Carbs: 1 gram;** Carbohydrates: 2.5 grams; Fiber: 1.5 grams; Protein: 7 grams; Fat: 5 grams; Calories: 83
Makes 8 (3-spear) servings; Prep time: 15 minutes; Cook time: 15 minutes

Cook and wrap the asparagus early in the day, but don't dress it until just before
serving. To distribute the dressing evenly over the asparagus, use a pastry brush,
or gently toss the drizzled, wrapped spears by rolling them over each other with
your fingertips.

24 asparagus spears, about 1½ pounds, trimmed

12 thin slices prosciutto di Parma (6 ounces), halved
   lengthwise

1½ tablespoons extra virgin olive oil

2 teaspoons grated lemon zest

1 teaspoon fresh lemon juice

¼ teaspoon salt

Pinch pepper

1 Bring a large pot of lightly salted water to a boil. Add
asparagus and cook until crisp-tender, 2 to 3 minutes.
Drain and transfer to a bowl filled with ice water, cool
about 2 minutes, then pat dry.

2 Wrap each asparagus spear with one piece of prosciutto.
Place lengthwise on a serving tray.

3 Combine oil, zest, lemon juice, salt, and pepper in a
bowl; mix well. Use a pastry brush to coat wrapped
spears with dressing. Serve immediately.

VERDEMOLE

 PER SERVING **Net Carbs: 1 gram**; Carbohydrates: 2 grams; Fiber: 1 gram; Protein: 1 gram; Fat: 1 gram; Calories: 17
Makes 12 servings; Prep time: 20 minutes; Cook time: 10 minutes, plus 30 minutes chilling

This twist on that south-of-the-border favorite, guacamole, marries asparagus and broccoli to yield a fresh, flavorful spread. Serve it with low-carb tortilla chips.

1 pound asparagus, trimmed

2 cups broccoli florets

1 serrano chile, seeded and chopped, or 2 jalapeño peppers, seeded and chopped (1 tablespoon)

½ cup coarsely chopped fresh cilantro

3 tablespoons sour cream

⅛ teaspoon salt

¼ teaspoon ground cumin

⅛ teaspoon pepper

2 tablespoons fresh lime juice

1 Bring a large pot of salted water to a boil. Add asparagus and broccoli, return to a boil, and cook until tender, 5 to 7 minutes. Drain. Place vegetables in a food processor with serrano or jalapeños and cilantro. Pulse to combine, scraping down the sides; repeat until finely chopped.

2 Add sour cream, salt, cumin, pepper, and lime juice; pulse for 30 seconds to combine. Transfer to a serving bowl. Cover and chill for 30 minutes before serving. This recipe can be prepared up to 3 days ahead of time and stored, refrigerated, in an airtight container.

Atkins Tip: It's best to wear rubber gloves when working with hot chiles to prevent irritation.

Verdemole

SWEET AND SPICY NUTS

 PER SERVING **Net Carbs: 2 grams;** Carbohydrates: 5 grams; Fiber: 3 grams; Protein: 4 grams; Fat: 17.5 grams; Calories: 182
Makes 8 (¼-cup) servings; Prep time: 10 minutes; Cook time: 1 hour

These flavorful nuts freeze beautifully, and are well worth keeping on hand for
unexpected guests. They also make a lovely hostess gift during the holiday season;
present them in a glass jar tied with a festive ribbon.

1 egg white

1 tablespoon water

3 packets sugar substitute

½ teaspoon salt

½ teaspoon pepper

½ teaspoon ground cumin

½ teaspoon ground cinnamon

¼ teaspoon cayenne pepper

2 cups mixed nuts (pecans, almonds, macadamias,
cashews, walnuts)

1 Heat oven to 275°F. Line a baking sheet with foil; spray
with cooking spray.

2 Mix egg white, water, sugar substitute, salt, pepper,
cumin, cinnamon, and cayenne in a large bowl. Add
nuts; mix until evenly coated.

3 Spread nuts in a single layer on prepared baking sheet.
Bake until golden brown, 50 minutes to 1 hour.

LEMON-FENNEL BISCOTTI

 PER SERVING **Net Carbs: 1 gram;** Carbohydrates: 3 grams; Fiber: 2 grams; Protein: 5.5 grams; Fat: 3 grams; Calories: 60
Makes 24 servings; Prep time: 25 minutes; Cook time: 50 minutes

Serve these savory biscotti with soups, or use them like crackers for dips, soft
cheeses, or pâtés. Like traditional (high-carb) biscotti, these are dry enough to with-
stand dunking without falling apart. Try them with warm Bagna Cauda (page 42),
Chorizo Cheese Bake (page 45), or Sesame-Tofu Dip (page 60).

2 cups Atkins Quick Quisine™ Bake Mix, plus more for
working dough

1½ teaspoons baking powder

½ teaspoon pepper

2 teaspoons fennel seeds

½ teaspoon salt

3 large eggs

5 tablespoons unsalted butter, melted and cooled

1 tablespoon grated lemon zest

1 Heat oven to 375°F. Whisk bake mix, baking powder,
pepper, fennel seeds, and salt in a medium bowl. Whisk
together eggs, butter, and zest in a small bowl. Stir
wet ingredients into dry ingredients until they form a
soft dough.

2 Gather the dough together with your hands and
place it on a surface lightly dusted with bake mix.
Knead gently for a few seconds to form a smooth ball.
Press dough into a sausage shape, about 12 inches
long. (The dough is very tender, so you may find it
easier to squeeze and pull it than to roll it.) Transfer
dough to a baking sheet. Press down on the dough to
flatten it to about 3½ inches wide. Bake until slightly
risen and dry looking, about 25 minutes.

3 Remove from oven. When just cool enough to handle,
cut diagonally into 24 slices no more than ½-inch thick.
Return slices to baking sheet and bake 10 minutes. Turn
over with a spatula. Return to oven and bake until dried
and very crisp, 5 to 10 minutes more.

SESAME-CRUSTED TUNA OVER ASIAN GREENS

 PER SERVING **Net Carbs: 1.5 grams;** Carbohydrates: 2.5 grams; Fiber: 1 gram; Protein: 27 grams; Fat: 12.5 grams; Calories: 235
Makes 6 servings; Prep time: 15 minutes; Cook time: 6 minutes

*Serve top-quality tuna red in the center—rare—for maximum tenderness and flavor.
To accommodate guests who prefer their fish more well-done, either return a few
slices to the skillet or cook one of the fillets longer than the other.*

1 tablespoon unseasoned rice vinegar

1 tablespoon fresh lemon juice

1 tablespoon soy sauce

½ teaspoon granulated sugar substitute

3 tablespoons canola oil, divided

2 teaspoons dark sesame oil

Salt and pepper

2 (12-ounce) tuna steaks, about 1 inch thick

¼ cup sesame seeds

3 cups mixed Asian greens, such as mizuna and tatsoi
or mixed baby greens

1 Combine the vinegar, lemon juice, soy sauce, and sugar
substitute in a small bowl. Whisk in 1 tablespoon canola
oil and sesame oil. Season with salt and pepper to taste.

2 Season tuna with salt and pepper. Place sesame seeds
on a large plate. Press all sides of tuna steaks into seeds
to coat.

3 Heat remaining 2 tablespoons canola oil in a large
nonstick skillet over medium-high heat. Add tuna; cook
until fish is browned but still pink in the center, about 3
minutes per side. Transfer tuna to a cutting board.

4 Toss greens with ⅓ cup dressing. Place a small mound
of greens on each of 6 first course plates. Cut tuna
into 18 slices, each ¼-inch thick. Place three slices on
each plate. Drizzle remaining dressing over the tuna
and serve.

STUFFED PROSCIUTTO PILLOWS

 PER SERVING **Net Carbs: 2 grams;** Carbohydrates: 3.5 grams; Fiber: 1.5 grams; Protein: 10 grams; Fat: 19.5 grams; Calories: 228
Makes 6 (2-piece) servings; Prep time: 15 minutes; Cook time: 5 minutes

*This starter is best served warm over mixed greens (as in this recipe) or alone as
finger food.*

PROSCIUTTO PILLOWS:
12 thin slices prosciutto di Parma (6 ounces)

6 ounces goat cheese, cut into 12 slices

3 tablespoons drained and chopped sun-dried
tomatoes in oil, divided

SALAD:
3 tablespoons extra virgin olive oil

1½ tablespoons balsamic vinegar

1½ tablespoons prepared pesto sauce

¼ teaspoon salt

¼ teaspoon pepper

6 cups mixed salad greens

1 FOR PROSCIUTTO PILLOWS: Place one slice prosciutto
on a work surface. Top with a slice of goat cheese,
1 inch from short end. Top with ¾ teaspoon sun-dried
tomatoes. Fold end of prosciutto over cheese and roll
up, folding in edges to enclose cheese. Repeat with
remaining prosciutto, cheese, and tomatoes. (May
be made up to this point one day in advance. Wrap
tightly and refrigerate. Bring to room temperature
before proceeding.)

2 Heat oven to 300°F. Arrange pillows on a shallow
baking pan, seam side down; cover with foil. Bake just
until warm, 5 minutes.

3 FOR SALAD: Whisk oil, vinegar, pesto, salt, and pepper
in a large bowl. Add greens; toss.

4 To serve, divide greens among 6 plates and top with
2 pillows.

Sesame-Crusted Tuna Over Asian Greens

SHORT-CUT PIGS IN A BLANKET

PER SERVING **Net Carbs: 4 grams**; Carbohydrates: 8 grams; Fiber: 4 grams; Protein: 11.5 grams; Fat: 16.5 grams; Calories: 208
Makes 8 (3-piece) servings; Prep time: 15 minutes; Cook time: 10 minutes

This kitschy 1950s favorite never fails to make guests smile. Our revised recipe trims
the carbs by using low-carb white bread instead of pie dough.

6 slices low-carb white bread

2 tablespoons butter, melted

24 miniature cocktail franks

¼ cup Dijon mustard

1 Heat oven to 350°F. Trim crusts from bread slices; brush both sides lightly with melted butter. Cut each slice into four strips. Roll one frank into each strip, and secure with a toothpick.

2 Arrange franks on a baking sheet. Bake until wrapping is golden brown, 14 to 16 minutes. Serve hot with mustard for dipping.

ROAST BEEF WITH HORSERADISH CREAM

 PER SERVING **Net Carbs: 2.5 grams;** Carbohydrates: 4.5 grams; Fiber: 2 grams; Protein: 9.5 grams; Fat: 15 grams; Calories: 195
Makes 20 (2-piece) servings; Prep time: 35 minutes, plus 2 to 24 hours marinating; Cook time: 30 minutes

You can prepare this elegant hors d'oeuvre with ease by doing a little each night the week before the party. Each numbered step below can be completed on successive days. Do the final assembly just before serving.

BEEF:

3 tablespoons Dijon mustard

6 garlic cloves, minced (1 tablespoon)

1 tablespoon chopped fresh rosemary

½ teaspoon pepper

¼ cup olive oil

1½ pounds beef tenderloin

1 teaspoon salt

TOAST POINTS:

10 slices low-carb rye bread, crusts removed

HORSERADISH CREAM:

½ cup sour cream

¼ cup mayonnaise

2 tablespoons prepared horseradish, squeezed dry

2 tablespoons chopped fresh chives

Salt and pepper

Additional chopped fresh chives, for garnish

1 FOR BEEF: Combine mustard, garlic, rosemary, and pepper in a bowl. Whisk in oil until a paste forms. Rub over beef. Transfer beef to a resealable plastic bag. Refrigerate at least 2 and up to 24 hours.

2 Heat oven to 450°F. Wipe excess marinade from beef and season with salt. Place on a wire rack on a rimmed baking sheet. Roast until an instant-read thermometer inserted into the center registers 135°F for medium rare, about 30 minutes. Let stand 10 minutes before cutting into very thin slices.

3 FOR TOAST POINTS: Reduce the oven temperature to 375°F. Cut each slice of bread in an X to make 4 bread triangles. Arrange triangles in a single layer on a large baking sheet. Bake until toasted and crisp, 8 to 10 minutes. Cool. (Toast points may be stored at room temperature in an airtight plastic bag for several days and recrisped in the oven, as needed.)

4 FOR HORSERADISH CREAM: Combine sour cream, mayonnaise, horseradish, and chives in a bowl. Mix well. Season with salt and pepper to taste.

5 Arrange toast points on a work surface. Top each with a folded slice of beef. Top each slice of beef with a rounded ¼ teaspoon of horseradish cream. Sprinkle with chopped chives to garnish.

SESAME-TOFU DIP

 PER SERVING **Net Carbs: 1 gram;** Carbohydrates: 1 gram; Fiber: 0 grams; Protein: 2.5 grams; Fat: 6 grams; Calories: 69
Makes 12 servings; Prep time: 10 minutes

This flavorful dip, which tastes much like hummus, also makes a satisfying sauce for grilled meats, poultry, fish, and vegetables. The dip may be made a day or two in advance, and will thicken as it stands. To thin, simply whisk in a little water.

16 ounces silken tofu

3 tablespoons fresh lemon juice

1 teaspoon salt

1 teaspoon sesame oil

¼ cup canola oil

Blend tofu, lemon juice, salt and sesame oil in a food processor until smooth. With processor on, slowly add canola oil in a steady stream until it is incorporated. (Mixture should have the consistency of thick mayonnaise.)

Roast Beef with Horseradish Cream

ENTRÉES

The focus of the entire meal—the king of the table—is the entrée. Whether you choose beef, lamb, pork, veal, poultry, or fish, a spectacular main dish makes any celebration unforgettable.

Roast Salmon with Fennel and Herbs, page 87

STANDING RIB ROAST WITH ONIONS AND LEEKS

 PER SERVING **Net Carbs: 6 grams;** Carbohydrates: 7 grams; Fiber: 1 gram; Protein: 44 grams; Fat: 31 grams; Calories: 490
Makes 8 servings; Prep time: 15 minutes; Cook time: 2 hours

The less you do to this cut of meat, the better—it is quite glorious simply seasoned and roasted. Meat drippings turn the leeks and onions into an indulgent condiment.

3 leeks, white and light-green parts only

2 medium onions, sliced (1½ cups)

2 teaspoons ground coriander

1 teaspoon dried basil

1 teaspoon dried oregano

1 teaspoon onion powder

1½ teaspoons salt

½ teaspoon pepper

1 (6½- to 7-pound) standing rib roast (3 ribs), trimmed

1 Heat oven to 400°F. Cut the leeks in half lengthwise, then widthwise into 1-inch pieces. Rinse well to remove sand. Place in a bowl with onions.

2 Combine coriander, basil, oregano, onion powder, salt, and pepper in a small bowl; mix well. Rub mixture over rib roast and place in a roasting pan.

3 Roast the beef 45 minutes. Add leeks and onions to pan. Return to oven and roast, stirring vegetables occasionally, until an instant-read thermometer inserted into the center of beef registers 135°F for medium-rare, about 70 to 75 minutes longer.

PRIME RIB ROAST BEEF WITH RED WINE SAUCE

 PER SERVING **Net Carbs: 2 grams;** Carbohydrates: 3 grams; Fiber: 1 gram; Protein: 32 grams; Fat: 25 grams; Calories: 390
Makes 8 servings; Prep time: 20 minutes; Cook time: 1 hour 30 minutes, plus 10 minutes resting

Ask your butcher to remove the bones from a three-rib standing rib roast for this special-occasion dish.

2 tablespoons pepper

1 tablespoon paprika

1 tablespoon garlic powder

2 teaspoons salt

1 (4½- to 5-pound) boneless standing rib roast beef, trimmed and tied

2 carrots, chopped

2 celery stalks, chopped (1 cup)

2 medium onions, chopped (1½ cups)

3 sprigs fresh thyme

1 sprig fresh rosemary

1 bay leaf

1 (14½-ounce) can lower sodium beef broth

1¼ cups red wine

2 tablespoons unsalted butter

1 Heat oven to 450°F. Lightly oil a roasting pan.

2 Combine pepper, paprika, garlic powder, and salt in a small bowl; mix well. Rub mixture over roast and set in roasting pan. Add carrots, celery, onions, thyme, rosemary, and bay leaf to pan.

3 Roast the beef 25 minutes. Reduce temperature to 375°F; pour beef broth into the pan. Cook until an instant-read thermometer inserted into the center of beef registers 135°F for medium-rare, 55 to 60 minutes longer. Transfer beef to a cutting board and tent loosely with foil. Let stand 10 minutes before slicing.

4 Strain the pan juices, vegetables, and herbs through a wire mesh sieve into a medium saucepan. Skim off excess fat. Add wine. Bring the mixture to a boil over high heat; cook to reduce slightly, 5 minutes. Remove from heat and whisk in butter until melted.

ZINFANDEL POT AU FEU

PER SERVING **Net Carbs: 13 grams;** Carbohydrates: 15 grams; Fiber: 2 grams; Protein: 69 grams; Fat: 35 grams; Calories: 710

3 4 Makes 8 servings; Prep time: 25 minutes; Cook time: 4 hours

This very elegant dish is served in a light but intensely flavorful broth. The dish looks especially nice if you can find baby carrots with a bit of the greens left on.

6 pounds beef short ribs (about 16 ribs)

1 teaspoon salt

½ teaspoon pepper

2 (14½-ounce) cans lower sodium beef broth

2½ cups red zinfandel wine

1 medium onion, quartered

2 sprigs fresh thyme

2 tablespoons tomato paste

24 pearl onions, peeled

16 garlic cloves

16 baby carrots, peeled

4 leeks, white and light-green part only, trimmed and split lengthwise and widthwise, if needed

2 celery stalks, halved lengthwise and cut across in 2-inch pieces

1 Heat a large pot over medium-high heat. Season ribs with salt and pepper. Working in batches, brown ribs on all sides, turning frequently, 5 to 6 minutes. Remove from pot and pour off excess fat. Return pot to the heat and add broth, wine, onion, thyme, and tomato paste. Bring to a boil and scrape up any browned bits from the bottom of the pot. Add ribs, reduce heat to medium-low, and cover and simmer until meat is very tender, about 3 hours.

2 Transfer ribs to a bowl. Discard quartered onion and thyme; skim fat from surface of broth. Add pearl onions, garlic, carrots, leeks, and celery to the pot. Bring to a simmer; cover and cook until vegetables are tender, about 30 minutes.

3 Meanwhile, remove meat from the bones and trim excess fat. Return meat to pot and cook until heated through, about 10 minutes.

4 To serve, divide meat among 8 large, shallow soup plates. Surround with equal amounts of onion, garlic, carrots, leek, and celery. Fill plates with broth.

Zinfandel Pot au Feu

BACON-WRAPPED FILET MIGNON

PER SERVING **Net Carbs: 3 grams;** Carbohydrates: 3 grams; Fiber: 0 grams; Protein: 46 grams; Fat: 79 grams; Calories: 910

Makes 8 servings; Prep time: 15 minutes; Cook time: 24 minutes

These tender steaks are seared on the stove to give them a dark crust, then finished in the oven. You can brown the steaks and make the sauce early in the day, refrigerate, then bring them to room temperature and finish cooking just before serving.

8 (8-ounce) filet mignons (each about 1½ inches thick)

1 teaspoon salt

¼ teaspoon pepper

8 slices bacon

3 tablespoons unsalted butter, divided

1 medium shallot, finely chopped (¼ cup)

4 garlic cloves, minced (2 teaspoons)

1 cup heavy cream

½ teaspoon dried basil

2 ounces blue cheese, crumbled (½ cup)

1 Heat oven to 425°F. Season filets with salt and pepper. Wrap 1 slice of bacon around the sides of each filet and secure with a toothpick.

2 Melt 2 tablespoons of the butter in a 12-inch nonstick skillet over medium-high heat. Add filets to skillet and cook on all sides until browned, for a total of 5 to 6 minutes. Transfer to a rimmed baking sheet. Roast until an instant-read thermometer inserted in the center of each filet registers 135°F for medium-rare, 10 to 12 minutes, or to desired doneness. Remove toothpicks.

3 While filets cook, wipe out skillet and melt remaining tablespoon butter over medium heat. Add shallot and garlic; cook, stirring occasionally, until they begin to soften, 1 to 2 minutes. Increase heat to medium-high; add cream and basil. Bring to a boil and cook until reduced by half, 3 to 4 minutes. Add blue cheese; cook, stirring, until melted, about 1 minute. Serve over filets.

Atkins Tip: When searing meats (or any kind of food, for that matter), don't crowd the skillet; food given plenty of space browns more easily.

Bacon-Wrapped Filet Mignon

BEEF TENDERLOIN WITH DIJON HERB CRUST

 PER SERVING **Net Carbs: 2 grams;** Carbohydrates: 2 grams; Fiber: 0 grams; Protein: 78 grams; Fat: 36 grams; Calories: 670
Makes 8 servings; Prep time: 40 minutes, plus 8 hours marinating; Cook time: 45 minutes

The beef will cook more quickly and evenly if you let it stand at room temperature for 30 minutes before roasting. To ease cleanup, line the pan with foil.

¼ cup Dijon mustard

¼ cup chopped fresh parsley

2 tablespoons chopped fresh rosemary

2 teaspoons chopped fresh thyme

12 garlic cloves, minced (2 tablespoons)

1 medium shallot, finely chopped (2 tablespoons)

1½ teaspoons salt

½ teaspoon pepper

¼ cup olive oil

1 (5½-pound) whole beef tenderloin, trimmed and tied

1 Combine mustard, parsley, rosemary, thyme, garlic, shallot, salt, and pepper in a bowl; stir well. Stir in oil. Coat beef completely with mustard mixture. Set beef on a foil-lined baking sheet; cover loosely with foil. Refrigerate 8 hours or overnight.

2 Heat oven to 450°F. Remove beef from the refrigerator and bring to room temperature, about 30 minutes. Roast until an instant-read thermometer inserted in the thickest portion registers 135° for medium-rare, about 45 minutes.

CLASSIC BRISKET

 PER SERVING **Net Carbs: 6 grams;** Carbohydrates: 8.5 grams; Fiber: 2.5 grams; Protein: 40.5 grams; Fat: 60.5 grams; Calories: 757
Makes 8 servings; Prep time: 10 minutes; Cook time: 4 hours 10 minutes

As the brisket simmers on the stove for four hours, it fills the house with an enticing aroma. The dish takes very little work. It can be made weeks in advance and frozen, or days ahead and refrigerated.

2 tablespoons paprika

2 tablespoons dried oregano

1 teaspoon ground cumin

1½ teaspoons salt

½ teaspoon pepper

1 (4-pound) center-cut brisket, trimmed

2 celery stalks, chopped (1 cup)

1 medium onion, chopped (¾ cup)

1 cup water

1 (28-ounce) can crushed tomatoes with basil

1 Combine paprika, oregano, cumin, salt, and pepper in a bowl. Rub the spice blend over both sides of brisket.

2 Heat a Dutch oven over medium high heat. Add brisket and cook, turning once, until browned, about 8 minutes. Add celery and onion and cook 1 minute. Add water. Reduce heat to medium-low, cover, and simmer 3 hours.

3 Stir in tomatoes. Cook until brisket is tender, about 1 hour longer. Transfer brisket to a cutting board and let stand 10 minutes. Cut brisket across the grain into thin slices. Use a spatula to return sliced meat to Dutch oven. Simmer gently, uncovered, over medium heat until brisket is very tender and sauce has thickened a bit, about 1 hour longer.

Atkins Tip: Don't skip the step of slicing the meat and cooking it another hour. That's when the flavor of the sauce really permeates the meat and the brisket becomes incredibly tender. Cooking the dish uncovered helps to thicken the sauce.

BEEF FILET WITH PANCETTA AND SPINACH

 PER SERVING **Net Carbs: 1 gram;** Carbohydrates: 2 grams; Fiber: 1 gram; Protein: 46 grams; Fat: 24 grams; Calories: 410
Makes 10 servings; Prep time: 35 minutes; Cook time: 50 minutes, plus 10 minutes resting

This attractive tenderloin makes an impressive centerpiece for a gathering.

1 tablespoon olive oil

15 cloves garlic, minced (2½ tablespoons)

¼ pound thinly sliced pancetta, cut into strips

8 cups lightly packed fresh baby spinach leaves

Salt and pepper

1 (4-pound) beef tenderloin, trimmed of all excess fat

¼ pound sliced provolone cheese

3 tablespoons pine nuts, toasted

6 to 8 (12-inch) lengths kitchen string

1 Heat oven to 400°F. Heat oil in a large skillet over medium-high heat. Add garlic and stir until softened, 1 minute. Add pancetta; cook until it begins to brown. Add spinach; cook until leaves are wilted and moisture has evaporated, about 5 minutes. Season with salt and pepper to taste.

2 Using a very sharp knife cut through the tenderloin lengthwise about three-quarters of the way and open it up like a book. Cover with plastic wrap. Use the bottom of a heavy skillet to gently pound beef just enough to flatten it. Remove plastic wrap. Season both sides of meat with salt and pepper.

3 Lay a row of provolone slices evenly down beef, leaving a 1-inch border around the edges so filling doesn't ooze out during cooking. Spoon spinach mixture over cheese. Starting with a long edge, roll beef to encase the filling. Tie the roll every few inches with string to keep it even and compact.

4 Cook roll on a pan fitted with a rack until an instant-read thermometer inserted into the center of the beef registers 135°F for medium-rare, about 50 minutes.

5 Let roll rest 10 minutes. Remove string, slice, and serve.

CHIPOTLE BRAISED SHORT RIBS

 PER SERVING **Net Carbs: 9 grams;** Carbohydrates: 12.5 grams; Fiber: 3.5 grams; Protein: 89 grams; Fat: 52 grams; Calories: 880
Makes 6 servings; Prep time: 15 minutes; Cook time: 3 hours 25 minutes

Unsweetened chocolate lends many Mexican dishes depth of flavor. It is nothing like the chocolate we associate with candy. Chipotle powder is available in your supermarket's spice rack.

1 tablespoon olive oil

6 pounds beef short ribs

1½ teaspoons salt

¾ teaspoon pepper

12 cloves garlic, minced (2 tablespoons)

1 large onion, chopped (1 cup)

2 teaspoons ground chipotle powder

2 teaspoons ground cumin

1 teaspoon dried oregano

1 (28-ounce) can whole plum tomatoes, chopped

1 tablespoon fresh lime juice

1 ounce unsweetened chocolate, chopped

1 tablespoon granular sugar substitute

1 Heat oven to 350°F. Heat oil in a 12-inch skillet over medium-high heat. Season ribs with salt and pepper. Cook one-third of ribs in skillet, turning often, until well browned on all sides, 6 minutes. Transfer to a large roasting pan. Repeat with remaining ribs.

2 Add garlic and onion to skillet; cook 1 minute. Add chipotle, cumin, and oregano. Cook until fragrant, 30 seconds. Stir in tomatoes and their juice, lime juice, chocolate, and sugar substitute. Use a wooden spoon to scrape up any browned bits from bottom of skillet. Reduce the heat to medium-low, cover, and simmer 5 minutes.

4 Pour tomato mixture over ribs, spreading evenly with a spatula. Cover pan tightly with foil. Bake until ribs are very tender, 2½ to 3 hours.

PORK LOIN WITH FENNEL AND SAGE

PER SERVING **Net Carbs: 10 grams;** Carbohydrates: 14 grams; Fiber: 4 grams; Protein: 54 grams; Fat: 38 grams; Calories: 620
Makes 8 servings; Prep time: 18 minutes, plus 8 hours marinating; Cook time: 1 hour 35 minutes, plus 10 minutes resting

This dish is done largely ahead of time. Choose your favorite mushrooms to roast with the pork. Cremini and oyster mushrooms are flavorful and retain their meaty texture.

4 teaspoons fennel seeds

1 tablespoon salt

2 teaspoons garlic powder

1 teaspoon ground sage

1 teaspoon dried oregano

1 teaspoon crushed red pepper flakes

½ teaspoon dry mustard powder

3 tablespoons olive oil, divided

1 (6-pound) bone-in center-cut pork loin roast

1½ pounds mushrooms, coarsely chopped

3 heads fennel, trimmed and thinly sliced

8 shallots, peeled and thinly sliced

1 Combine fennel seeds, salt, garlic powder, sage, oregano, red pepper flakes, and mustard in a small bowl; mix well. Set aside 2 teaspoons of the spice mixture. Stir 2 tablespoons of the oil into the remaining mixture to form a paste. Spread paste evenly over pork; cover and refrigerate 8 hours or overnight.

2 Heat oven to 450°F. Place remaining tablespoon oil in a large roasting pan. Place pan in oven until oil is hot, about 6 minutes. Place pork in pan and return pan to oven. Cook 15 minutes. Reduce oven temperature to 375°F; continue cooking another 30 minutes.

3 Combine mushrooms, fresh fennel, and shallots; sprinkle with reserved 2 teaspoons spice mixture, tossing gently to coat. Add vegetable mixture to roasting pan; continue cooking, stirring occasionally, until an instant-read thermometer inserted in the thickest portion of pork registers 145°F to 150°F for medium, about 50 minutes.

4 Let pork rest 10 minutes before carving. Serve with pan juices and vegetables.

Pork Loin with Fennel and Sage

PORK LOIN WITH GREEN HERB CRUST

 PER SERVING **Net Carbs: 2 grams;** Carbohydrates: 3 grams; Fiber: 1 gram; Protein: 46 grams; Fat: 33 grams; Calories: 500
Makes 8 servings; Prep time: 20 minutes; Cook time: 55 minutes, plus 10 minutes resting

The green herb crust not only imparts great flavor, it also makes the dish look very appetizing. Arrange a platter of overlapping slices when serving this hot or cold as part of a buffet.

½ cup chopped fresh parsley

⅓ cup chopped fresh basil

3 tablespoons chopped fresh oregano

2 teaspoons garlic powder

1 teaspoon ground cumin

2 teaspoons salt

¾ teaspoon pepper

1 (4-pound) boneless pork loin, trimmed and tied

2 tablespoons extra virgin olive oil

1 medium onion, sliced (1 cup)

4 garlic cloves, sliced

1 Heat oven to 450°F. Lightly oil a baking sheet.

2 Combine parsley, basil, oregano, garlic powder, cumin, salt, and pepper in a small bowl; mix well. Rub pork loin with oil. Press herb mixture all over pork to coat.

3 Arrange onion and garlic slices in a line down center of baking sheet and set pork directly on top.

4 Roast the pork 15 minutes. Reduce oven temperature to 375°F; roast until an instant-read thermometer inserted into center of pork registers 145°F to 150°F, 35 to 40 minutes longer. Let pork rest 10 minutes before slicing. Serve with onion and garlic.

MAPLE-MUSTARD GLAZED BAKED HAM

 PER SERVING **Net Carbs: 0.5 gram;** Carbohydrates: 0.5 gram; Fiber: 0 grams; Protein: 53.5 grams; Fat: 27 grams; Calories: 469
Makes 10 servings; Prep time: 15 minutes; Cook time: 1 hour 30 minutes

It only takes four ingredients and 15 minutes of prep time to make this special—and very tasty—entrée. To maximize tenderness, thinly slice the ham.

Maple-Mustard Glazed Baked Ham

1 (8-pound) fully cooked ham

8 whole cloves

⅓ cup sugar-free pancake syrup

3 tablespoons Dijon mustard

1 Heat oven to 325°F. Use a sharp knife to lightly score the entire surface of ham in a diamond pattern; insert cloves. Place ham on a rack in a shallow roasting pan.

2 Mix syrup and mustard in a small bowl until blended. Brush mixture over ham. Bake until an instant-read thermometer inserted deep into ham registers 140°F, 1½ to 2 hours. Baste ham occasionally with glaze during baking.

LECHON ASADO (CUBAN-STYLE ROAST PORK)

 PER SERVING **Net Carbs: 2 grams;** Carbohydrates: 2 grams; Fiber: 0 grams; Protein: 71 grams; Fat: 38 grams; Calories: 650
Makes 12 servings; Prep time: 30 minutes, plus 8 hours marinating; Cook time: 3 hours, plus 10 minutes resting

This Cuban holiday classic is traditionally made with a suckling pig. To make this special occasion dish more accessible—but equally delicious—we've substituted picnic shoulder. Long marination and slow cooking give this less expensive cut a wonderful flavor.

1 head garlic, separated into cloves and peeled

1 cup fresh lemon juice

½ cup fresh lime juice

½ cup packed fresh cilantro leaves

1 large onion, chopped (1 cup)

2 tablespoons grated orange zest

2 teaspoons dried oregano

1 tablespoon salt

1½ cups extra virgin olive oil

1 (6- to 7-pound) pork picnic shoulder, bone-in and skin on

1 Combine garlic, lemon juice, lime juice, cilantro, onion, zest, oregano, and salt in a blender. Process until puréed, about 2 minutes. Add oil; pulse to combine.

2 Pierce skin of pork all over with the tip of a sharp knife. Place pork in a large bowl, add garlic mixture, and turn several times to coat with marinade. Cover with plastic wrap. Refrigerate 8 to 24 hours, turning occasionally.

3 Heat oven to 500°F. Place pork, skin side up, in a roasting pan. Reduce oven temperature to 350°F. Roast, brushing occasionally with some marinade for the first hour, until skin is crisp and an instant-read thermometer inserted into thickest part of pork registers 145°F to 150°F, about 3 hours. Let rest 10 minutes before carving.

CRANBERRY-GINGER PORK

 PER SERVING **Net Carbs: 1 gram;** Carbohydrates: 2 grams; Fiber: 1 gram; Protein: 87 grams; Fat: 29 grams; Calories: 640
Makes 6 servings; Prep time: 5 minutes; Cook time: 8 to 10 hours

Slow cookers aren't just for saving time on weeknights. Start the roast in the morning, and by the time you're done with holiday preparations, the pork will be ready and waiting. This robust dish combines tart, sweet, smoky, and spicy flavors.

1 (4-pound) bone-in pork loin roast

1 cup fresh or frozen cranberries, coarsely chopped

¼ cup sugar-free pancake syrup

1 canned chipotle en adobo, chopped

2 teaspoons grated fresh ginger

½ teaspoon salt

¼ teaspoon pepper

Mix cranberries, syrup, chipotle, ginger, salt, and pepper in a slow cooker. Place roast on top and rub with mixture. Cover and cook on low 8 to 10 hours.

Atkins Tip: Canned chipotles en adobo are smoked jalapeño peppers in a spicy tomato-based sauce. They can be found in the ethnic food section of most supermarkets. You'll rarely need the whole can (even though it seems tiny) as chipotles are muy caliente. Freeze the extra in small portions in ice cube trays, then transfer to a freezer-proof plastic bag.

ORANGE-HERB PORK ROAST

PER SERVING **Net Carbs: 1 gram;** Carbohydrates: 1 gram; Fiber: 0 grams; Protein: 30 grams; Fat: 10 grams; Calories: 290
Makes 6 servings; Prep time: 25 minutes; Cook time: 1 hour 10 minutes

A savory rub of orange peel, sage, thyme, and garlic goes well with pork, but can also be used on chicken or turkey. Serve with sautéed green beans.

ORANGE-HERB PORK:

1 tablespoon chopped fresh sage, or 1 teaspoon dried

4 garlic cloves, minced (2 teaspoons)

2 teaspoons grated orange zest

1 teaspoon dried thyme

½ teaspoon salt

½ teaspoon pepper

2 pounds boneless pork loin, trimmed

1½ cups water, divided

BOURBON SAUCE:

1 cup lower sodium chicken broth

½ cup bourbon

½ cup heavy cream

1 FOR ORANGE-HERB PORK: Heat oven to 375°F. Coat a shallow roasting pan with cooking spray. Combine sage, garlic, zest, thyme, salt, and pepper on a cutting board. Mince with a sharp knife, then mash with the flat side of knife (or use a mini food processor) to make a paste. Rub paste over surface of pork.

2 Place pork fat-side down in roasting pan. Add 1 cup water to pan; roast 30 minutes. Turn pork over; add remaining ½ cup water to pan if dry. Roast until an instant-read thermometer inserted into center of pork registers 145°F to 150°F, 30 to 40 minutes longer. Transfer pork to cutting board; cover loosely with foil and let stand while making sauce.

3 FOR BOURBON SAUCE: Add chicken broth to pan. Bring to a boil over medium-high heat, scraping up any browned bits. Add bourbon and cream. Cook, stirring frequently, until sauce reduces to ¾ cup, or lightly coats the back of a spoon, about 10 minutes.

4 Cut roast into ¼-inch thick slices. Serve with sauce.

LEMON-SAGE PORK STEW

PER SERVING **Net Carbs: 6.5 grams;** Carbohydrates: 8.5 grams; Fiber: 2 grams; Protein: 62 grams; Fat: 26.5 grams; Calories: 534
Makes 8 servings; Prep time: 15 minutes; Cook time: 3 hours

Like most stews, this improves in flavor as it sits. Make up to three days in advance, refrigerate, and reheat before serving.

5 pounds pork shoulder, cut into 1½-inch pieces

Salt and pepper

4 tablespoons olive oil

4 tablespoons unsalted butter

6 garlic cloves, minced (1 tablespoon)

4 (14½ ounce) cans lower sodium beef broth

½ pound baby carrots

½ pound frozen or fresh pearl onions (2 cups)

2 celery stalks, cut into ½-inch pieces on the diagonal

¼ cup fresh sage, thinly sliced

3 tablespoons lemon zest

3 tablespoons fresh lemon juice

1 Season pork with salt and pepper. Heat oil and butter in a large heavy-bottomed pot set over high heat. Cook pork in batches, browning well on all sides, about 8 minutes. Add garlic and sauté until fragrant, about 30 seconds.

2 Return pork to pan. Add broth, turn heat down to low, and simmer covered until pork is fork-tender, about 2 hours. Add vegetables and cook until softened, about 20 minutes longer.

3 Transfer pork and vegetables to a platter. Increase heat to high and cook liquid until reduced by half, about 10 minutes. Return pork to pot and simmer just until heated through, about 10 minutes. Stir in sage, zest, and lemon juice and serve.

ROAST RACK OF LAMB

PER SERVING **Net Carbs: 2 grams;** Carbohydrates: 2 grams; Fiber: 0 grams; Protein: 41 grams; Fat: 15 grams; Calories: 310

Makes 6 servings; Prep time: 5 minutes; Cook time: 30 minutes, plus 10 minutes resting

Ask your butcher to "french" the rack of lamb—a technique that removes the fat and membrane that covers the rib bones, making them more attractive.

3 racks of lamb (18 bones, total), frenched

1 teaspoon salt

½ teaspoon pepper

1 tablespoon butter

2 tablespoons chopped fresh parsley

2 tablespoons chopped fresh mint

2 teaspoons chopped fresh rosemary leaves, plus sprigs for garnish

4 garlic cloves, minced (2 teaspoons)

4 tablespoons Dijon mustard

1 Heat oven to 400°F. Season lamb with salt and pepper. Melt butter in a large nonstick skillet set over medium-high heat. Sear lamb on both sides until golden, 5 to 6 minutes total.

2 Mix parsley, mint, rosemary, and garlic in a small bowl. When lamb is cool enough to handle, brush with mustard. Pat herb mixture onto mustard.

3 Place lamb in a roasting pan. Roast until an instant-read thermometer inserted in the thickest portion of the lamb registers 135°F for medium-rare, 20 to 25 minutes. Let rest 10 minutes. Slice between the bones to separate chops. Garnish with rosemary sprigs.

WINE-BRAISED LAMB SHANKS WITH TOMATOES

PER SERVING **Net Carbs: 5 grams;** Carbohydrates: 6 grams; Fiber: 1 gram; Protein: 42 grams; Fat: 35 grams; Calories: 540

Makes 6 servings; Prep time: 15 minutes; Cook time: 2 hours 18 minutes

Don't discard even a drop of the delicious sauce, if you have any left over—it can be frozen or refrigerated and used on grilled chicken or meat.

2 tablespoons olive oil

6 lamb shanks (7 to 7½ pounds)

1½ teaspoons salt, divided

¾ teaspoon pepper, divided

6 garlic cloves, minced (1 tablespoon)

1 celery stalk, chopped (⅓ cup)

1 teaspoon dried basil

1 teaspoon dried oregano

1 teaspoon fennel seeds

1 (28-ounce) can crushed tomatoes

1 cup red wine

1 Heat oven to 350°F. Heat oil in a large pot over medium-high heat. Sprinkle lamb with 1 teaspoon of the salt and ½ teaspoon of the pepper. Add lamb to the pot in 2 batches, if necessary; cook until brown on all sides, turning often, about 8 minutes per batch. Transfer lamb to a roasting pan large enough to fit the shanks in a single layer.

2 Return skillet to medium-high heat. Add garlic, celery, basil, oregano, and fennel seeds to skillet; cook until fragrant, 30 seconds. Add tomatoes and wine; cook, scraping up any browned bits from bottom of skillet. Bring to a simmer and cook 2 minutes. Pour sauce over lamb in roasting pan.

3 Cover pan tightly with foil and place in center of oven. Roast lamb until very tender, about 2 hours. Remove lamb from sauce. Skim off excess fat from sauce. Serve each shank with ½ cup sauce.

MIDDLE EASTERN SPICE-CRUSTED LAMB

PER SERVING **Net Carbs: 0 grams;** Carbohydrates: 0.5 gram; Fiber: 0.5 gram; Protein: 46 grams; Fat: 13 grams; Calories: 316

Makes 8 servings; Prep time: 10 minutes; Cook time: 45 minutes, plus 10 minutes resting

This succulent roast gets its flavor from a rub of traditional Middle Eastern spices. Make double the quantity of the spice mix and store the extra in an airtight container for up to six months to add instant flavor to grilled or roasted meats.

2 teaspoons ground coriander

1 teaspoon ground cumin

1 teaspoon ground cinnamon

1 teaspoon salt

½ teaspoon pepper

1 (4-pound) boneless leg of lamb, tied

Chives, for garnish

1 Heat oven to 450°F. Combine coriander, cumin, cinnamon, salt, and pepper in a small bowl and mix well. Rub spice mixture over surface of lamb. Place lamb in oven; roast 15 minutes. Reduce oven temperature to 350°F; roast until an instant-read thermometer inserted into several thick spots registers 135°F for medium-rare, about 35 minutes longer.

2 Transfer lamb to a cutting board, cover loosely with foil, and let stand 10 minutes. Cut across lamb, making ¼-inch slices. Garnish with chives.

CROWN ROAST OF LAMB FLORENTINE

 PER SERVING **Net Carbs: 4 grams;** Carbohydrates: 6 grams; Fiber: 2 grams; Protein: 49 grams; Fat: 28 grams; Calories: 480
Makes 8 servings; Prep time: 30 minutes; Cook time: 70 to 75 minutes, plus 5 minutes resting

The preparation for this glorious dish is really quite simple. To prevent overbrowning
the rib tips, cover them loosely with foil.

STUFFING:

1 (2-pound) head cauliflower, broken into florets

1 tablespoon extra virgin olive oil

12 garlic cloves, minced (2 tablespoons)

1 (10-ounce) bag fresh spinach, washed and dried

8 ounces mozzarella cheese, shredded (1¾ cups)

¼ cup grated Parmesan cheese

Salt and pepper

CROWN ROAST:

3 tablespoons Dijon mustard

6 garlic cloves, minced (1 tablespoon)

2 tablespoons extra virgin olive oil

1 tablespoon chopped fresh rosemary

1½ teaspoons salt

½ teaspoon pepper

1 (24-chop) crown roast of lamb

1 Heat oven to 425°F. Cover a rimmed baking sheet with foil and lightly oil it.

2 FOR STUFFING: Bring a large pot of lightly salted water to a boil. Add cauliflower and cook 3 minutes; drain. Heat oil in a large nonstick skillet over medium-high heat. Add garlic; cook until fragrant, about 30 seconds. Add spinach; cook until wilted, about 3 minutes. Add blanched cauliflower; cook, stirring often, until slightly browned, about 4 minutes. Remove from heat and cool 5 minutes. Stir in cheeses. Season with salt and pepper to taste.

3 FOR CROWN ROAST: Combine mustard, garlic, olive oil, rosemary, salt, and pepper in a small bowl; mix well. Place lamb on baking sheet and rub mustard mixture over inside and outside of lamb. Fill center of roast with the cauliflower mixture.

4 Roast the lamb 20 minutes. Reduce oven temperature to 375°F; roast until an instant-read thermometer inserted into the thickest portion of the lamb registers 135°F to 140°F for medium-rare, 30 to 35 minutes longer. Let stand 5 to 10 minutes before carving.

GREEK-STYLE BONELESS LEG OF LAMB

 PER SERVING **Net Carbs: 1 gram;** Carbohydrates: 2 grams; Fiber: 1 gram; Protein: 38 grams; Fat: 30 grams; Calories: 433
Makes 8 servings; Prep time: 20 minutes, plus 4 hours marinating; Cook time: 40 minutes

Don't save this dish just for the holidays—it's a snap to throw together. In fact, it's so
easy, you can cook it on the grill for a simple midweek meal.

12 garlic cloves, minced (2 tablespoons)

⅓ cup extra virgin olive oil

3 tablespoons fresh lemon juice

2 tablespoons dried oregano

1 teaspoon dried thyme

1 (4- to 5-pound) boneless, butterflied leg of lamb, trimmed

1½ teaspoons salt

½ teaspoon pepper

1 Combine garlic, olive oil, lemon juice, oregano, and thyme in a large bowl; mix well. Add lamb and turn to coat. Cover with plastic wrap and refrigerate, turning occasionally, at least 4 or up to 24 hours.

2 Heat oven to 425°F. Remove lamb from marinade. Sprinkle lamb with salt and pepper. Place lamb on a wire rack on a baking sheet covered with foil. Roast the lamb until browned and an instant-read thermometer inserted into several thick spots registers 135°F for medium-rare, 35 to 40 minutes.

VEAL WITH GOAT CHEESE AND ROAST PEPPERS

PER SERVING **Net Carbs: 3 grams;** Carbohydrates: 3 grams; Fiber: 0 grams; Protein: 32 grams; Fat: 33 grams; Calories: 440
Makes 12 servings; Prep time: 45 minutes; Cook time: 1 hour 35 minutes

You can season, stuff, roll, and tie this roast up to one day ahead of time. Simply keep it covered and refrigerated until you're ready to cook and serve it.

1 red bell pepper, stem removed, halved, and seeded

1 yellow bell pepper, stem removed, halved, and seeded

1 (9-ounce) log goat cheese, softened

2 eggs, lightly beaten

¼ cup freshly chopped parsley

1 tablespoon chopped fresh tarragon

1 teaspoon chopped fresh thyme

6 garlic cloves, minced (1 tablespoon)

1 medium shallot, chopped (2 tablespoons)

1 tablespoon fresh lemon juice

3 teaspoons salt, divided

¾ teaspoon pepper, divided

4 pounds veal scallopine

¼ cup extra virgin olive oil

Kitchen string

1 Heat broiler. Place bell pepper halves, cut-side down, on a foil-lined baking sheet. Broil until skins are blistered, about 10 minutes. Place peppers in a resealable plastic bag; seal and let stand 10 minutes. Peel peppers; cut remainder into thin strips and set aside. Reduce oven temperature to 450°F.

2 Combine cheese, eggs, parsley, tarragon, thyme, garlic, shallot, lemon juice, and 1 teaspoon of the salt in a medium bowl; stir with a rubber spatula to combine.

3 Sprinkle veal with 1 teaspoon salt and ¼ teaspoon pepper. Spread cheese mixture evenly over roast, leaving a ½-inch border around the edges. Roll the roast, jelly-roll style, starting with a long edge; secure with kitchen string. Rub the roast with oil and sprinkle with the remaining teaspoon salt and ½ teaspoon pepper. Place roast on the rack of a broiler pan.

4 Roast until an instant-read thermometer inserted in the thickest portion of meat registers 140°F, about 1 hour 15 minutes. Let roast stand 10 minutes before slicing.

Shiitake and Fontina-Stuffed Veal Breast

SHIITAKE AND FONTINA–STUFFED VEAL BREAST

PER SERVING **Net Carbs: 13 grams;** Carbohydrates: 16 grams; Fiber: 3 grams; Protein: 61 grams; Fat: 18 grams; Calories: 510

3 4

Makes 6 servings; Prep time: 45 minutes; Cook time: 3 hours, plus 20 minutes resting

Have your butcher cut a pocket between the ribs and meat of the veal breast.
Roasting it bone-in keeps the meat succulent—and makes a great presentation.

2 tablespoons extra virgin olive oil

½ pound shiitake mushrooms, stems discarded,
  caps sliced

1 small onion, chopped (½ cup)

4 garlic cloves, minced (2 teaspoons)

Salt and pepper

1 tablespoon fresh lemon juice

2 tablespoons chopped parsley leaves

3 tablespoons chopped fresh sage leaves or
  3 teaspoons dried, divided

6 to 7 pounds center-cut veal breast (6 rib bones)

¼ pound very thinly sliced proscuitto di Parma

¼ pound thinly sliced fontina cheese

6 carrots, peeled

1 (14½-ounce) can lower sodium chicken broth

1 cup dry white wine

Toothpicks

1 Heat oven to 350°F. Heat oil in a large skillet over
season lightly with salt and pepper. Cook, stirring often,
until mushrooms begin to brown, about 10 minutes.
Stir in lemon juice, parsley, and 2 tablespoons of the
fresh sage (or 2 teaspoons dried).

2 Season breast well with salt and pepper. Place a layer
of prosciutto, then fontina in the pocket. Spoon in
mushrooms. Seal the pocket with toothpicks (count
how many you use so you'll be sure to remove all of
them before serving).

3 Line the bottom of a large roasting pan with carrots.
Pour in broth. Place veal on top of carrots, cover pan
securely with foil, and roast for 1½ hours. Remove foil.
Roast uncovered until veal is very tender and browned,
about 1½ hours more.

4 Transfer veal and carrots to a platter; let rest 20 minutes.
Meanwhile, tilt roasting pan and skim off fat, leaving
juices behind. Place pan over high heat and add wine.
Cook, scraping up the browned bits from the bottom of
the pan, until wine is reduced by about half; strain.

5 Remove toothpicks. Sprinkle roast with remaining
tablespoon sage. Pour pan sauce over roast or serve
on the side. Use a very sharp knife to slice the roast
between the rib bones; run your knife between the
bones and the meat, lift meat from bones, and serve.

Atkins Tip: The carrots in this dish serve double duty:
they naturally sweeten the pan sauce with unbeatable
roast carrot flavor, and serve as a "rack" for the breast,
ensuring that the veal roasts—instead of poaches—in
the broth. Unfortunately, they also add quite a few
carbs. If you're in OWL, but eager to try this recipe,
simply enjoy it without the side of carrots.

ROAST CHICKEN WITH WILD MUSHROOM JUS

PER SERVING **Net Carbs: 4 grams;** Carbohydrates: 5 grams; Fiber: 1 gram; Protein: 62 grams; Fat: 15 grams; Calories: 420

`3` `4` Makes 8 servings; Prep time: 25 minutes; Cook time: 2 hours 42 minutes

It's hard to resist the enticing perfume of porcini mushrooms. In this recipe, you make a porcini butter to rub under and over the chicken skin, which thoroughly infuses the chicken with the mushroom's earthy sweet scent and flavor.

1 ounce dried porcini mushrooms, divided

8 tablespoons (1 stick) unsalted butter, softened, divided

1½ teaspoons salt

½ teaspoon pepper

1 (7½- to 8½-pound) roaster chicken

1 large onion, chopped (1 cup)

2 carrots, peeled and chopped

2 celery stalks, chopped

1 (14½-ounce) can lower sodium chicken broth

8 garlic cloves, minced (4 teaspoons)

4 ounces white mushrooms, thinly sliced

4 ounces shiitake mushroom, stems removed, thinly sliced

1 teaspoon dried oregano

Kitchen string

1 Heat oven to 425°F. Lightly coat a large roasting pan with cooking spray.

2 Grind ½ ounce of the porcini mushrooms to a fine powder in a spice mill or coffee grinder; transfer to a bowl. Add 6 tablespoons of the butter, salt, and pepper. Mix well with a spoon until combined.

3 Rinse chicken and pat dry with paper towels. Tuck the wing tips underneath the bird. Insert fingertips under the skin on the breast and the leg to loosen the skin. Rub half of the butter mixture under the skin and over the breast meat and leg meat of the chicken. Rub the remaining butter mixture over the skin. Tie the chicken legs together with kitchen string. Place the remaining ½ ounce porcini mushrooms, onion, carrots, and celery in the prepared roasting pan. Set chicken on top of vegetables. Pour in chicken broth.

4 Roast the chicken 25 minutes. Reduce oven temperature to 375°F; cook, basting every 30 minutes with pan juices, until an instant-read thermometer inserted into the thickest part of the thigh registers 165°F, about 2 hours longer. Strain pan juices into a measuring cup and skim off excess fat.

5 Meanwhile, melt remaining 2 tablespoons butter in a large nonstick skillet over medium-high heat. Add garlic; cook until fragrant, 30 seconds. Add the white mushrooms, shiitake mushrooms, and oregano; cook, stirring occasionally, until golden brown, 7 to 8 minutes. Stir in pan juices and bring to a boil; cook until liquid is slightly reduced and mushrooms are tender, 4 minutes.

Atkins Tip: By omitting the carrots, this recipe becomes suitable for the weight-loss phases of Atkins.

ROAST DUCK BREAST WITH SYRAH SAUCE

PER SERVING **Net Carbs: 3 grams;** Carbohydrates: 3 grams; Fiber: 0 grams; Protein: 57 grams; Fat: 32 grams; Calories: 600

Makes 6 servings; Prep time: 10 minutes; Cook time: 40 minutes

Duck breasts are a terrific option for entertaining, since they appeal to guests who love red meat as well as those who prefer to eat poultry.

3 magret duck breasts, about 3 pounds total

Salt and pepper

1 large shallot, minced (⅓ cup)

2 garlic cloves, minced (1 teaspoon)

2 cups Syrah wine

1 cup lower sodium beef broth

¼ cup heavy cream

1 packet sugar substitute

2 tablespoons unsalted butter

1 Heat oven to 400°F. Cover a rimmed baking sheet with parchment paper or foil; set aside.

2 Using a sharp knife, score the skin of each duck breast in a crosshatch pattern; season breasts on all sides with salt and pepper. Heat a heavy skillet over medium-high heat. Add two duck breasts, skin-side down, and cook until browned, 2 to 3 minutes. Turn breasts over and cook 1 minute longer; transfer to baking sheet. Repeat with remaining duck breast.

3 Transfer baking sheet to oven; roast duck until an instant-read thermometer inserted into thickest part of breast registers 130°F to 135°F for medium-rare, 15 to 18 minutes. Cover pan loosely with foil and set aside.

4 Meanwhile, pour off all but 2 tablespoons of fat from the skillet. Heat over medium heat. Add shallot and garlic; cook, stirring occasionally, until softened, 2 to 3 minutes. Add wine; increase heat to high, bring to a boil, and reduce by half, about 10 minutes. Add broth and return to a boil. Continue boiling until the mixture is reduced to ¾ cup, 10 to 12 minutes. Strain the mixture through a fine sieve set over a bowl, pressing on the solids with a rubber spatula. Return sauce to skillet over medium heat. Add cream and sugar substitute; simmer 2 minutes. Remove from heat, whisk in butter, and season with salt and pepper to taste.

5 To serve, cut duck diagonally across the grain into thin slices, divide among 6 plates, and spoon sauce over.

Roast Duck Breast with Syrah Sauce
Broccolini with Shallot-Lemon Butter, page 106

SOUTHWESTERN TURKEY

PER SERVING **Net Carbs: 2 grams;** Carbohydrates: 2 grams; Fiber: 0 grams; Protein: 54 grams; Fat: 48 grams; Calories: 660
Makes 12 servings; Prep time: 20 minutes; Cook time: 3 hours 30 minutes plus 10 minutes resting

The beautiful reddish-brown color and subtle spicy flavor of this turkey make it an appealing change from the more traditionally prepared bird. To keep the heat mild, use only one or even a half of a chipotle in the butter, or omit the chipotle in the sauce altogether.

SOUTHWESTERN TURKEY:

¾ cup unsalted butter, softened

3 tablespoons chopped fresh cilantro

1 tablespoon ground cumin

1 tablespoon salt

1½ teaspoons grated lime zest

1½ teaspoons fresh lime juice

8 garlic cloves, minced (4 teaspoons), divided

2 chipotles en adobo, minced

1 (12- to 14-pound) turkey, giblets removed

SPICY GRAVY:

2 tablespoons unsalted butter

1 small onion, chopped (½ cup)

2 garlic cloves, minced (1 teaspoon)

1 chipotle en adobo, minced

2 cups heavy cream

2 teaspoons fresh lime juice

Salt

1 FOR SOUTHEWESTERN TURKEY: Heat oven to 450°F. Combine butter, cilantro, cumin, salt, zest, juice, garlic, and chipotles in a medium bowl. Beat with an electric mixer at medium speed until well blended and smooth.

2 Insert fingers between skin and flesh of turkey to loosen skin; rub butter mixture under the skin of the turkey. Place turkey, breast-side up, on a wire rack in a roasting pan. Cook, basting with pan drippings, 20 minutes. Reduce oven temperature to 350°F; continue cooking, basting every 30 minutes, until an instant-read thermometer inserted in the thickest portion of turkey breast registers 165°F, 3¼ to 3½ hours. Let turkey stand 10 minutes before slicing.

3 FOR SPICY GRAVY: Melt butter in a medium saucepan over medium-high heat. Add onion and garlic; sauté until they begin to soften, about 2 minutes. Add chipotle and cream; bring to a boil. Reduce heat and simmer until liquid is reduced by half, about 25 to 30 minutes.

4 Skim off and discard fat from pan drippings. Add remaining pan drippings (you should have about ¾ cup) to the cream mixture; cook an additional minute. Remove from heat. Stir in lime juice; season with salt to taste. Serve along with turkey.

Atkins Tip: Every Thanksgiving, the turkey call-in hotlines get some of the same few problems. Here is a reminder to help avoid some common mistakes:

- Remember to take the package containing the neck and gizzards out of the cavity of the bird. Check both the front and back cavities.

- Before you turn your oven on, adjust the racks and be sure your roasting pan—and the height of the bird—fit.

- Make sure your bird is completely thawed. A large bird may take three days in the refrigerator to thaw. Never thaw on the counter.

Spice-Roasted Cornish Game Hens

SPICE-ROASTED CORNISH GAME HENS

PER SERVING **Net Carbs: 1 gram;** Carbohydrates: 2 grams; Fiber: 1 gram; Protein: 69 grams; Fat: 63 grams; Calories: 868
Makes 6 servings; Prep time: 15 minutes; Cook time: 1 hour 10 minutes

These birds are a snap to make. Prepare them the day before, wrap well, and refrigerate, then roast just before serving.

8 cloves garlic, minced (4 teaspoons)

3 tablespoons extra virgin olive oil

2 tablespoons peeled grated fresh ginger

2 teaspoons grated orange zest

2 teaspoons paprika

1½ teaspoons ground cumin

1 teaspoon ground coriander

1 teaspoon fennel seeds, crushed

½ teaspoon ground cinnamon

1½ teaspoons salt

½ teaspoon pepper

6 (1½-pound) Cornish game hens

Mixed olives, orange slices, and parsley sprigs, for garnish

Kitchen string

1 Heat oven to 400°F. Set a wire rack on a large, rimmed baking sheet and lightly coat with oil.

2 Combine garlic, oil, ginger, zest, paprika, cumin, coriander, fennel seeds, cinnamon, salt, and pepper in a bowl; mix well to form a paste.

3 Insert fingers between skin and flesh to loosen the skin over the breasts and legs. Rub three-quarters of the spice paste under the skin onto the breasts and legs. Rub remaining paste on outer skin. Tuck the wing tips under the bird. Tie the legs together with kitchen string; place hens on rack.

4 Roast the hens 45 minutes. Baste occasionally and cook until an instant-read thermometer inserted into the thickest part of the thigh registers 165°F, about 20 to 25 minutes. Garnish with olives, orange slices, and parsley.

TRICOLOR PEPPERCORN-ROASTED GOOSE

 PER SERVING **Net Carbs: 3 grams;** Carbohydrates: 4 grams; Fiber: 1 gram; Protein: 78 grams; Fat: 30 grams; Calories: 620
Makes 8 servings; Prep time: 15 minutes; Cook time: 3 hours, plus 10 minutes resting

What could be more festive than a Christmas goose? It's as easy to make as any other whole bird, but the meat has a rich taste that sets it apart. And, you can enjoy the crisp skin without sabotaging your weight control efforts; just remove the high carb carrots and onions before serving.

4 tablespoons (½ stick) unsalted butter, softened

1 tablespoon cracked black peppercorns

1 tablespoon cracked white peppercorns

1 tablespoon cracked green peppercorns

1 tablespoon fresh thyme leaves

1 teaspoon paprika

1¼ teaspoons salt

1 (10- to 12-pound) whole goose, trimmed of excess fat

2 heads garlic

4 carrots, chopped

4 celery stalks, chopped (2 cups)

3 large onions, chopped (3 cups)

1 cup lower sodium chicken broth, or water

Thyme sprigs, for garnish

1 Heat oven to 375°F. Combine butter, peppercorns, thyme, paprika, and salt in a bowl; mix well. Pat goose skin dry with a paper towel. Rub with the butter mixture.

2 Separate garlic into individual cloves; peel cloves.

3 Place garlic, carrots, celery, onions, and broth or water in the bottom of a large roasting pan. Place goose on top of the vegetables. Roast, basting occasionally, until skin is golden brown and juices in the cavity run clear, 2½ to 3 hours. If the bottom of the pan gets dry, add more water. Remove goose from oven; let rest 10 minutes before carving. Scoop garlic cloves from pan with a slotted spoon and serve with goose. Discard onion, carrot, and celery. Garnish with thyme sprigs.

Turkey with Spinach Cornbread Stuffing

TURKEY WITH SPINACH CORNBREAD STUFFING

 PER SERVING **Net Carbs: 11 grams;** Carbohydrates: 19 grams; Fiber: 8 grams; Protein: 74 grams; Fat: 54.5 grams; Calories: 890
Makes 12 servings; Prep time: 40 minutes; Cook time: 4 hours 5 minutes, plus 10 minutes resting

Instead of purchasing chicken broth by the 14½-ounce can, look for larger containers and freeze any you have left over.

SPINACH CORNBREAD STUFFING:

1 (8½-ounce) package Atkins Quick Quisine™ Deluxe Corn Muffin & Bread Mix

½ cup water

⅓ cup heavy cream

⅓ cup vegetable oil

4 large eggs, divided

6 slices bacon

2 medium onions, chopped (1½ cups)

8 garlic cloves, minced (4 teaspoons)

2 (10-ounce) bags fresh spinach, stems trimmed, leaves coarsely chopped

2 cups lower sodium chicken broth

Salt and pepper

TURKEY:

4 tablespoons unsalted butter, softened

1 tablespoon salt, plus more to taste

2 teaspoons pepper, plus more to taste

1 teaspoon ground sage

18 cloves garlic, chopped (3 tablespoons)

1 (14-pound) turkey

2 cups lower sodium chicken broth

GRAVY:

1 cup lower sodium chicken broth

1 cup heavy cream

1 tablespoon ThickenThin™ not/Starch thickener

Salt and pepper

1 FOR SPINACH CORNBREAD STUFFING: Heat oven to 425°F. Whisk cornbread mix, water, cream, oil, and 2 of the eggs in a medium bowl until combined. Pour batter into a lightly greased 8-inch-square baking pan; bake until golden brown, about 30 minutes. Cool in pan 10 minutes. Remove from pan; cool completely on a wire rack. Cut cornbread into 1-inch cubes; place cubes in a large bowl. Set aside.

2 Cook bacon in a large nonstick skillet over medium heat until crisp. Remove bacon from pan; cool and crumble. Add bacon to cornbread. Add onions to the drippings left in the skillet; sauté until translucent, 4 minutes. Add garlic; add spinach in batches, waiting for each batch to wilt slightly before adding more. Cook until spinach is wilted and tender, 10 to 15 minutes, stirring frequently. Add spinach mixture to cornbread.

3 Whisk 2 cups broth and the remaining 2 eggs in a medium bowl. Pour over cornbread mixture; toss gently to combine. Season with salt and pepper.

4 FOR TURKEY: Heat oven to 450°F. Combine butter, salt, pepper, sage, and garlic, stirring well. Insert fingers between skin and meat of turkey to loosen skin; rub butter mixture on meat. Sprinkle skin with salt and pepper. Place turkey in a roasting pan, breast-side up. Place 4 cups stuffing inside the turkey cavity. Roast for 30 minutes. Add broth to pan; baste turkey with pan drippings. Reduce oven temperature to 350°F; continue cooking, basting every 30 minutes, until an instant-read thermometer inserted in the thickest part of the breast registers 165°F, 2 hours 50 minutes more. Bake any dressing left over after stuffing the turkey in a 7- by 11-inch baking dish at 350°F for 30 minutes, while the turkey finishes cooking. Let turkey stand 20 minutes before carving.

5 FOR GRAVY: Place roasting pan over medium-high heat; add broth and cream. Scrape browned bits from bottom of pan. Bring to a boil, reduce heat, and simmer until liquid has reduced by half, about 10 minutes. Sprinkle thickener over pan drippings; whisk until combined. Cook until thick and smooth, about 1 minute. Season with salt and pepper to taste. Serve gravy with turkey.

Atkins Tip: If you have passed phase 2, feel free to use Atkins Quick Quisine™ Corn Muffin & Bread Mix—but remember to adjust the nutritional information for this recipe accordingly (Per Serving: Net Carbs: 16 grams; Carbohydrates: 23 grams; Fiber: 7 grams; Protein: 73 grams; Fat: 47 grams; Calories: 910).

BOUILLABAISSE

PER SERVING **Net Carbs: 10.5 grams;** Carbohydrates: 11.5 grams; Fiber: 1 gram; Protein: 46 grams; Fat: 10 grams; Calories: 326

Makes 8 servings; Prep time: 20 minutes; Cook time: 45 minutes

Saffron-tinged broth the color of sunsets is redolent with the flavors of the sea. Feel free to substitute other kinds of shellfish, such as lobster or clams.

3 tablespoons extra virgin olive oil

8 garlic cloves, chopped (4 teaspoons)

2 tomatoes, seeded and chopped (1½ cups)

1 large onion, chopped (1 cup)

½ small fennel bulb, cored and thinly sliced (½ cup)

1 bay leaf

½ teaspoon crushed saffron threads

5 (8-ounce) bottles clam juice

1 pound cod, skinned and cut into 8 (2-inch) pieces

2 pounds mussels, scrubbed and debearded

1 pound large shrimp, peeled and deveined

1 pound sea scallops

Salt and pepper

1 Heat oil in a large pot over medium-high heat. Add garlic, tomatoes, and onion; cook, stirring occasionally, until onion is soft, 5 to 6 minutes. Add fennel, bay leaf, and saffron; cook 1 minute longer. Add clam juice; bring to a boil. Reduce heat to medium-low. Cover and simmer 8 minutes.

2 Increase heat to medium and add cod; cover and cook until cod is just cooked through, 4 to 5 minutes. Remove cod with a slotted spoon. Add mussels to pot, cover and cook 2 minutes. Stir in shrimp and scallops; cook until shellfish is cooked through, 6 to 8 minutes. Season with salt and pepper to taste.

3 Place a piece of cod in each of 8 bowls. Top each with broth and shellfish mixture. Serve immediately.

Bouillabaisse

GREEN ROASTED SHRIMP

 PER SERVING **Net Carbs: 2.5 grams;** Carbohydrates: 4 grams; Fiber: 1.5 grams; Protein: 35 grams; Fat: 10 grams; Calories: 253
Makes 8 servings; Prep time: 25 minutes; Cook time: 8 minutes

These festive-looking shrimp make a glorious main course—or use smaller shrimp
to make an appetizer. Marinate the shrimp up to two hours before roasting.

2 cups tightly packed fresh basil leaves

Grated zest of 1 lemon

⅓ cup chopped fresh chives

¼ cup extra virgin olive oil

2 tablespoons fresh oregano

2 garlic cloves

½ teaspoon fennel seeds

¼ teaspoon red pepper flakes

2 teaspoons salt

3 pounds extra-large shrimp, (16 to 20 per pound),
   peeled and deveined

1 Adjust oven racks so that one is in the upper third and
one is in the lower third. Heat oven to 500°F. Lightly oil
2 baking sheets.

2 Combine basil, lemon zest, chives, oil, oregano,
garlic, fennel seeds, pepper flakes, and salt in a blender;
process to a bright green paste, 1 to 2 minutes.

3 Place shrimp in a large bowl. Pour in basil mixture; toss
well to coat. Arrange shrimp in a single layer on the
prepared baking sheets.

4 Place one pan in the upper third of the oven and one in
the lower third. Roast until shrimp are pink, curled, and
cooked through, switching the pans once, 7 minutes.
Serve immediately or at room temperature.

ROAST SALMON WITH FENNEL AND HERBS

 PER SERVING **Net Carbs: 2.5 grams;** Carbohydrates: 3.5 grams; Fiber: 1 gram; Protein: 65 grams; Fat: 26 grams; Calories: 518
Makes 8 servings; Prep time: 15 minutes; Cook time: 1 hour

For the most spectacular presentation, leave the head and tail on (as shown on
page 62), although the fish tastes just as good (and may fit in your oven better!)
without it. If you can't get both marjoram and oregano, they can substitute for one
another in equal amounts.

1 (7- to 8-pound) whole salmon, cleaned, head and
   tail on

3 tablespoons extra virgin olive oil

1½ teaspoons salt

½ teaspoon pepper

½ medium fennel bulb, thinly sliced (1 cup)

1 small onion, thinly sliced (½ cup)

5 lemon slices

4 orange slices

6 sprigs fresh marjoram

6 sprigs fresh oregano

4 sprigs fresh thyme

1 Heat oven to 450°F. Lightly oil a large rimmed
baking sheet.

2 Use a sharp knife to make 5 deep crosswise cuts (down
to, but not through, the bone) on each side of salmon.
Rub salmon inside and out with oil, salt, and pepper.
Transfer salmon to baking sheet. Stuff the cavity with
layers of fennel, onion, lemon, orange, marjoram,
oregano, and thyme.

3 Roast salmon until the flesh flakes easily when pierced
with a fork, 50 to 60 minutes. Serve warm, at room
temperature, or chilled.

ROAST SNAPPER PROVENÇAL

PER SERVING **Net Carbs: 5.5 grams;** Carbohydrates: 6.5 grams; Fiber: 1 gram; Protein: 41.5 grams; Fat: 20 grams; Calories: 383

Makes 6 servings; Prep time: 20 minutes; Cook time: 12 minutes

Simple and lovely, this dish couldn't be easier to assemble. The olive salad may be prepared a week in advance, but buy the fish the day of your party.

OLIVE SALAD:

1 cup pitted kalamata olives, sliced

1 cup pitted, pimiento-stuffed Spanish olives, sliced

2 teaspoons extra virgin olive oil

1 teaspoon grated lemon zest

1 teaspoon fresh lemon juice

SNAPPER:

6 (6- to 8-ounce) red snapper fillets, skin on

1½ teaspoons salt, divided

½ teaspoon pepper, divided

18 whole fresh basil leaves

4 plum tomatoes, sliced

4 garlic cloves, thinly sliced

3 tablespoons fresh lemon juice

¼ cup extra virgin olive oil

2 tablespoons thinly sliced fresh basil leaves

1 FOR OLIVE SALAD: Combine kalamata olives, Spanish olives, oil, zest, and juice in a small bowl; mix well.

2 FOR SNAPPER: Heat oven to 450°F. Lightly oil a large, rimmed baking sheet.

3 Season snapper with 1 teaspoon of the salt and ¼ teaspoon of the pepper; arrange skin-side down in a single layer on baking sheet. Arrange 3 basil leaves in a straight line down center of each fillet. Top basil with 4 overlapping tomato slices. Sprinkle garlic slices over tomatoes. Drizzle with lemon juice and oil. Sprinkle with remaining ½ teaspoon salt and ¼ teaspoon pepper.

4 Roast until snapper is opaque and flakes easily with a fork, about 12 minutes. Transfer snapper to a serving platter or individual dinner plates. Sprinkle with the sliced basil leaves. Divide olive salad among plates.

LOBSTER MEDALLIONS WITH VANILLA CREAM

PER SERVING **Net Carbs: 3 grams;** Carbohydrates: 3 grams; Fiber: 0 grams; Protein: 23 grams; Fat: 20 grams; Calories: 310

Makes 12 servings; Prep time: 35 minutes; Cook time: 3 hours 20 minutes

The idea of vanilla sauce on lobster may seem unusual, but it is actually a classic French combination, with a flavor that is out of this world.

1½ cups white wine

1 large shallot, finely chopped (⅓ cup)

2 garlic cloves, minced (1 teaspoon)

1 vanilla bean

1½ cups heavy cream

2 teaspoons fresh lemon juice

½ packet sugar substitute

6 tablespoons unsalted butter, divided

Salt and pepper to taste

6 (6- to 8-ounce) pre-cooked, shelled lobster tails

1 Combine wine, shallot, and garlic in a medium saucepan. Using a paring knife, slit vanilla bean

lengthwise; use the back of the knife blade to scrape out the seeds. Add seeds and bean pod to saucepan. Bring to a boil over medium-high heat; cook until liquid is reduced to ½ cup, 10 to 12 minutes.

2 Add cream, lemon juice, and sugar substitute and return to a boil. Reduce heat to medium; simmer until reduced to 1½ cups, about 10 minutes. Remove from heat; discard vanilla bean. Whisk in 2 tablespoons of the butter until melted. Season with salt and pepper to taste; keep warm.

3 Melt remaining butter in a large nonstick skillet over medium-high heat. Add lobster and cook, tossing often, until hot, 2 to 3 minutes. Season with salt and pepper. Cut tails crosswise into ½-inch-thick rounds. Spoon sauce onto plates and top with lobster.

Rosemary Roasted Sweet Potatoes, page 92

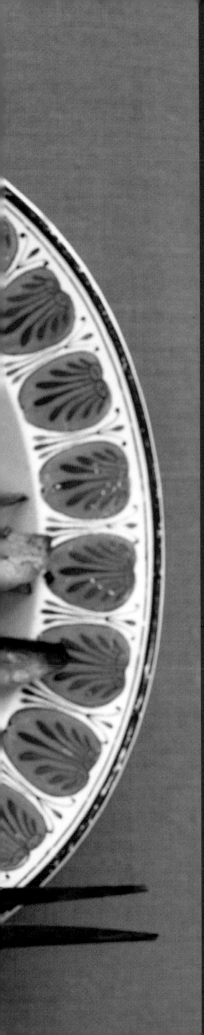

VEGETABLES & SIDE DISHES

Variety is the secret to successful menu planning. Select side dishes with flavors that harmonize with your entrée. But also be sure to consider the colors on your plate—the more hues included, the broader the range of nutrients you'll be serving—plus, your meal will be more visually appealing.

ROSEMARY-ROASTED SWEET POTATOES

3 4 PER SERVING **Net Carbs: 13 grams;** Carbohydrates: 16 grams; Fiber: 3 grams; Protein: 2 grams; Fat: 2.5 grams; Calories: 90
Makes 12 servings; Prep time: 10 minutes; Cook time: 30 minutes

The dramatic, unexpected look of long sweet potato "spears" adds to the pleasure of this naturally sweet, nutrient-packed dish (shown on page 90).

3 sweet potatoes (2 pounds), peeled, cut lengthwise into ¼-inch-thick spears

2 tablespoons macadamia nut (or canola) oil

1 tablespoon chopped fresh rosemary

½ teaspoon ground cumin

1 teaspoon salt

⅛ teaspoon cayenne

1 Heat oven to 425°F. Place oven racks in the upper third and lower third of oven. Lightly oil 2 rimmed baking sheets.

2 Combine potato spears, oil, rosemary, cumin, salt, and cayenne in a large bowl; toss well to coat. Arrange potatoes in a single layer on baking sheets.

3 Roast potatoes, rotating pans and tossing potatoes every 10 minutes, until lightly golden and tender, about 30 minutes.

Atkins Tip: To cut potatoes into spears, first halve them lengthwise. Place the flat, cut side down on the board, and halve lengthwise again. With a flat side again facing down, cut each wedge lengthwise into 1/4-inch-thick slices.

PUMPKIN-NUT BAKE

 PER SERVING **Net Carbs: 4.5 grams;** Carbohydrates: 6 grams; Fiber: 1.5 grams; Protein: 9.5 grams; Fat: 19 grams; Calories: 222
Makes 10 servings; Prep time: 15 minutes; Cook time: 1 hour

This sweet baked side dish has the appealing aroma and flavor of holiday "pumpkin pie" spices. It can be baked ahead of time and served at room temperature or rewarmed in a 200°F oven.

12 large eggs, beaten

2 cups canned pumpkin purée

8 ounces mascarpone cheese, lightly whipped

½ cup sugar-free pancake syrup

¼ teaspoon ground nutmeg

¼ teaspoon ground allspice

½ teaspoon salt

¼ cup pecans, chopped

1 Heat oven to 350°F. Butter a 9- by 13-inch baking pan.

2 Beat eggs with an electric mixer at high speed until thick, about 5 minutes.

3 Whisk pumpkin in a large bowl until smooth; gradually whisk in eggs, mascarpone, syrup, nutmeg, allspice, and salt. Pour mixture into baking pan. Bake 45 minutes.

4 Sprinkle chopped pecans evenly over top. Return to oven and bake until eggs are set and nuts are toasted, 15 minutes more. Cool slightly before cutting.

Atkins Tip: If you can't find mascarpone cheese, you can substitute 4 ounces of cream cheese softened in ½ cup of cream.

SOUTHWESTERN CORNBREAD

PER SERVING **Net Carbs: 9 grams;** Carbohydrates: 12 grams; Fiber: 3 grams; Protein: 9 grams; Fat: 10 grams; Calories: 160
Makes 12 servings; Prep time: 15 minutes; Cook time: 25 minutes

Don't be misled by the name of this dish—the flavors of the cornbread adapt well
to many different menus, not just Tex-Mex. It's a great accompaniment to roast
meats and poultry, and it is wonderful for mopping up pan juices.

1 (8½-ounce) package Atkins Quick Quisine™ Deluxe
   Corn Muffin & Bread Mix

½ cup chopped fresh cilantro

½ small red onion, chopped (½ cup)

1 teaspoon grated lime zest

½ cup water

⅓ cup vegetable oil

⅓ cup heavy cream

2 large eggs, lightly beaten

1 Heat oven to 350°F. Lightly oil an 8-inch square
baking pan.

2 Whisk bake mix, cilantro, onion, and zest in a large
bowl. Add water, oil, heavy cream, and eggs; mix
with a wooden spoon until smooth.

3 Pour batter into pan. Bake until bread is set and a
toothpick inserted in center comes out clean, about
25 minutes. Cool in pan on a wire rack. Cut into 12
portions. Serve warm or at room temperature.

Southwestern Cornbread

ROASTED ARTICHOKE GRATIN

 PER SERVING **Net Carbs: 4 grams;** Carbohydrates: 8 grams; Fiber: 4 grams; Protein: 5 grams; Fat: 7 grams; Calories: 110
Makes 8 servings; Prep time: 10 minutes; Cook time: 40 minutes

This dish couldn't be easier to make, or more perfect for entertaining. Prepare the
artichokes a day ahead and store in the refrigerator in an oven-to-table glass dish.
Bring to room temperature and continue with step 3.

2 (9-ounce) boxes frozen artichoke hearts, thawed

9 garlic cloves, minced (1½ tablespoons)

2 tablespoons chopped fresh basil leaves

2 tablespoons chopped fresh parsley

2 tablespoons extra virgin olive oil

1 tablespoon fresh lemon juice

⅓ cup shredded fontina cheese (1½ ounces)

¼ cup shredded Taleggio cheese (1 ounce)

¼ cup grated Parmesan cheese, preferably Parmigiano-
Reggiano

1 Heat oven to 400°F. Lightly oil a 6-cup oval gratin dish.

2 Combine artichoke hearts, garlic, basil, parsley, oil, and
lemon juice in a bowl; toss well. Pour into the prepared
gratin dish. Roast, 20 minutes, stirring occasionally.

3 Remove from oven. Sprinkle fontina, Taleggio, and
Parmesan cheeses evenly over the top. Return to oven.
Roast until cheeses melt and begin to brown, about 20
minutes longer.

Atkins Tip: You'll save yourself a tremendous amount
of work by purchasing frozen artichokes; preparing
fresh artichokes can be time-consuming and costly.
Plus, you'll be hard-pressed to find fresh artichokes in
the grocery store come holiday time.

ASPARAGUS WITH BROWNED BUTTER

 PER SERVING **Net Carbs: 3 grams;** Carbohydrates: 5 grams; Fiber: 2 grams; Protein: 3 grams; Fat: 6 grams; Calories: 80
Makes 10 servings; Prep time: 10 minutes; Cook time: 7 minutes

Allowing butter to brown when melted gives it a lovely nutty flavor and a warm,
irresistible aroma. Be sure you don't overcook it, however, or the butter will scorch.

3 bunches asparagus (3 pounds), trimmed and cut into
2-inch pieces

5 tablespoons unsalted butter

2 teaspoons balsamic vinegar

1 teaspoon fresh lemon juice

Salt and pepper

1 Bring a large pot of salted water to a boil over high
heat. Add asparagus and cook 3 minutes; drain.

2 Melt butter in a large nonstick skillet over medium-high
heat, swirling occasionally, until butter begins to brown,
2 to 3 minutes. Add vinegar and lemon juice carefully,
as hot butter may splatter; cook 1 minute longer. Stir
in asparagus; cook and toss until hot, 1 to 2 minutes.
Season with salt and pepper to taste.

Roasted Artichoke Gratin

ROASTED ASPARAGUS

PER SERVING **Net Carbs: 3 grams;** Carbohydrates: 6 grams; Fiber: 3 grams; Protein: 3 grams; Fat: 7 grams; Calories: 96
Makes 6 servings; Prep time: 5 minutes; Cook time: 15 minutes

Roasting brings out the natural sweetness in most vegetables and intensifies the
flavor. This recipe may be doubled for a crowd.

2 bunches asparagus (2 pounds), trimmed

3 tablespoons extra virgin olive oil

1¼ teaspoons salt

½ teaspoon pepper

1 Heat oven to 400°F. Line a baking sheet with foil.

2 Combine asparagus, oil, salt, and pepper in a bowl; mix
well. Arrange asparagus in a single layer on prepared
baking sheet.

3 Bake, shaking pan occasionally, until asparagus is tender
and lightly crisped, 10 to 12 minutes.

CREAMED SPINACH

 PER SERVING **Net Carbs: 4 grams;** Carbohydrates: 6 grams; Fiber: 2 grams; Protein: 2 grams; Fat: 18 grams; Calories: 190
Makes 6 servings; Prep time: 20 minutes; Cook time: 12 minutes

While this recipe works with frozen spinach, for a special occasion, use fresh spinach leaves. Their brighter flavor is the just-right accompaniment to roast beef, steak, and the holiday turkey.

4 (12-ounce) bunches fresh spinach, stems trimmed, leaves well rinsed

1 cup heavy cream

2 tablespoons unsalted butter

Pinch ground nutmeg

Salt and pepper

1 Add enough water to a large pot so it is 3 inches full; bring to a boil. Add spinach and cook, stirring occasionally, until wilted, 2 to 3 minutes. Drain and cool 5 minutes; squeeze out excess water.

2 Combine cream, butter, and nutmeg in a small saucepan over medium-high heat; bring to a boil. Cook until reduced by one-third, 6 to 7 minutes.

3 Return the large saucepan to the stove over medium heat. Add the spinach; cook 1 minute, stirring frequently. Add cream mixture and cook until hot, 1 to 2 minutes. Season with salt and pepper to taste.

Atkins Tip: Don't let the idea of washing the spinach deter you—it can be fast and easy. Place the spinach in your largest bowl, cover with tap water and swirl it around once or twice. Let it stand until the water is perfectly still, then lift the leaves out of the water and place them in a colander, leaving the sand behind. The leaves will be clean and ready to cook.

BRAISED CELERY AND LEEKS

PER SERVING **Net Carbs: 10 grams;** Carbohydrates: 12 grams; Fiber: 2 grams; Protein: 2 grams; Fat: 9 grams; Calories: 130
Makes 8 servings; Prep time: 15 minutes; Cook time: 1 hour 5 minutes

Cooked celery is better with the tough outer fibers removed. Cut a half inch off the base of the stalk and use a knife to pull off the stringy fibers toward the top of the stalk.

4 medium leeks (1¾ pounds), light green and white parts only, outer layer removed

8 celery stalks, cut crosswise in half

1 (14½-ounce) can lower sodium chicken broth

6 tablespoons unsalted butter, cut into ½-inch pieces

Salt and pepper

1 Heat oven to 375°F. Trim roots from leeks far enough to expose the edible white end, but keep root intact. (It will hold the leek together.) Cut leeks in half lengthwise and wash in cold water to remove any dirt. Transfer to a roasting pan. Add celery to pan. Pour chicken broth and ½ cup water over vegetables. Dot the vegetables with butter. Cover pan tightly with aluminum foil. Poke a few holes in the foil to allow steam to escape.

2 Bake vegetables 45 minutes. Uncover and bake until vegetables are tender and sauce has reduced slightly, 20 minutes. Season with salt and pepper to taste.

ESCAROLE WITH PANCETTA

PER SERVING **Net Carbs: 3 grams;** Carbohydrates: 6 grams; Fiber: 3 grams; Protein: 4 grams; Fat: 13 grams; Calories: 160
Makes 8 servings; Prep time: 5 minutes; Cook time: 20 minutes

Escarole, like radicchio and endive, is a kind of chicory. Its somewhat bitter flavor mellows when cooked. If you can't find pancetta, you may substitute regular bacon, which has a more smoky flavor.

6 ounces pancetta (Italian bacon), cut into ⅓-inch dice

2 tablespoons extra virgin olive oil

1 large onion, finely chopped (1 cup)

4 garlic cloves, thinly sliced

2 heads escarole, cleaned and coarsely chopped

1½ teaspoons salt

½ teaspoon pepper

1 Heat a large skillet over medium heat. Add pancetta and cook until lightly browned, 4 minutes. Add oil and onion; cook until softened, 5 minutes, stirring occasionally. Add garlic and cook 1 minute.

2 Add escarole, salt, and pepper; mix well. Cook, stirring occasionally, until tender, 10 minutes.

Escarole with Pancetta

Braised Cabbage

BRAISED CABBAGE

 PER SERVING **Net Carbs: 7 grams;** Carbohydrates: 10 grams; Fiber: 3 grams; Protein: 6 grams; Fat: 9 grams; Calories: 140
Makes 12 servings; Prep time: 12 minutes; Cook time: 40 minutes

The deep purple color of the cabbage wedges makes a dramatic presentation—
and signals the presence of valuable phytonutrients.

2 small heads red cabbage (4 pounds)

¼ cup unsalted butter

1 cup lower sodium chicken broth

½ cup white wine

2 tablespoons cider vinegar

1 teaspoon salt

¼ teaspoon pepper

3 tablespoons olive oil, divided

6 ounces thinly sliced prosciutto di Parma, about 9 slices

6 tablespoons chopped fresh parsley

½ teaspoon caraway seeds

1 Cut each head of cabbage into 6 wedges, slicing through the root so wedges stay intact.

2 Divide butter between two large skillets and melt over medium-high heat. Arrange cabbage wedges in a single layer in the skillets; cook 2 minutes. Add broth, wine, vinegar, salt, and pepper; bring to a boil. Reduce heat; cover and simmer until cabbage is tender, about 30 minutes.

3 Heat 1 tablespoon of the oil in a large skillet over medium-high heat. Add 3 slices prosciutto; cook until crisp, about 1 minute per side. Place on paper towels to drain. Repeat. When cool enough to touch, crumble prosciutto.

4 Sprinkle cabbage wedges with parsley, caraway seeds, and prosciutto.

BUTTER-BRAISED TURNIPS

 PER SERVING **Net Carbs: 3 grams;** Carbohydrates: 5 grams; Fiber: 2 grams; Protein: 1 gram; Fat: 6 grams; Calories: 70
Makes 8 servings; Prep time: 10 minutes; Cook time: 40 minutes

*Braised turnips are creamy and mild, and a delightful alternative to the same-old
(high-carb) potatoes.*

5 white turnips (1¾ pounds), peeled and cut into
½-inch cubes

1 cup lower sodium chicken broth

4 tablespoons (½ stick) unsalted butter

½ teaspoon granular sugar substitute (optional)

⅛ teaspoon ground nutmeg

Salt and pepper

1 Combine turnips, chicken broth, butter, sugar substitute, and nutmeg in a 12-inch skillet over medium heat.

2 Bring to a simmer and cook, stirring occasionally, until the liquid evaporates and the turnips are shiny, tender, and beginning to brown slightly, about 40 minutes. Season with salt and pepper to taste.

SAUSAGE DRESSING

 PER SERVING **Net Carbs: 8 grams;** Carbohydrates: 14 grams; Fiber: 6 grams; Protein: 18 grams; Fat: 14 grams; Calories: 248
Makes 12 servings; Prep time: 40 minutes; Cook time: 40 minutes

*This recipe makes a bit more than 10 cups of the dressing, plenty to stuff a large
(20- to 24-pound) turkey. You can also stuff a smaller bird and bake the remaining
dressing in a casserole dish. If you use less than the full amount of stuffing in the
dish, be sure to adjust your cooking time.*

16 slices low-carb white bread

6 tablespoons unsalted butter

2 medium onions, diced (1½ cups)

4 ribs celery, diced (2 cups)

4 garlic cloves, sliced

1 tablespoon vegetable oil

1 pound sweet Italian sausage, bulk or removed
from casing

3 tablespoons minced fresh sage leaves, or
1 tablespoon dried

2 teaspoons fresh thyme leaves, or ¾ teaspoon dried

2½ cups lower sodium chicken broth

Salt and pepper

3 large eggs, well beaten

1 Heat oven to 400°F. Butter a 9- by 13-inch glass baking dish or casserole.

2 Cut bread into ½-inch cubes. Place in a large bowl.

3 Melt butter in a large skillet over medium heat. Cook onions, celery, and garlic until soft, about 7 minutes. Transfer to bowl with bread. Return skillet to medium-high heat. Add oil and sausage; cook, breaking up chunks as you stir, until sausage is lightly browned, about 6 minutes.

4 Add sausage, sage, thyme, and broth to bread mixture and toss well. Season with salt and pepper to taste. Stir in beaten eggs. Transfer to baking dish. Bake until lightly browned on top, about 40 minutes. Let rest at least 10 minutes before serving.

Atkins Tip: Be sure to cut the bread into ½-inch cubes, as small pieces yield a better texture for the stuffing.

SAUSAGE-SAGE STUFFING

 PER SERVING **Net Carbs: 4.5 grams;** Carbohydrates: 9 grams; Fiber: 4.5 grams; Protein: 25 grams; Fat: 24.5 grams; Calories: 352
Makes 12 servings; Prep time: 20 minutes, plus 10 minutes marinating; Cook time: 50 minutes

This stuffing gets its savory flavor from ground pork and sage, with a little sweetness
from fennel seeds. Thanks to low-carb rye bread, you can enjoy it in OWL.

8 slices low-carb rye bread

2 pounds ground pork

1 teaspoon fennel seeds

½ teaspoon salt

6 tablespoons unsalted butter, divided

3 celery stalks, chopped (1½ cups)

1 large onion, chopped (1 cup)

4 teaspoons ground sage

1 (14½-ounce) can lower sodium chicken broth

3 eggs, beaten

½ cup chopped fresh parsley

1 Heat oven to 350°F. Butter a 9-inch-square baking dish.

2 Cut bread into ½-inch cubes; transfer to a large bowl.

3 Heat a large skillet over medium-high heat. Add pork, fennel seeds, and salt; cook until browned, 6 to 7 minutes; drain off excess fat. Add to bowl with bread cubes.

4 Wipe out skillet, and return to medium-high heat. Melt 3 tablespoons of the butter. Add celery and onion; cook until softened, 5 minutes. Stir in sage; cook 2 minutes. Stir in broth. Pour entire mixture over bread cubes and toss gently. Add eggs and parsley; mix well. Transfer to baking dish.

5 Dot top of stuffing with remaining 3 tablespoons butter. Bake 20 minutes, toss, and bake another 20 minutes.

WILD MUSHROOM STUFFING

 PER SERVING **Net Carbs: 8.5 grams;** Carbohydrates: 14.5 grams; Fiber: 6 grams; Protein: 14 grams; Fat: 13 grams; Calories: 220
Makes 10 servings; Prep time: 40 minutes; Cook time: 1 hour 10 minutes

You can use any mixture of mushrooms for this dish. Try substituting port for the
Madeira. The alcohol in the wine cooks off, leaving behind a rich wine flavor.

3 tablespoons unsalted butter

3 small shallots, sliced (⅓ cup)

9 garlic cloves, minced (1½ tablespoons)

2 pounds assorted wild mushrooms, coarsely chopped

1 teaspoon salt

¼ teaspoon pepper

½ cup Madeira wine

9 slices low-carb white bread, torn into 1½-inch pieces

¼ cup chopped fresh parsley

2 teaspoons chopped fresh thyme

1 cup lower sodium chicken broth

½ cup heavy cream

1 egg, lightly beaten

1 Heat oven to 350°F. Butter an 7- by 11-inch baking dish.

2 Melt butter in a large skillet over medium-high heat. Add shallots and garlic; sauté 2 minutes. Add mushrooms, salt, and pepper; cook until moisture released by the mushrooms evaporates, about 8 minutes. Add wine; cook until liquid evaporates, about 6 minutes. Remove from heat.

3 Place mushroom mixture in a large bowl. Add bread, parsley, and thyme; toss gently. Whisk broth, cream, and egg in a small bowl. Pour over mushroom mixture and toss to coat. Transfer mixture to baking dish. Bake until golden and set, about 45 minutes.

Fried Okra

FRIED OKRA

PER SERVING **Net Carbs: 3 grams;** *Carbohydrates: 6 grams; Fiber: 3 grams; Protein: 6 grams; Fat: 8.5 grams; Calories: 121*
Makes 8 servings; Prep time: 15 minutes; Cook time: 20 minutes

In this classic Southern treat, the okra is firm and the batter coating is crisp. For best results, use a thermometer to ensure you're frying at 350°F. The okra will cook evenly and the coating will stay golden brown. If you'd like to make the okra a few hours in advance, reheat it in a 300°F oven.

½ cup Atkins Quick Quisine™ Bake Mix

2 teaspoons chili powder

1 teaspoon ground cumin

¾ teaspoon salt

¼ teaspoon cayenne

1 pound okra, rinsed, ends trimmed, cut into ¼-inch-thick slices

2 large eggs, lightly beaten

2½ cups canola oil

1 Combine bake mix, chili powder, cumin, salt, and cayenne in a large bowl; mix well.

2 Toss half of the okra in beaten eggs. Lift okra, let excess egg drip off, and transfer to bowl with bake mix. Toss, shake off excess coating, and transfer to a large plate. Repeat to coat remaining okra.

3 Heat oil in a 2-quart saucepan over medium heat until it reaches 350°F on a deep-fry or candy thermometer. Add one-quarter of okra to oil; cook, until golden and tender, 4 to 5 minutes, stirring occasionally. Transfer okra to a large baking sheet covered with paper towels. Repeat, cooking three more batches. Serve warm.

ROAST CARROTS WITH CINNAMON AND CUMIN

PER SERVING **Net Carbs: 4 grams;** Carbohydrates: 7 grams; Fiber: 3 grams; Protein: 1 gram; Fat: 7 grams; Calories: 89

Makes 6 servings; Prep time: 5 minutes; Cook time: 20 minutes

Sweet carrots combine with aromatic spices to make an ideal accompaniment to roast meats. Prepare them the day ahead, then pop them in the oven along with your roast, allowing extra cooking time.

1 (1-pound) bag baby carrots

3 tablespoons extra virgin olive oil

¾ teaspoon ground cinnamon

¼ teaspoon ground cumin

Salt and pepper

1 Heat oven to 450°F. Lightly oil a rimmed baking sheet.

2 Combine carrots, oil, cinnamon, and cumin in a bowl; toss well. Arrange carrots on baking sheet in a single layer. Roast in upper third of oven, shaking pan occasionally, until carrots are tender and lightly golden, about 20 minutes. Season with salt and pepper to taste.

GLAZED CARROTS

PER SERVING **Net Carbs: 7 grams;** Carbohydrates: 9 grams; Fiber: 2 grams; Protein: 1 gram; Fat: 3.5 grams; Calories: 74

Makes 12 servings; Prep time: 15 minutes; Cook time: 12 minutes

Cut these carrots on a sharp diagonal to give them a dramatic look. Cooking them with a touch of sugar-free pancake syrup infuses them with a lovely maple flavor.

14 carrots, peeled, sliced in half lengthwise and cut on the diagonal into 1-inch pieces

4 tablespoons (½ stick) unsalted butter

2½ tablespoons sugar-free pancake syrup

1 teaspoon salt

½ cup water

1¼ teaspoons grated orange zest

1 Combine carrots, butter, syrup, salt, and water in a medium skillet with a tightly fitting lid. Bring to a boil, then lower heat; cover and simmer for 2 minutes.

2 Uncover pan and continue to cook until all water is evaporated and carrots are tender, about 3 more minutes. (Add more water and cook a few more minutes if carrots are not tender enough.) Stir in zest, cook 30 seconds more, and serve.

BRUSSELS SPROUTS WITH LEMON

PER SERVING **Net Carbs: 3 grams;** Carbohydrates: 5 grams; Fiber: 2 grams; Protein: 2 grams; Fat: 11 grams; Calories: 120

Makes 4 servings: 4; Prep time: 10 minutes; Cook time: 15 minutes

Overcooked Brussels sprouts account for why many people dislike these tiny cabbages. Cook them only until crisp-tender—you'll taste the difference!

1 pint Brussels sprouts, outer leaves removed, bottoms trimmed, halved

4 tablespoons (½ stick) unsalted butter

½ teaspoon salt

2 tablespoons lemon juice

1 tablespoon lemon zest

1 Add water to a medium pot to come 1½ inches up the side of the pot. Add sprouts and bring to a boil over high heat. Cover and steam until tender, about 10 minutes. Remove from pot with a slotted spoon and set aside.

2 Melt butter in a large skillet over medium-high heat. Add salt and cook until butter browns slightly, 2 to 3 minutes. Add lemon juice and zest; cook 30 seconds. Stir in sprouts; cook, shaking pan occasionally, until warmed through, 1 to 2 minutes.

SAUTÉED BRUSSELS SPROUTS

 PER SERVING **Net Carbs: 3 grams;** Carbohydrates: 5 grams; Fiber: 2 grams; Protein: 3.5 grams; Fat: 5 grams; Calories: 78
Makes 8 servings; Prep time: 15 minutes; Cook time: 17 minutes

To clean Brussels sprouts for sautéeing, remove the outermost leaves, rinse under cold water, and pat dry. Choose sprouts that are brightly colored, and avoid those with yellowing leaves. For the greatest freshness, buy them on the stalk.

4 slices bacon, cut into ½-inch pieces

2 pints Brussels sprouts, outer leaves trimmed, halved

6 garlic cloves, sliced

1 teaspoon chopped fresh thyme

½ cup water

Salt and pepper

1 Heat a large nonstick skillet over medium heat. Add bacon; cook until browned and slightly crisped, 6 to 7 minutes, stirring occasionally. Stir in Brussels sprouts, garlic, and thyme; cook 2 minutes, stirring occasionally.

2 Pour in water. Cook, stirring occasionally, until water has evaporated and Brussels sprouts are crisp-tender, 8 to 10 minutes. Season with salt and pepper to taste.

CAULIFLOWER-PEA PANCAKES

PER SERVING **Net Carbs: 10 grams;** Carbohydrates: 14 grams; Fiber: 4 grams; Protein: 8.5 grams; Fat: 4.5 grams; Calories: 123

3 4 Makes 8 (1-pancake) servings; Prep time: 10 minutes; Cook time: 4 minutes

These pancakes make a fine alternative to potato latkes. Since cauliflower does not have the starch that potatoes do, be sure to stir the batter frequently to keep the eggs and vegetables combined.

1 large head cauliflower (2¼ pounds), cut into pieces

6 eggs, lightly beaten

2 sheets whole-wheat matzo, finely ground (½ cup)

1 small onion, coarsely grated

1½ teaspoons salt

½ teaspoon pepper

1 cup frozen peas, thawed

1 Chop cauliflower into fine pieces in a food processor. Add eggs, matzo, onion, salt, pepper, and peas. Pulse to combine.

2 Heat a nonstick griddle or skillet over medium heat. For each pancake, scoop up ¼ cup batter, place on griddle, and flatten with a spatula to a 3-inch diameter. Cook until golden, 1 to 2 minutes per side.

Cauliflower-Pea Pancakes

CAULIFLOWER–SOUR CREAM PURÉE

 PER SERVING **Net Carbs: 4 grams;** Carbohydrates: 7 grams; Fiber: 3 grams; Protein: 3 grams; Fat: 7 grams; Calories: 90
Makes 6 servings; Prep time: 10 minutes; Cook time: 10 minutes

Variations of this addictively tasty, creamy purée have become a standard in the
low-carb cook's repertoire. Make this dish in advance and simply reheat in the oven
in a buttered casserole.

1 head cauliflower, (2 pounds), cut into florets
   (8 cups)

2 tablespoons sour cream

2 tablespoons heavy cream

1½ tablespoons unsalted butter

1 teaspoon salt

1 Bring a large pot of salted water to a boil over high
heat. Add cauliflower florets; cook until tender, 10 to 12
minutes. Drain.

2 Purée cauliflower in a food processor, adding florets in
batches. Add sour cream, heavy cream, butter, and salt;
process until smooth and well combined. Reheat gently,
if necessary.

COLLARD GREENS WITH HAM AND ONIONS

 PER SERVING **Net Carbs: 3 grams;** Carbohydrates: 6 grams; Fiber: 3 grams; Protein: 4 grams; Fat: 15 grams; Calories: 170
Makes 12 servings; Prep time: 35 minutes; Cook time: 1 hour 50 minutes

Look for one-pound bags of prewashed chopped fresh collard greens in the supermarket—they're a great time-saver. The prewashing gets rid of most of the soil and
grit, but for food-safety reasons, rinse them again at home.

1 tablespoon olive oil

1 small onion, chopped (½ cup)

4 ounces ham, diced (1½ cups)

2 pounds fresh collard greens, trimmed and coarsely
   chopped

1 teaspoon salt

1 teaspoon crushed red pepper flakes

2 cups lower sodium chicken broth

½ cup white wine

¼ cup apple cider vinegar

1 (6-ounce) piece salt pork

½ cup (1 stick) unsalted butter, cut into small pieces

1 Heat oil in a Dutch oven or a large heavy skillet with a
tight-fitting lid over medium-high heat. Add onion and
ham; sauté until lightly browned, about 4 minutes.
Stir in collards, salt, and red pepper flakes; sauté until
slightly wilted, about 4 minutes. Add broth, wine,
vinegar and salt pork; stir to combine. Bring mixture to
a boil. Reduce heat, cover, and cook 1½ hours, stirring
occasionally.

2 Uncover and add butter. Cook an additional 10
minutes, with cover off, stirring occasionally. Discard
salt pork.

Atkins Tip: Collard greens are a popular vegetable
in the southern United States. Don't discard the pot
liquor after cooking. It is rich in nutrients—especially
Vitamin A and calcium—and perfect for dipping
Southwestern Cornbread, page 93.

BROCCOLINI WITH SHALLOT-LEMON BUTTER

 PER SERVING **Net Carbs: 6 grams;** Carbohydrates: 7.5 grams; Fiber: 1.5 grams; Protein: 3.5 grams; Fat: 7.5 grams; Calories: 109
Makes 6 servings; Prep time: 5 minutes; Cook time: 10 minutes

Broccolini has slender stems and flowering buds similar to, but more delicate than, standard broccoli florets. It's both milder and sweeter than broccoli.

3 bunches broccolini (1½ pounds), trimmed

4 tablespoons (½ stick) unsalted butter

1 small shallot, finely chopped (2 tablespoons)

1 tablespoon fresh lemon juice

Salt and pepper

1 Bring a large pot of salted water to a boil. Add broccolini; cook until bright green and crisp-tender, about 3 minutes. Drain, rinse under cold water, and drain again.

2 Melt butter in a large skillet over medium-high heat. Add shallot; cook until shallot is lightly golden and butter begins to brown, 2 to 3 minutes. Add lemon juice; cook 10 seconds. Add broccolini; cook and toss until hot, 1 to 2 minutes. Season with salt and pepper to taste.

BROCCOLI FLORETS WITH LEMON BUTTER SAUCE

 PER SERVING **Net Carbs: 2 grams;** Carbohydrates: 4 grams; Fiber: 2 grams; Protein: 2 grams; Fat: 9 grams; Calories: 105
Makes 10 servings; Prep time: 10 minutes; Cook time: 15 minutes

This simple lemon butter sauce, also known as beurre blanc, is prepared by the classic French method of gradually whisking pieces of butter into liquid to make a thickened sauce. Mustard, chopped herbs, or citrus zest, which are often added as flavor variations, are equally good with blanched vegetables.

2 large heads broccoli, cut into bite-size florets

1 small shallot, finely chopped (2 tablespoons)

¼ cup white wine

2 tablespoons fresh lemon juice

½ cup (1 stick) cold, unsalted butter, cut into small bits

Salt and pepper

1 Bring a large pot of salted water to a boil. Add broccoli; cook until crisp-tender, 5 to 7 minutes. Drain; and return to pot to keep warm while you prepare the sauce.

2 Cook shallot, wine, and lemon juice in a small saucepan over medium heat. Simmer until reduced to 2 tablespoons. Reduce heat to low; whisk in a few pieces of butter until nearly melted. Gradually add remaining butter, whisking constantly until sauce is smooth. Dress broccoli florets with sauce. Season with salt and pepper to taste.

Atkins Tip: Many green vegetables, including broccoli, zucchini, asparagus, and green beans, attain their most vivid color when cooked until crisp-tender. When the color begins to break down and turn gray, the vegetables lose nutrients and flavor.

Broccolini with Shallot-Lemon Butter

BROCCOLI RABE, GARLIC, AND HOT RED PEPPER

 PER SERVING **Net Carbs: 5.5 grams;** Carbohydrates: 6 grams; Fiber: 0.5 gram; Protein: 4 grams; Fat: 11 grams; Calories: 140
Makes 10 servings; Prep time: 15 minutes; Cook time: 7 minutes

This is the dish so often served at your favorite Italian restaurant. Add more or less
red pepper to taste—but remember, a pinch goes a long way. A little spice offers a
good balance to the bitterness of the vegetable.

3 bunches broccoli rabe (3 pounds), stems trimmed

½ cup extra virgin olive oil

7 garlic cloves, thinly sliced

¼ teaspoon crushed red pepper flakes

Salt and pepper

1 Bring a large pot of salted water to a boil. Add
broccoli rabe and return to a boil; cook until bright
green and crisp-tender, about 3 minutes. Drain and
rinse under cold water. Squeeze out as much excess
liquid as possible.

2 Return pot to stove and heat oil over medium-high
heat. Add garlic and red pepper flakes; cook until
the garlic is lightly golden, 1 to 2 minutes, stirring
occasionally. Add broccoli rabe; cook, stirring often,
until hot and well mixed, 1 to 2 minutes. Season with
salt and pepper to taste.

Atkins Tip: To clean broccoli rabe, trim off the woody
ends (usually about an inch) and rinse under cold
water. Be prepared for the flavor of broccoli rabe—it
has more of a bitter bite than broccoli. This is best
paired with a sweetly flavored main dish, like Classic
Brisket, page 67, or Cranberry-Ginger Pork, page 71.

ROASTED VEGETABLE RATATOUILLE

PER SERVING **Net Carbs: 17 grams;** Carbohydrates: 21 grams; Fiber: 4 grams; Protein: 4 grams; Fat: 15.5 grams; Calories: 229
Makes 8 servings; Prep time: 35 minutes; Cook time: 50 minutes

Although these vegetables are fine in any phase of Atkins, they lose water and shrink
when cooked, so a full-size portion is higher in Net Carbs than is recommended
during Induction and OWL.

1 large eggplant (about 1½ pounds), cut into 1-inch cubes

2 zucchini (¾ pound), sliced in half lengthwise and cut
across in ½-inch slices

2 yellow squash (¾ pound), sliced in half lengthwise
and cut across in ½-inch slices

1 green bell pepper, seeded, cut into ¾-inch dice

1 red bell pepper, seeded, cut into ¾-inch dice

9 tablespoons olive oil, divided

Salt

6 garlic cloves, sliced

2 medium onions chopped (2 cups)

1 (28-ounce) can crushed tomatoes

2 bay leaves

1 teaspoon dried thyme

½ teaspoon pepper

1 tablespoon balsamic vinegar

¼ cup thinly sliced basil leaves

1 Heat oven to 425°F. Toss eggplant, zucchini, squash,
and bell peppers with 6 tablespoons of the olive oil and
1 teaspoon of the salt. Divide vegetables between two
baking sheets. Roast, until lightly brown and very soft,
about 40 minutes, stirring occasionally.

2 Heat a large deep pot over medium-high heat. Add
the remaining 3 tablespoons oil. Add garlic and onions;
cook, until they begin to brown, about 6 minutes
stirring occasionally,

3 Add tomatoes, bay leaves, thyme, pepper, vinegar, and
roasted vegetables to pot. Bring to a simmer and cook
10 minutes. Discard bay leaves. Season with salt to
taste. Garnish with sliced basil, and serve.

LEEKS IN VINAIGRETTE

PER SERVING **Net Carbs: 12 grams;** Carbohydrates: 13.5 grams; Fiber: 1.5 grams; Protein: 6.5 grams; Fat: 17.5 grams; Calories: 234

3 4   Makes 8 servings; Prep time: 20 minutes; Cook time: 40 minutes

Serve the leeks as a side dish to your main course or as an elegant first course.

4 slices bacon

3 large eggs

8 leeks, trimmed, halved lengthwise, and rinsed

1½ cups lower sodium chicken broth

2 tablespoons fresh lemon juice

1½ tablespoons white wine vinegar

1 tablespoon Dijon mustard

¼ cup extra virgin olive oil

Salt and pepper

1 tablespoon chopped fresh parsley

1 Heat a large skillet over medium-high heat. Add bacon and cook until crisp, 6 to 7 minutes. Remove bacon from skillet, drain on a plate lined with paper towels. Crumble and set aside. Set aside the skillet with drippings.

2 Place eggs in a small saucepan; cover with water. Bring to a boil and immediately remove from the heat. Cover and let stand 10 minutes. Rinse eggs with cold water. Peel eggs and coarsely chop. Set aside.

3 Return pan with bacon drippings to medium-high heat. Add leeks, cut sides up; cook 1 minute. Add broth; bring to a boil. Reduce heat and simmer until tender, 25 to 30 minutes. Remove leeks from pan with a slotted spoon; discard cooking liquid.

4 Whisk together lemon juice, vinegar, and mustard. Whisking constantly, slowly drizzle in oil; season with salt and pepper to taste. Drizzle dressing over leeks; sprinkle with bacon, egg, and parsley.

Leeks in Vinaigrette

Roasted Spiced Delicata Squash

ROASTED SPICED DELICATA SQUASH

PER SERVING **Net Carbs: 9 grams;** Carbohydrates: 11 grams; Fiber: 2 grams; Protein: 2 grams; Fat: 7 grams; Calories: 110
Makes 6 servings; Prep time: 5 minutes; Cook time: 25 minutes

Speckled orange, pale yellow, and green, the beautiful skin of delicata squash is thin enough to eat. The squash is shaped somewhat like a zucchini. A substitute is the round (and similarly speckled) dumpling squash.

3 medium delicata squash (2½ pounds), halved
lengthwise and seeded

3 tablespoons macadamia nut (or canola) oil

1 teaspoon ground coriander

½ teaspoon ground cumin

½ teaspoon ground cinnamon

¼ teaspoon ground ginger

1 teaspoon salt

⅛ teaspoon cayenne pepper

1 Heat oven to 450°F. Lightly oil 2 rimmed baking sheets; set aside.

2 Cut squash across in ½-inch-thick half-moons. Toss with oil.

3 Combine coriander, cumin, cinnamon, ginger, salt, and cayenne; toss with squash. Arrange squash slices in a single layer on baking sheets. Roast, tossing once, until tender and lightly browned, 22 to 25 minutes.

SWEET POTATO–PUMPKIN PURÉE

PER SERVING **Net Carbs: 17.5 grams;** Carbohydrates: 22 grams; Fiber: 4.5 grams; Protein: 4 grams; Fat: 16 grams; Calories: 242

3 4 Makes 8 servings; Prep time: 20 minutes; Cook time: 1 hour 5 minutes, plus 45 minutes standing

This dish will surely satisfy nostalgic cravings for the marshmallow-topped sweet potatoes of yesteryear. This version, however, is a bit more sophisticated.

TOPPING:

3 egg whites

3 tablespoons granular sugar substitute

½ cup pecan halves, toasted and chopped

PURÉE:

2 medium sweet potatoes (1½ pounds), peeled and cut into 1-inch cubes (5 cups)

¼ cup unsalted butter

½ cup heavy cream

2 tablespoons granular sugar substitute

½ teaspoon salt

½ teaspoon ground cinnamon

½ teaspoon pumpkin pie spice

1 (15-ounce) can pumpkin purée

1 Heat oven to 250°F. Lightly butter a baking sheet.

2 FOR TOPPING: Place egg whites in a medium mixing bowl; beat with an electric mixer at high speed until foamy. Gradually add sugar substitute; continue mixing just until soft peaks form. Spoon onto prepared baking sheet and spread with a spatula to a ¼-inch thickness. Bake 35 minutes. Turn oven off; let meringue stand in oven for 45 minutes. Crush meringue and place in a bowl. Add pecans; toss gently to combine.

3 FOR PURÉE: Place sweet potatoes in a medium saucepan. Cover with water to 2 inches above potatoes; bring to a boil. Cook until tender, 20 minutes drain. Return saucepan to medium-high heat. Add potatoes and all remaining ingredients; stir to combine. Mash with a potato masher until smooth; cook until heated through, about 1 minute. Transfer potato mixture to a serving bowl; cover with topping.

CANDIED GINGER SWEET POTATOES

PER SERVING **Net Carbs: 18 grams;** Carbohydrates: 21 grams; Fiber: 3 grams; Protein: 2 grams; Fat: 4.5 grams; Calories: 130

3 4 Makes 8 servings; Prep time: 20 minutes; Cook time: 45 minutes

Substituting sugar-free pancake syrup for maple syrup in this holiday classic saves 6 grams of Net Carbs per serving.

4 sweet potatoes, (about 2 pounds), peeled and cut into 1-inch slices

⅓ cup sugar-free pancake syrup

1 tablespoon peeled and grated fresh ginger, chopped

3 tablespoons cold unsalted butter, cut into small pieces

1 Heat oven to 350°F. Butter an 8- by 10-inch baking dish.

2 Cook potatoes in boiling salted water until almost tender, 8 to 10 minutes. Drain.

3 Combine syrup and ginger in a small saucepan. Cook over low heat until syrup is warm and the flavors have blended, about 3 minutes.

4 Arrange potatoes in a single layer in baking dish. Pour syrup mixture over potatoes. Dot with butter. Cover with aluminum foil and bake until potatoes are very soft, about 40 minutes.

Atkins Tip: Make this dish a day or two ahead and store tightly wrapped in the refrigerator. Bring to room temperature, then reheat in the oven with your other holiday dishes (at any temperature below 400°F).

LATKES

 PER SERVING **Net Carbs: 5.5 grams;** Carbohydrates: 13.5 grams; Fiber: 8 grams; Protein: 15.5 grams; Fat: 19 grams; Calories: 285
Makes 8 (2-latke) servings; Prep time: 10 minutes, plus 10 minutes cooling; Cook time: 20 minutes

Latkes—on Atkins? Sure! These "potato" pancakes really taste like potatoes, thanks to Instant Mashers, a low-carb potato-flavored powder available at www.atkins.com. The latkes puff slightly as they cook (much like high-carb pancakes) and remain soft and fluffy inside.

2 cups water

3 tablespoons olive oil

1 (5.9-ounce) package Dixie Carb Counters™ Instant Mashers, Classic Flavor

2 large eggs

1 cup Atkins Quick Quisine™ Bake Mix, divided

¼ cup finely chopped fresh chives

1 teaspoon salt

¼ teaspoon pepper

6 tablespoons canola oil

1 Bring water and olive oil to a boil in a medium saucepan over medium-high heat. Whisk in Instant Mashers. Reduce heat to medium-low and cook, stirring with a wooden spoon, until thickened, 1 to 2 minutes. Transfer to a large bowl. Let cool 10 minutes.

2 Stir in eggs, ½ cup of the bake mix, chives, salt, and pepper; mix well. Spread remaining ½ cup bake mix on a plate. Drop a level ¼ cup of Instant Mashers mixture into the bake mix. Turn each lump to coat, and pat into a 3-inch disk. Prepare and cook each batch before forming the next.

3 Heat 4 tablespoons of oil in a large nonstick skillet over medium heat. Add the first batch of latkes and cook until golden and slightly puffed, about 4 minutes, turning once. Form the next batch of latkes. Add 1 tablespoon more oil to skillet and cook latkes. Repeat with the remaining oil and latkes. Keep the cooked latkes warm in a 200°F oven.

GREEN BEANS AMANDINE

 PER SERVING **Net Carbs: 6 grams;** Carbohydrates: 12 grams; Fiber: 6 grams; Protein: 4 grams; Fat: 11 grams; Calories: 150
Makes 8 servings; Prep time: 10 minutes; Cook time: 10 minutes

Cook the beans up to two days in advance and store in the refrigerator. By cooking the almonds in the butter, you infuse all the butter—which will coat the beans—with a warm, nutty flavor.

1½ teaspoons salt, divided

2 pounds green beans, trimmed on an angle

4 tablespoons (½ stick) unsalted butter

3 tablespoons sliced almonds

Salt and pepper

1 Bring a large pot of salted water to a boil. Add green beans and return to a boil. Cook until crisp-tender, 3 minutes; drain.

2 Melt butter with almonds in a large skillet over medium heat. Cook until butter is lightly browned and almonds are fragrant, 4 to 5 minutes. Add green beans to skillet and cook, tossing, until hot, about 2 minutes. Season with salt and pepper to taste.

Green Bean, Pepper, and Onion Sauté

GREEN BEAN, PEPPER, AND ONION SAUTÉ

 2 3 4 PER SERVING **Net Carbs: 9 grams;** Carbohydrates: 11 grams; Fiber: 2 grams; Protein: 2 grams; Fat: 7 grams; Calories: 110
Makes 8 servings; Prep time: 20 minutes; Cook time: 25 minutes

*Caramelized baby onions add a soft, sweet note to the snap of green beans in this
very pretty dish. Cook the green beans and onions ahead of time, through step 2,
and when it's time to serve dinner, finish with step 3.*

1 pound green beans, trimmed

3 tablespoons unsalted butter

1½ cups frozen small white onions

6 garlic cloves, minced (1 tablespoon)

½ teaspoon dried thyme

1 red bell pepper, cut into ¼-inch-thick strips

1 green bell pepper, cut into ¼-inch-thick strips

1 tablespoon red wine vinegar

⅓ cup chopped hazelnuts

Salt and pepper

1 Bring a large pot of salted water to a boil. Add the green beans and cook until bright green and crisp-tender, about 3 minutes; drain.

2 Melt butter in a large skillet over medium-high heat. Add onions, garlic, and thyme. Cook, stirring occasionally, until lightly browned, 8 to 10 minutes. Stir in peppers and vinegar; cook, stirring occasionally, until softened, 7 to 8 minutes.

3 Stir in green beans and hazelnuts; cook until beans are hot and hazelnuts are lightly toasted, 2 to 3 minutes. Season with salt and pepper to taste.

GREEN BEANS WITH GINGER-PECAN BUTTER

 PER SERVING **Net Carbs: 3 grams;** Carbohydrates: 6 grams; Fiber: 3 grams; Protein: 2 grams; Fat: 7 grams; Calories: 90
Makes 6 servings; Prep time: 20 minutes; Cook time: 7 minutes

Butter flavored with ginger and toasted pecans gives vegetables holiday flavor and flair. The nuts add valuable nutrients along with loads of flavor and crunch. You can make the seasoned butter ahead of time and refrigerate until ready to use.

1 pound of green beans, trimmed and halved

¼ cup pecans, toasted and finely chopped

2 tablespoons butter, softened

1½ teaspoon finely grated fresh ginger

¼ teaspoon salt

1 Bring a large pot of salted water to boil. Add green beans and cook until crisp-tender, about 5 minutes; drain.

2 Mix pecans, butter, ginger, and salt together in a small bowl.

3 Return beans to pot; add butter mixture. Cook over low heat, stirring, until beans are hot and butter has melted, about 1 minute.

Atkins Tip: You can start this recipe up to three days ahead of time. Cook beans, plunge in a bowl of ice water until cold, then pat dry and refrigerate until ready to use.

GREEN BEAN SUCCOTASH WITH KIELBASA

PER SERVING **Net Carbs: 8 grams;** Carbohydrates: 13 grams; Fiber: 5 grams; Protein: 7 grams; Fat: 9 grams; Calories: 150
Makes 8 servings; Prep time: 15 minutes plus 10 minutes cooling; Cook time: 20 minutes

We've used edamame (green soy beans) in place of the high-carb lima beans usually found in succotash. Look for shelled, blanched edamame in the freezer section of your supermarket.

1 red bell pepper, halved and seeded

2 teaspoons salt, divided

2 pounds fresh green beans, trimmed and cut into
    1-inch pieces

1 cup frozen edamame, thawed

½ cup corn kernels

3 tablespoons extra virgin olive oil, divided

¾ cup kielbasa, cut into ½-inch dice

2 tablespoons fresh lemon juice

3 shallots, chopped (⅓ cup)

¼ teaspoon pepper

¼ cup chopped fresh chives

1 Heat broiler. Place bell pepper halves cut-sides down on a foil-lined baking sheet. Broil until skins are blistered, about 10 minutes. Place peppers in a resealable plastic bag; seal and let stand 10 minutes. Peel peppers, discarding skins; chop remainder and set aside.

2 Bring a medium saucepan half-filled with water to a boil. Add 1 teaspoon of the salt, green beans, and edamame; steam until green beans are crisp-tender, about 3 minutes. Add corn; cook an additional 30 seconds. Drain; rinse with cold water and drain again.

3 Place 1 tablespoon of the oil in saucepan; return to medium-high heat. Add kielbasa; sauté until browned, about 4 minutes. Remove from heat. Add green bean mixture, remaining 2 tablespoons oil, lemon juice, shallots, pepper, and chives; toss well to combine. Serve warm.

ROASTED FENNEL WITH RED PEPPERS

 PER SERVING **Net Carbs: 6.5 grams;** Carbohydrates: 9 grams; Fiber: 2.5 grams; Protein: 1.5 grams; Fat: 5 grams; Calories: 79
Makes 6 servings; Prep time: 10 minutes; Cook time: 40 minutes

Fennel has a sweet and very mild licorice flavor. It should not be confused with fresh anise, which has a more assertive licorice taste. The feathery fronds that top fennel stalks make a lovely garnish and can add subtle flavor to broths and soups.

2 fennel bulbs (2¼ pounds), trimmed and cut into
 ¼-inch-thick wedges

2 red bell peppers, cut into ¼-inch-thick strips

2 tablespoons extra virgin olive oil

1 teaspoon dried oregano

1 teaspoon salt

¼ teaspoon pepper

1 Heat oven to 425°F. Lightly oil a rimmed baking sheet.

2 Combine fennel, bell pepper, oil, oregano, salt, and pepper in a large bowl; toss well to coat. Transfer fennel mixture to the prepared baking sheet; roast, stirring occasionally, until vegetables are tender and lightly browned, about 40 minutes.

Roasted Fennel with Red Peppers

KALE GRATIN WITH CREAMY MUENSTER SAUCE

 PER SERVING **Net Carbs: 4 grams;** Carbohydrates: 5 grams; Fiber: 1 gram; Protein: 4 grams; Fat: 8 grams; Calories: 110
Makes 10 servings; Prep time: 20 minutes; Cook time: 10 minutes

Kale, a member of the cabbage family, is a nutrient powerhouse: it's loaded with antioxidants and vitamins A, C, and K.

1 bunch kale (1 pound), tough stems discarded, washed (12 cups)

4 tablespoons (½ stick) unsalted butter

½ cup low-carb bread crumbs

2 tablespoons Atkins Quick Quisine™ Bake Mix

1 cup lower sodium chicken broth, heated

4 ounces Muenster cheese, shredded (1 cup)

½ teaspoon salt

½ teaspoon pepper

½ teaspoon freshly grated nutmeg

1 Heat oven to 425°F. Butter an 8-inch-square baking dish. Slice kale leaves crosswise into ½-inch-thick strips.

2 Cook kale in a large pot of lightly salted boiling water until tender, 10 minutes. Drain in a colander and rinse with cold water. Press with the back of a spoon to remove excess water. Chop finely.

3 Melt 2 tablespoons of the butter in a medium saucepan over medium heat, add bread crumbs and stir until browned, 2 to 3 minutes. Transfer to a small bowl.

4 In same skillet, melt remaining 2 tablespoons butter over medium-high heat. Whisk in bake mix and cook until bubbly, about 1 minute. Whisk in hot broth and bring to a boil. Cook, whisking until very thick, about 2 minutes. Add ½ cup of cheese, salt, pepper, and nutmeg; heat until cheese is melted. Stir in kale. Spread evenly in prepared baking dish. Top with buttered bread crumbs and remaining ½ cup cheese. Bake until golden brown, 15 to 20 minutes.

Atkins Tip: To make a ½-cup of low-carb bread crumbs, leave two slices of low-carb bread out on the counter until it's dry or toast it briefly in a low oven. Grind the stale bread in a food processor.

KALE WITH BACON AND GARLIC

 PER SERVING **Net Carbs: 7 grams;** Carbohydrates: 8.5 grams; Fiber: 1.5 grams; Protein: 7.5 grams; Fat: 6 grams; Calories: 115
Makes 6 servings; Prep time: 15 minutes; Cook time: 20 minutes

The strong flavors of garlic and bacon are a great match for kale.

1 bunch kale (1 pound), tough stems discarded, washed and coarsely chopped (12 cups)

4 ounces sliced bacon, cut crosswise into ½-inch pieces

1 large onion, chopped (1 cup)

¼ teaspoon crushed red pepper flakes

6 garlic cloves, minced (1 tablespoon)

1 tablespoon red wine vinegar

½ cup grated Parmesan cheese, preferably Parmigiano-Reggiano

1 Cook kale in a large pot of salted boiling water, until tender, about 10 minutes. Drain, reserving ½ cup of cooking water. Rinse kale under cold water and pat dry.

2 Heat a large skillet over medium heat, add the bacon and cook until crisp, 6 to 7 minutes. Remove bacon from the skillet and drain on a plate covered with paper towels. Reduce heat to low; add onion and pepper flakes to bacon drippings. Cook until onion is tender and lightly golden, 10 minutes. Add garlic and cook 1 minute. Drain off excess fat.

3 Return kale, reserved cooking water, and vinegar to skillet. Mix well and cook until heated through, 1 to 2 minutes. Transfer to a serving dish; sprinkle with cheese.

Kale with Pears and Onions

KALE WITH PEARS AND ONIONS

PER SERVING **Net Carbs: 14 grams;** Carbohydrates: 17 grams; Fiber: 3 grams; Protein: 4 grams; Fat: 6 grams; Calories: 130

3 4 Makes 6 servings; Prep time: 15 minutes; Cook time: 30 minutes

Sweet sautéed pears add an unexpected light note and counterpoint to kale. The kale can be blanched up to three days ahead.

1 bunch kale (1 pound), tough stems discarded, washed and coarsely chopped (12 cups)

3 tablespoons olive oil

1 medium onion, thinly sliced (1 cup)

1 medium pear, cored and cut into ¼-inch-thick wedges

¼ teaspoon curry powder

⅛ teaspoon ground nutmeg

½ teaspoon salt

¼ teaspoon pepper

1 Cook kale in a large pot of lightly salted water until bright green and wilted, about 3 minutes. Drain, cool 10 minutes and squeeze out excess liquid.

2 Heat oil in a large nonstick skillet over medium-high heat. Add onion and cook, stirring occasionally, until lightly golden, 6 to 7 minutes. Stir in pear and cook until crisp-tender, 2 to 3 minutes. Add curry powder and nutmeg and cook until fragrant, about 30 seconds.

3 Add kale, salt, and pepper to skillet. Cook stirring frequently, until tender, 3 to 4 minutes.

Mixed Berry and Ricotta–Stuffed Crêpes, page 121

BRUNCH

For overnight guests or to extend the pleasure of your party for one more day, you'll find these brunch dishes are the stuff of sweet dreams. Choices like family-friendly Blueberry-Pecan Pancakes and Raspberry Cream Cheese Bread Pudding as well as chic bistro-style dishes like Frisée with Lardons and Poached Eggs mean you will have something sure to please everyone.

SAVORY ITALIAN TART

PER SERVING **Net Carbs: 5 grams;** Carbohydrates 7.5 grams; Fiber: 2.5 grams; Protein: 21.5 grams; Fat: 25 grams; Calories: 334
Makes 8 servings; Prep time: 25 minutes; Cook time: 40 minutes

An elegant addition to a luncheon or buffet table, this flavorful dish is packed with classic Mediterranean ingredients, including olives, ricotta, Italian sausage, and herbs.

2 teaspoons Atkins Quick Quisine™ Bake Mix

1 pound asparagus, trimmed

6 ounces hot Italian sausage, removed from casing

2 large eggs, lightly beaten

1 (16-ounce) container ricotta cheese (2 cups)

8 ounces Jarlsberg cheese, shredded (2¾ cups), divided

2 plum tomatoes, seeded and chopped

1 teaspoon dried Italian herbs

½ teaspoon pepper

½ cup sliced black or green olives

1 Heat oven to 375°F. Lightly coat bottom and sides of an 11-inch tart pan with removable bottom with cooking spray. Sift bake mix evenly onto bottom and sides of pan; set aside.

2 Bring a large saucepan of salted water to a boil over medium-high heat. Add asparagus and cook until crisp-tender, 2 to 3 minutes (depending on thickness of spears). Drain; cover with cold water to stop cooking. Drain well. Cut 2½ inches off the asparagus tips for top of tart and set aside. Slice stalks into ¼-inch pieces.

3 Heat a large heavy skillet over medium heat. Crumble sausage into skillet; cook until lightly browned, stirring occasionally, 5 minutes. Add asparagus stalks. Cook until asparagus is tender, 2 minutes. Remove from heat.

4 In a large bowl, combine eggs and ricotta. Stir in 2½ cups of the Jarlsberg cheese, tomatoes, sausage mixture, Italian herbs, and pepper; mix well.

5 Spread mixture evenly into tart pan, smoothing top. Place on a large baking sheet and bake for 25 minutes. Remove from oven. Arrange reserved asparagus tips, spoke style, in center of tart, pressing in slightly. Sprinkle with remaining ¼ cup Jarlsberg cheese and olives. Bake until the tip of a knife inserted near the center comes out clean, about 5 minutes. Let stand 15 minutes. Remove from pan and serve.

ITALIAN SAUSAGE PATTIES

PER SERVING **Net Carbs: 0.5 gram;** Carbohydrates: 1 gram; Fiber: 0.5 gram; Protein: 19.5 grams; Fat: 24 grams; Calories: 303
Makes 8 (2-patty) servings; Prep time: 20 minutes, plus 1 hour chilling; Cook time: 16 minutes

These flavorful patties make a tasty alternative to the usual breakfast bacon or ham. Make extras and freeze them, uncooked and individually wrapped.

3 garlic cloves, minced (1½ teaspoons)

1 tablespoon dried sage

1 teaspoon dried oregano

½ teaspoon onion powder

¼ teaspoon ground allspice

¼ teaspoon dried thyme

1¾ teaspoons salt

¾ teaspoon pepper

2 pounds ground pork

1 Combine garlic, sage, oregano, onion powder, allspice, thyme, salt, and pepper in a large bowl; mix thoroughly. Add pork to the bowl; use your hands to evenly mix and distribute spices through meat. Cover with plastic wrap. Refrigerate 1 hour.

2 With wet hands, shape mixture into 16 ¼-inch-thick patties. Do not overwork the meat.

3 Heat a nonstick skillet over medium-high heat. Working in batches, add the sausage patties and cook, turning once, until browned and cooked through, about 8 minutes.

Savory Italian Tart

MIXED BERRY AND RICOTTA–STUFFED CRÊPES

PER SERVING **Net Carbs: 5 grams;** Carbohydrates: 6 grams; Fiber: 1 gram; Protein: 3 grams; Fat: 4 grams; Calories: 70

3 4 Makes 24 (1-crêpe) servings; Prep time: 15 minutes; Cook time: 1 hour 12 minutes

Make the crêpe batter several hours in advance and keep it tightly covered in the refrigerator. Crêpes are shown on page 118.

FILLING:

1½ pints strawberries, stems removed, berries quartered (3 cups)

1 pint blueberries (2 cups)

1 (16-ounce) container ricotta cheese

4 teaspoons granular sugar substitute

CRÊPES:

4 tablespoons unsalted butter, divided

1 cup Atkins Quick Quisine™ Bake Mix

¼ cup whole-wheat flour

1 tablespoon granular sugar substitute

2 cups reduced-carb whole-milk dairy beverage

2 large eggs, lightly beaten

1 FOR FILLING: Combine strawberries, blueberries, ricotta, and sugar substitute in a bowl; mix well.

2 FOR CRÊPES: Melt 2 tablespoons butter in the microwave. Combine bake mix, flour, and sugar substitute in a large bowl. Add dairy beverage, melted butter, and eggs, stirring until combined.

3 Heat an 8-inch nonstick skillet over medium-low heat until hot. Rub with a little bit of butter. Add 2 tablespoons batter, tilting the pan to coat the bottom and form a disk. Cook until lightly browned, about 1½ minutes. Carefully flip crêpe with a spatula; cook 1 minute longer. Transfer to a large plate. Repeat with the remaining batter.

4 Arrange 6 crêpes on a work surface. Spoon 3 tablespoons filling down the center of each and roll them up. Repeat with remaining filling and crêpes.

EGGS BENEDICT WITH BÉARNAISE SAUCE

PER SERVING **Net Carbs: 5 grams;** Carbohydrates: 5.5 grams; Fiber: 0.5 gram; Protein: 21.5 grams; Fat: 47 grams; Calories: 539
Makes 6 servings; Prep time: 30 minutes; Cook time: 25 minutes

These poached eggs sit on Canadian bacon and tomato slices and are topped with rich, classic béarnaise sauce.

BÉARNAISE SAUCE:

1 shallot, minced (2 tablespoons)

2 tablespoons white wine vinegar or tarragon vinegar

⅔ cup dry white wine

½ teaspoon whole black peppercorns, cracked

7 sprigs fresh tarragon, leaves chopped, stems reserved

4 large egg yolks

1 cup (2 sticks) unsalted butter, melted

¾ teaspoon salt

Pinch cayenne

EGGS:

1 tablespoon unsalted butter

12 slices Canadian bacon (about 8 ounces)

2 large beefsteak tomatoes (cut in 12 ⅓-inch-thick slices)

Salt and pepper

¼ cup white vinegar

12 large eggs

1 FOR BÉARNAISE SAUCE: In a small saucepan, combine shallot, vinegar, wine, peppercorns, and tarragon stems. Simmer over medium-low heat until liquid is reduced to ¼ cup, about 15 minutes.

2 Strain reduced wine mixture into the top of a double boiler. Whisk in egg yolks and continue whisking until mixture becomes foamy and thick, about 2 minutes. Remove the top of the double boiler and turn off the flame. Place the top of the double boiler back over the hot water and very slowly whisk in butter. Whisk in salt, cayenne, and chopped tarragon. Hold sauce over the hot water or in an insulated thermos until ready to use. Do not reheat.

3 FOR EGGS: Heat oven to 200°F. Melt butter in a large skillet set over medium-high heat. Working in two batches, cook bacon until lightly browned. Place in oven to keep warm. Season tomato slices with salt and pepper to taste and, working again in two batches, warm tomatoes in the skillet. Keep warm in the oven.

4 Bring an inch of water to a bare simmer in a large skillet. Add vinegar. Break eggs into small cups and gently pour six at a time into the water. Cook eggs just until the whites are firm, about 2 minutes. Lift eggs out with a slotted spoon and place on a plate covered with paper towels to absorb water. Cook remaining eggs in same manner.

5 To assemble, place two tomato slices on each plate. Top each with a slice of bacon and an egg. Spoon a tablespoon of béarnaise over each and top with pepper.

Eggs Benedict with Béarnaise Sauce

SMOKED SALMON AND CHIVE OMELET

 PER SERVING Net Carbs: 2 grams; Carbohydrates: 2.5 grams; Fiber: 0.5 gram; Protein: 16.5 grams; Fat: 27 grams; Calories: 322
Makes 2 servings; Prep time: 10 minutes; Cook time: 6 minutes

This recipe makes one omelet large enough for two. To serve a crowd, multiply the recipe as many times as you wish, then cook each omelet only to the point of adding the filling and folding it over. Finish cooking by transferring them to a foil lined baking sheet in a 200°F oven, where they can be held for up to 45 minutes.

1 ounce smoked salmon, chopped (2 slices)

1 tablespoon cream cheese, softened

4 large eggs, beaten

2 tablespoons heavy cream

1 teaspoon Dijon mustard

1 tablespoon chopped fresh chives

½ teaspoon salt

⅛ teaspoon pepper

1½ tablespoons butter

1 Combine salmon and cream cheese in a small bowl and mix well. Combine eggs, cream, mustard, chives, salt, and pepper in a separate bowl; mix well.

2 Melt butter in an 8½-inch skillet set over medium heat. Pour in the egg mixture; cook, occasionally lifting the edges with a spatula to allow raw egg to run under, until underside is lightly browned and top is still slightly wet, 4 to 5 minutes. Spoon cream cheese mixture onto half of the omelet, fold the unfilled half over it, and cook 30 seconds. Turn and cook until egg is set, 45 seconds to 1 minute longer.

FRISÉE WITH LARDONS AND POACHED EGGS

 PER SERVING Net Carbs: 3 grams; Carbohydrates: 7 grams; Fiber: 4 grams; Protein: 9 grams; Fat: 17 grams; Calories: 220
Makes 8 servings; Prep time: 20 minutes; Cook time: 10 minutes

This classic French bistro salad is as refreshing for the brunch table as it is for a first dinner course. The gently poached egg yolk, when burst with a fork, becomes part of the salad dressing. Lardon is the French word for diced and fried bacon.

2 tablespoons sherry vinegar

1 tablespoon Dijon mustard

1 shallot, minced (2 tablespoons)

¾ teaspoon salt

¼ teaspoon pepper

⅓ cup macadamia nut or walnut oil

6 slices thick-cut bacon, cut into 1½- by ¼-inch rectangles

2 bunches frisée or white chicory, cut into 2-inch pieces (12 cups)

3 tablespoons white vinegar

8 large eggs

Salt and pepper

1 Whisk sherry vinegar, mustard, shallot, salt, and pepper in a small bowl. Add the oil in a slow, steady stream, whisking continuously until well combined.

2 Cook bacon in a medium skillet set over medium-high heat, stirring occasionally, until crisp, 6 to 7 minutes.

3 Toss frisée with vinegar mixture in a large bowl. Divide among 8 plates and top with bacon.

4 Meanwhile, bring an inch of water to a bare simmer in a large skillet. Add the vinegar. Break eggs into small cups and gently pour into the water. Cook eggs just until the whites are firm, about 2 minutes. Lift eggs out with a slotted spoon and place on a plate covered with paper towels to absorb water. Place one egg on top of each salad. Season with salt and pepper to taste.

DUBLINER CHEESE TART

PER SERVING **Net Carbs: 2 grams;** Carbohydrates: 3 grams; Fiber: 1 gram; Protein: 13 grams; Fat: 24 grams; Calories: 270
Makes 6 servings; Prep time: 20 minutes; Cook time: 30 minutes

Sliced into six pieces, this traditional Irish tart can be enjoyed as a main course with
with a cup of tea and a salad; cut into twelve smaller slices, serve it as a side dish
with a roast.

1 teaspoon Atkins Quick Quisine™ Bake Mix

1 tablespoon unsalted butter

4 scallions, thinly sliced (¼ cup)

1 garlic clove, minced (½ teaspoon)

3 slices Canadian bacon, cut into thin strips (⅓ cup)

8 medium mushrooms, thinly sliced (2 cups)

½ teaspoon dried basil

½ teaspoon dried thyme

¼ teaspoon dried sage

¼ teaspoon dried oregano

⅛ teaspoon dried rosemary

3 large eggs

¾ cup heavy cream

1 teaspoon whole-grain mustard

4 ounces grated cheddar cheese (1½ cups)

1 medium plum tomato, cut into 6 slices

Fresh thyme, for garnish

1 Heat oven to 350°F. Butter bottom, sides, and rim of a 9-inch quiche pan or pie plate. Sift bake mix over bottom, sides and rim of pan; set aside.

2 Melt butter in a large skillet set over medium heat. Add scallions and garlic; cook, stirring occasionally, until scallions begin to soften, about 1 minute. Add bacon; cook, stirring occasionally, until bacon begins to brown, about 3 minutes. Add mushrooms, basil, thyme, sage, oregano, and rosemary; cook, stirring occasionally, until mushrooms are softened, 5 to 7 minutes. Set aside.

3 Whisk eggs, heavy cream, and mustard in a medium bowl until thoroughly blended.

4 Spoon mushroom mixture into the pan, sprinkle with cheese, and pour in egg mixture. Arrange tomato slices on top. Bake until tart is slightly puffed and golden brown and a knife inserted near center comes out clean, 25 to 30 minutes. Serve warm or at room temperature. Garnish with fresh thyme.

ZUCCHINI BREAD

PER SERVING **Net Carbs: 6.5 grams;** Carbohydrates: 9 grams; Fiber: 2.5 grams; Protein: 7 grams; Fat: 12 grams; Calories: 170
Makes 12 servings; Prep time: 15 minutes; Cook time: 45 minutes, plus cooling time

Instead of serving slices of this as a traditional brunch loaf, bake the batter in
muffin tins (just reduce the baking time) to accompany a dinner entrée.

¾ cup whole-wheat pastry flour

½ cup Atkins Quick Quisine™ Bake Mix

1 teaspoon salt

1 teaspoon baking powder

½ cup (1 stick) unsalted butter, softened

½ cup sour cream

4 large eggs

1 large zucchini, grated (2 cups)

2 tablespoons grated onion

⅓ cup grated Parmesan cheese

1 Heat oven to 350°F. Lightly butter a 9- by 5-inch loaf pan.

2 Whisk pastry flour, bake mix, salt, and baking powder in a small bowl to combine. Place butter in a medium mixing bowl; beat at high speed with an electric mixer until light and fluffy. Beat in sour cream; add eggs, one at a time, beating well after each addition. Stir in zucchini and onion. Reduce mixer to low speed; add flour mixture gradually, beating until just combined.

3 Pour batter into prepared pan; sprinkle cheese over top. Bake until golden brown and set, about 45 minutes. Cool in pan 10 minutes. Remove from pan; cool completely on a wire rack.

Dubliner Cheese Tart

TURKEY, GRUYÈRE, AND ONION SPOONBREAD

 PER SERVING **Net Carbs: 10 grams;** Carbohydrates: 13 grams; Fiber: 3 grams; Protein: 19 grams; Fat: 26 grams; Calories: 360
Makes 12 servings; Prep time: 20 minutes; Cook time: 42 minutes

Spoonbread is a traditional side dish in the South. With the addition of leftover turkey and cheese, it becomes a brunch or lunch entrée. It's also a great way to use up that leftover Thanksgiving turkey!

¼ cup unsalted butter

1 medium onion, thinly sliced (¾ cup)

1 (8½-ounce) package Atkins Quick Quisine™ Deluxe Corn Muffin & Bread Mix

1 cup heavy cream

½ cup water

½ cup sour cream

⅓ cup vegetable oil

3 eggs, separated

1 teaspoon salt

6 ounces shredded Gruyère cheese (1½ cups)

1½ cups chopped cooked turkey breast (cut in ¼- to ½-inch pieces)

1 Heat oven to 350°F. Coat a 9- by 13-inch baking dish with butter or oil.

2 Melt butter in a large skillet over medium heat. Add onion; cook, stirring often, until golden, 10 to 12 minutes. Remove from heat.

3 Place cornbread mix in a large bowl. Add cream, water, sour cream, oil, egg yolks, and salt; stir well to combine. Stir in cheese. Beat egg whites at high speed with an electric mixer until stiff peaks form. Gently fold egg whites into cornbread mixture.

4 Sprinkle turkey evenly in the prepared dish; top with cornbread mixture. Sprinkle onions evenly over top. Bake until golden, about 30 minutes.

BACON-CHEDDAR BISCUITS

 PER SERVING **Net Carbs: 3.5 grams;** Carbohydrates: 5.5 grams; Fiber: 2 grams; Protein: 6 grams; Fat: 13.5 grams; Calories: 164
Makes 14 servings: Prep time: 20 minutes; Cook time: 18 minutes

These breakfast biscuits are equally tasty when made with bits of sausage or ham instead of bacon, or with Brie or blue cheese instead of cheddar.

4 slices bacon, cut into ½-inch pieces

1 cup Atkins Quick Quisine™ Bake Mix

¼ cup whole-wheat flour

1¼ teaspoons baking powder

½ teaspoon granular sugar substitute

4 tablespoons (½ stick) cold unsalted butter, cut into small pieces

1 cup plus 1 tablespoon heavy cream

½ cup shredded sharp cheddar cheese (2 ounces)

1 Heat oven to 350°F. Lightly butter a baking sheet.

2 Cook bacon in a medium skillet over medium-high heat until crisp, 6 to 7 minutes.

3 Combine bake mix, whole-wheat flour, baking powder, and sugar substitute in a medium bowl; mix well. Cut butter into dry mixture with a pastry cutter or 2 knives until it resembles coarse crumbs. Stir in 1 cup of the cream; mix until just combined. Stir in bacon and cheese. Turn dough out onto a work surface lightly dusted with bake mix. Knead dough 4 to 5 times until smooth. Pat into a ½-inch-thick 7-inch round. Use a 2-inch biscuit cutter to cut 11 rounds. Reroll the scraps and cut 3 more rounds.

4 Place the biscuit rounds on the prepared baking sheet. Brush the tops with remaining tablespoon cream. Bake until biscuits rise and are lightly golden, 16 to 18 minutes. Remove from oven. Cool on a wire rack 10 minutes before serving.

Blueberry-Pecan Pancakes

BLUEBERRY-PECAN PANCAKES

PER SERVING **Net Carbs: 5.5 grams;** Carbohydrates: 10.5 grams; Fiber: 5 grams; Protein: 14 grams; Fat: 12 grams; Calories: 194.5
Makes 8 (3-pancake) servings; Prep time: 10 minutes; Cook time: 30 minutes

No one would ever know these pancakes are lower in carbs than regular pancakes.
They look, taste, and even have the texture of everyone's favorite breakfast treat—
all while supporting your Atkins lifestyle.

4 tablespoons unsalted butter, melted

1½ cups Atkins Quick Quisine™ Bake Mix

2 packets sugar substitute

1 teaspoon baking powder

¼ teaspoon ground cinnamon

1½ cups reduced-carb whole-milk dairy beverage

2 large eggs, separated

½ teaspoon almond extract

1 cup fresh or thawed frozen blueberries

½ cup chopped pecans

1 Melt 2 tablespoons butter in the microwave. Combine bake mix, sugar substitute, baking powder, and cinnamon in a large bowl. Combine dairy beverage, melted butter, egg yolks, and almond extract in a separate bowl; mix well. Pour wet ingredients into the dry; stir to incorporate.

2 Beat egg whites with an electric mixer on high speed until stiff peaks form. Fold egg whites into batter until just combined. Stir in blueberries and pecans; let stand 5 minutes.

3 Melt 2 teaspoons butter in a large nonstick skillet set over medium heat. Drop a heaping tablespoon of batter onto skillet to form each pancake; cook until the tops of the pancakes are covered with bubbles, about 3 minutes. Flip pancakes and cook 3 minutes longer. Repeat with remaining batter and butter.

RASPBERRY CREAM CHEESE BREAD PUDDING

 PER SERVING **Net Carbs: 9 grams;** Carbohydrates: 15.5 grams; Fiber: 6.5 grams; Protein: 18 grams; Fat: 24 grams; Calories: 335
Makes 10 servings; Prep time: 20 minutes; Cook time: 1 hour 5 minutes

This loaf of stuffed bread is a decadent sweet treat. The pretty slices, with their creamy pink raspberry filling, make a beautiful presentation.

8 large eggs, beaten

1¼ cups heavy cream

⅓ cup granular sugar substitute

1 teaspoon vanilla extract

¼ teaspoon almond extract

1 teaspoon ground cinnamon

⅛ teaspoon ground nutmeg

1 (1-pound) loaf low-carb white bread, crusts removed and bread quartered

6 ounces cream cheese, softened

3 tablespoons no-sugar-added raspberry preserves

1 Heat oven to 350°F. Coat a 9- by 5-inch loaf pan with cooking spray.

2 Combine eggs, cream, sugar substitute, vanilla extract, almond extract, cinnamon, and nutmeg in a large bowl; mix well. Add bread pieces to custard and let soak 10 minutes, keeping bread submerged.

3 Meanwhile, combine cream cheese and preserves in a bowl; mix well with a fork.

4 Place half of bread mixture in bottom of loaf pan. Spread cream cheese mixture in a straight line on top of bread mixture leaving a ½-inch border at both ends. Top with remaining bread mixture. Pour any custard left in bowl over bread pudding.

5 Bake until puffed, browned, and set, 60 to 65 minutes. Let stand 5 minutes and serve.

OLD-FASHIONED SPICE DOUGHNUTS

PER SERVING **Net Carbs: 7.5 grams;** Carbohydrates: 11 grams; Fiber: 3.5 grams; Protein: 9 grams; Fat: 11 grams; Calories: 161
Makes 8 servings; Prep Time: 20 minutes; Cook time: 20 minutes

These doughnuts have old-fashioned flavor and a texture that is perfect for dunking.

1 cup plus 1 tablespoon Atkins Quick Quisine™ Bake Mix

⅓ cup whole-wheat flour

⅓ cup granular sugar substitute

1 teaspoon baking powder

1½ teaspoons ground cinnamon

¼ teaspoon ground nutmeg

¼ teaspoon ground allspice

¼ teaspoon ground ginger

⅛ teaspoon ground cloves

½ cup heavy cream

1 large egg, lightly beaten

3 cups plus 1 tablespoon canola oil, separated

1 Combine 1 cup of the bake mix, flour, sugar substitute, baking powder, cinnamon, nutmeg, allspice, ginger, and cloves in a large bowl; stir with a fork. Combine heavy cream, egg, and 1 tablespoon of the oil in a separate bowl; mix well. Add wet ingredients to dry and stir until a dough forms. Turn dough out onto a surface lightly dusted with 1 tablespoon bake mix. Knead until smooth, about 1 minute. Divide dough into 8 equal portions.

2 Roll each dough portion into an 8-inch-long cylinder; form into a ring and pinch the edges firmly to seal.

3 Heat remaining 3 cups oil in a 3-quart saucepan to 350°F on a deep-fry thermometer. Add doughnuts to the oil 3 at a time; fry, turning occasionally, until puffed and golden brown, about 3 minutes. Drain on a baking sheet lined with paper towels. Repeat with the remaining doughnuts.

SPICED BUNDT CAKE

PER SERVING **Net Carbs: 6 grams;** Carbohydrates: 13 grams; Fiber: 7 grams; Protein: 7 grams; Fat: 10 grams; Calories: 215
Makes 16 servings; Prep time: 20 minutes; Cook time: 50 minutes, plus 15 minutes to cool

This flavorful cake is good fresh out of the oven or toasted and topped with butter. For a truly stunning presentation, invest in a decorative bundt pan.

4 cups Atkins Quick Quisine™ Bake Mix

1 cup granular sugar substitute

1 cup chopped walnuts

3 tablespoons ground cinnamon

1 tablespoon ground allspice

1 tablespoon baking powder

¼ teaspoon ground nutmeg

2½ cups reduced-carb whole-milk dairy beverage

6 large eggs, separated

2 tablespoons vanilla extract

2 tablespoons walnut oil

1 Heat oven to 350°F. Lightly coat a 12-cup bundt pan with cooking spray.

2 Combine bake mix, sugar substitute, walnuts, cinnamon, allspice, baking powder, and nutmeg in a large bowl; mix well.

3 Combine dairy beverage, egg yolks, vanilla, and walnut oil in a bowl; mix well. Beat egg whites with an electric mixer on high speed until they hold stiff peaks, 4 to 5 minutes. Add yolk mixture to dry ingredients, stirring until well combined. Fold egg whites into the batter in three additions until just combined.

4 Pour batter into prepared pan. Bake until a cake tester inserted into center of cake comes out clean, about 50 minutes. Invert cake onto a wire rack. Cool at least 15 minutes before slicing.

Spiced Bundt Cake

EGG, CHEDDAR, AND CHORIZO ROULADE

PER SERVING **Net Carbs: 5.5 grams;** Carbohydrates: 7.5 grams; Fiber: 2 grams; Protein: 17 grams; Fat: 32.5 grams; Calories: 393
Makes 8 servings; Prep time: 16 minutes; Cook time: 40 minutes

This show-off brunch dish tastes outstanding and takes less than 20 minutes to prepare. For a less spicy version, use a mild dry sausage instead of chorizo.

ROULADE:

2 teaspoons vegetable oil

8 ounces smoked chorizo sausage, diced

½ teaspoon dried oregano

½ teaspoon ground cumin

½ teaspoon paprika

2 garlic cloves, minced (1 teaspoon)

½ cup heavy cream

7 large eggs, lightly beaten

½ teaspoon salt

⅛ teaspoon pepper

4 ounces grated cheddar cheese (1 cup)

1 medium avocado, pitted and diced

TOPPING:

1 cup sour cream

1 tablespoon chopped fresh cilantro

2 teaspoons fresh lime juice

Salt

1 FOR ROULADE: Heat oven to 325°F. Lightly oil a 9- by 13-inch baking dish. Line dish with parchment paper; lightly oil paper.

2 Heat oil in a large skillet set over medium-high heat. Add sausage; sauté until it begins to brown, about 2 minutes. Add oregano, cumin, paprika, and garlic; sauté 1 minute more. Remove from heat. Place sausage in a single layer in prepared dish.

3 Whisk cream, eggs, salt, and pepper in a small bowl to combine. Pour egg mixture over sausage. Bake until eggs are set, 28 to 30 minutes.

4 Remove eggs from dish. Sprinkle cheese over top of eggs, then sprinkle avocado evenly over cheese, leaving a ½-inch border around the edges. Starting with long edge, and using parchment paper as a guide, roll eggs up jelly-roll style. Let stand 2 minutes.

5 FOR TOPPING: Combine sour cream, cilantro, and lime juice, stirring well. Season with salt to taste. Slice the roulade and serve with sour cream topping.

Egg, Cheddar, and Chorizo Roulade

MUSHROOM SCONES

PER SERVING **Net Carbs: 2.5 grams;** Carbohydrates: 6 grams; Fiber: 3.5 grams; Protein: 10 grams; Fat: 12 grams; Calories:163
Makes 16 servings; Prep time: 25 minutes; Cook time: 21 minutes

These tender, savory scones are best straight from the oven. If you need to make them in advance, reheat in a 350°F oven for a few minutes before serving.

3 tablespoons vegetable oil

8 ounces shiitake mushrooms, stems removed and discarded, caps diced

¾ teaspoon dried thyme

2¼ cups Atkins Quick Quisine™ Bake Mix ,plus more for pressing out the dough

1 tablespoon baking powder

½ teaspoon salt

6 tablespoons cold unsalted butter, diced

2 large eggs

¾ cup heavy cream

1 Heat oven to 425°F. Lightly oil a baking sheet.

2 Heat oil in a large skillet set over medium-high heat. Add mushrooms and cook, stirring often, until nicely browned, about 6 minutes. Stir in thyme and remove from heat.

2 Whisk baking mix, baking powder, and salt in a medium bowl to combine. Cut butter into dry mixture with a pastry cutter or 2 knives until pieces are no larger than small peas. Stir in mushrooms. Whisk eggs and cream until smooth; measure and set aside 3 tablespoons. Pour remaining cream mixture over dry ingredients and stir until a soft dough forms.

3 Turn dough out onto a surface very lightly coated with baking mix. Knead dough with your hands a few times. Form into a ball. Press ball to an 8-inch square about ¾-inch thick. Cut dough into 16 squares. Transfer squares to baking sheet with a spatula.

4 Brush top of scones with reserved cream mixture. Bake in top third of oven until scones are nicely browned, about 15 minutes. Let cool on baking sheet 2 minutes. Serve warm or transfer to a wire rack to cool completely. Store in an airtight container for up to 1 day.

TOMATO-BASIL FRITTATA

PER SERVING **Net Carbs: 6 grams;** Carbohydrates: 7 grams; Fiber: 1 gram; Protein: 20.5 grams; Fat: 27.5 grams; Calories: 351
Makes 6 servings; Prep time: 15 minutes; Cook time: 15 minutes

When company is staying at your house, get a head start on this frittata by making separate containers of the egg mixture, the chopped onion and garlic, and the tomatoes the night before.

12 large eggs

⅓ cup heavy cream

¾ teaspoon salt

¼ teaspoon pepper

1 cup shredded mozzarella cheese (4 ounces)

½ cup chopped fresh basil

3 tablespoons extra virgin olive oil

1 large onion, chopped (1cup)

3 garlic cloves, minced (1½ teaspoons)

3 plum tomatoes, seeded and chopped

3 tablespoons grated Parmesan cheese

1 Heat broiler. Whisk eggs, heavy cream, salt, and pepper in a large bowl to combine. Stir in mozzarella cheese and basil.

2 Heat oil in a 10-inch ovenproof nonstick skillet set over medium-high heat. Add onion and garlic; cook, stirring occasionally, until starting to soften, 2 minutes. Add tomatoes; cook until giving off liquid, 2 minutes. Pour in egg mixture and stir once; cook, occasionally lifting sides with a spatula to let uncooked egg run underneath, until eggs begin to firm and sides begin to brown, 6 to 7 minutes. Sprinkle Parmesan cheese on top.

3 Place skillet under broiler; cook until eggs are set, puffed, and golden, 3 to 4 minutes. Slide frittata onto a serving platter. Serve hot, warm, or at room temperature.

Lemon-Berry Trifle, page 134

DESSERTS & SWEETS

From a glorious layer cake to a gooey chocolate treat, elegant parfaits and the most fabulous pies to irresistible cookies and homey treats, these desserts will win everyone over to a controlled-carb lifestyle.

LEMON-BERRY TRIFLE

PER SERVING **Net Carbs: 9.5 grams;** Carbohydrates: 12.5 grams; Fiber: 3 grams; Protein: 9 grams; Fat: 23 grams; Calories: 285
Makes 16 servings; Prep time: 25 minutes; Cook time: 32 minutes, plus 8 hours chilling

A layered trifle looks spectacular served in a clear, straight-sided 3½- to 4-quart trifle or serving bowl. Trifle bowls are usually footed, which adds to the stature and elegance of the dessert, as shown on page 132.

CAKE:

8 large eggs

¼ cup granular sugar substitute

1 tablespoon vanilla extract

1 cup Atkins Quick Quisine™ Bake Mix

½ cup no-sugar-added raspberry or strawberry jam

LEMON CUSTARD:

1½ cups heavy cream

1 cup plus 1 tablespoon fresh lemon juice

⅓ cup granular sugar substitute

4 eggs, lightly beaten

⅛ teaspoon salt

8 tablespoons (1 stick) unsalted butter

BERRIES:

1½ cups raspberries

2 cups blackberries

2 cups strawberries, quartered

WHIPPED CREAM:

1 cup heavy cream

1 tablespoon granular sugar substitute

½ teaspoon vanilla extract

1 FOR CAKE: Heat oven to 350°F. Butter a 9- by 12-inch jelly-roll pan. Beat eggs and sugar substitute in a large bowl with an electric mixer on high speed until thick and fluffy, about 9 minutes. Stir in extract. Add bake mix gradually, beating until just combined. Pour batter into pan. Bake in center of oven until a toothpick stuck in center of cake comes out clean, about 9 minutes. Cool in pan 5 minutes. Gently slide a flat spatula beneath cake and roll cake up and away from pan to remove. Cool completely on a wire rack. Cut cake across in half.

2 Spread jam on one half of cake. Set the other half on top, as though forming a sandwich. Cut the cake "sandwich" into long ½-inch wide strips; then cut across to make 2-inch long pieces.

3 FOR LEMON CUSTARD: Combine heavy cream, lemon juice, sugar substitute, eggs, and salt in a medium saucepan. Cook over medium-low heat, stirring constantly, until thick and bubbly, about 12 minutes. Remove from heat; stir in butter until completely melted. Place saucepan in a bowl filled with ice water until custard is completely cool. Stir occasionally.

4 FOR BERRIES: Toss berries together in a medium bowl. Set aside 1 cup for top of trifle.

5 FOR WHIPPED CREAM: Beat heavy cream in a large bowl with an electric mixer on high speed until stiff peaks form. Stir in sugar substitute and extract. Set aside 1 cup whipped cream; gently fold remaining whipped cream into lemon custard.

6 To assemble, set cake "sandwiches" in the trifle bowl end-to-end around the bottom edge, so that the jam filling forms a visible stripe. Fill the center with some of the end pieces of cake. (It's fine to have gaps in the bottom layer.) Spoon 1 cup lemon custard in the center; gently spread custard with the back of a spoon to cover the top of the cake lining the perimeter.

7 Lay a ring of berries over top of cake so they are visible from the outside of the bowl, then scatter more berries over the center. Continue adding layers of cake, custard, and berries, always starting with the perimeter ring. Finish by forming a mound with the reserved whipped cream and topping with the reserved berries. Cover loosely with plastic wrap. Refrigerate 8 hours.

Chocolate Mousse Mini Cheesecakes

CHOCOLATE MOUSSE MINI CHEESECAKES

PER SERVING **Net Carbs: 5.5 grams**; Carbohydrates: 7 grams; Fiber: 1.5 grams; Protein: 7 grams; Fat: 35 grams; Calories: 354
Makes 8 servings ; Prep time: 30 minutes; Cook time: 30 minutes, plus 4 hours chilling

Baking these individual cheesecakes in a water bath gives them a velvety mousse-like texture. Extra cheesecakes can be frozen and then thawed overnight in the refrigerator before serving.

2 (8-ounce) packages cream cheese, softened

3 ounces unsweetened chocolate, melted and cooled

½ cup granular sugar substitute

3 large eggs

¾ cup heavy cream

¾ teaspoon almond extract

½ teaspoon vanilla extract

Boiling water, for water bath

Mint sprigs, unsweetened chocolate shavings, and
  raspberries for garnish (optional)

1 Heat oven to 325°F. Place eight 6-ounce custard cups in a roasting pan; set aside.

2 Beat cream cheese in the large bowl of an electric mixer on medium speed, until lightened, scraping down sides of bowl as needed. Add chocolate and sugar substitute; beat until combined. Add eggs, one at a time, beating well after each addition. Add heavy cream and extracts, beating until completely smooth.

3 Pour mixture into prepared custard cups. Carefully pour enough boiling water into roasting pan to come halfway up sides of custard cups. Bake until mousse is puffed and center is just set, about 20 minutes.

4 Remove from oven, and cool in water bath for 10 minutes. Transfer custard cups to a wire rack; let cool to room temperature. Refrigerate until well chilled, 4 hours or overnight. Garnish with mint sprigs, chocolate shavings, and raspberries, if desired.

Atkins Tip: This is a fairly dense and rich dessert; if you like your cheesecake a little lighter, separate the eggs, add the yolks in step 2, then beat the whites to soft peaks and fold in at the end.

Mascarpone Parfait

MASCARPONE PARFAIT

PER SERVING **Net Carbs: 3 grams;** Carbohydrates: 3 grams; Fiber: 0 grams; Protein: 5 grams; Fat: 48 grams; Calories: 458
Makes 4 servings; Prep time: 15 minutes

This smooth, creamy dessert is ideal for the low-carb lifestyle. If you don't have parfait glasses, try serving the parfait in Champagne flutes.

1 cup heavy cream

1 (8-ounce) container mascarpone, slightly softened

1 tablespoon granular sugar substitute

Mint sprigs and lemon zest for garnish (optional)

1 Beat heavy cream in the large bowl of an electric mixer on medium-high speed until soft peaks form. Reduce speed to medium; add mascarpone and sugar substitute, beating just until smooth, 15 to 30 seconds.

2 Spoon mixture into four parfait glasses. Garnish with mint sprigs and lemon zest, if desired.

Atkins Tip: As a Pre-Maintenance and Lifetime Maintenance variation, try Pear and Raspberry Parfaits. Melt 1 teaspoon butter in a medium nonstick skillet set over medium-high heat. Sauté 1½ pears, cut into ½-inch dice, stirring occasionally, until lightly caramelized, 4 to 5 minutes. Cool and toss pears with 1 cup raspberries. Spoon evenly over parfaits. (This topping will increase carbohydrates to 16 grams, Net Carbs to 12.5 grams, fiber to 3.5 grams, protein to 6 grams, fat to 50 grams, and calories to 518.)

DOUBLE CHOCOLATE BROWNIES

PER SERVING **Net Carbs: 5 grams;** Carbohydrates: 7.5 grams; Fiber: 2.5 grams; Protein: 3.5 grams; Fat: 16 grams; Calories: 186

3 4

Makes 16 (1-brownie) servings; Prep time: 30 minutes; Cook time: 35 minutes

Be sure to thoroughly clean the mixing bowl and whisk attachment before whipping
your egg whites—even a trace of fat from the egg yolks can prevent the eggs from
forming peaks.

7 Atkins Endulge™ Chocolate Candy Bars, broken
   into pieces

1 ounce unsweetened chocolate, finely chopped

1 cup heavy cream

4 tablespoons unsalted butter

1 tablespoon vanilla extract

⅓ cup whole-wheat flour

¼ cup unsweetened cocoa powder

½ teaspoon baking powder

5 large eggs, separated

6 tablespoons granular sugar substitute

1 Heat oven to 350°F. Generously butter an 8-inch square
baking pan.

2 Combine chocolate bars and unsweetened chocolate in
a large bowl.

3 Heat heavy cream and butter in a small saucepan
over high heat. Bring to a boil, remove from heat, and
stir in extract. Pour cream mixture over chocolate and
stir until smooth, 1 to 2 minutes.

4 Combine flour, cocoa powder, and baking powder in a
bowl; set aside.

5 Combine egg yolks and sugar substitute in a mixing
bowl. Beat with the whisk attachment of an electric
mixer on high speed until thick and light yellow, 1 to 2
minutes. Stir yolk mixture into melted chocolate mixture.
Stir in dry ingredients until well combined.

6 With a clean bowl and whisk attachment, beat the
egg whites on high speed until stiff peaks form, 2 to
3 minutes. Stir one-third of egg whites into chocolate
mixture to lighten it. Gently fold in remaining egg
whites in two additions until combined. Pour batter
into prepared pan. Bake until a cake tester inserted
into center comes out with a slightly wet crumb, 25
to 28 minutes.

PUMPKIN MOUSSE

PER SERVING **Net Carbs: 4.5 grams;** Carbohydrates: 6 5 grams; Fiber: 2 grams; Protein: 2.5 grams; Fat: 17 grams; Calories:
180 Makes 8 servings; Prep time: 25 minutes; Cook time: 5 minutes, plus 2 hours chilling

Pumpkin pie spice and vanilla extract give this dessert a mellow, rounded flavor. The
mousse can also be used as a pie filling with a Pecan Crust (see page 144).

½ cup cold water

1 envelope unflavored gelatin

1½ teaspoons pumpkin pie spice

1 cup canned pumpkin purée

1½ cups heavy cream

3 tablespoons granular sugar substitute

1 tablespoon vanilla extract

1 Place water in a small saucepan; sprinkle gelatin over
water. Let stand until gelatin softens, 2 minutes.

2 Place saucepan over medium heat. Add pie spice to
gelatin mixture, whisking to combine. Bring to a boil;
cook until gelatin melts, about 1 minute, stirring often.
Remove from heat; cool completely.

3 Place pumpkin in a large bowl. Add gelatin mixture;
stir well to combine. Combine cream, sugar substitute,
and extract in a medium bowl; beat with an electric
mixer on high speed until stiff peaks form. Gently stir
one-third of cream into pumpkin mixture; gently fold in
remaining cream.

4 Divide mousse evenly among 8 parfait glasses. Cover
with plastic wrap and chill 2 hours.

PECAN-ORANGE MACAROONS

 PER SERVING **Net Carbs: 3 grams;** Carbohydrates: 6 grams; Fiber: 3 grams; Protein: 1.5 grams; Fat: 12 grams; Calories: 135
Makes 10 (3-cookie) servings; Prep time: 15 minutes; Cook time: 12 minutes

Tender and cakelike, these cookies owe their texture to toasted coconut. They can
be served warm or at room temperature.

1½ cups unsweetened shredded coconut

¼ cup pecans, lightly toasted and finely chopped

2 tablespoons heavy cream

¼ teaspoon orange extract

2 egg whites, room temperature

¼ teaspoon cream of tartar

½ cup granular sugar substitute

1 Heat oven to 350°F. Line two baking sheets with
parchment or waxed paper; set aside.

2 Combine coconut and pecans in a bowl. Add heavy
cream and extract; toss to combine.

3 Beat egg whites in the large bowl of an electric mixer
on high speed until thick and frothy. While mixer is
running, gradually add cream of tartar and sugar
substitute, beating until stiff peaks form. Fold egg
whites into coconut mixture until evenly combined.

4 Drop slightly rounded teaspoonfuls of mixture 1 inch
apart onto prepared baking sheets. Bake until lightly
browned on top and golden on bottom, 10 to 12
minutes. Cool cookies on baking sheet 1 minute;
transfer to a wire rack to cool completely. Store in an
airtight container.

Pecan-Orange Macaroons

PECAN THUMBPRINT COOKIES

PER SERVING Net Carbs: 5 grams; Carbohydrates: 4 grams; Fiber: 1.5 grams; Protein: 2 grams; Fat: 10 grams; Calories: 108
Makes 15 (2-cookie) servings; Prep time: 28 minutes, plus 30 minutes to freeze; Bake time: 20 minutes per batch

Use your favorite no-sugar-added fruit jam to fill the centers of these cookies.

2 cups pecan halves, toasted

½ cup Atkins Quick Quisine™ Bake Mix

¾ cup whole-wheat pastry flour

½ teaspoon baking powder

¼ teaspoon salt

¾ cup (1½ sticks) unsalted butter, softened

½ cup granular sugar substitute

2 large eggs

1 teaspoon vanilla extract

10 tablespoons no-sugar-added jam, any flavor

1 Combine pecans and bake mix in a food processor; process until nuts are finely ground. Whisk nut mixture, flour, baking powder, and salt in a small bowl to combine.

2 Beat butter and sugar substitute in the medium bowl of an electric mixer on high speed until smooth. Add eggs, one at a time, beating well after each addition. Stir in extract. Gradually add flour mixture; beat until combined.

3 Line a baking sheet with parchment paper. Drop dough by the tablespoonful onto prepared baking sheet, making 30 equal pieces. Place baking sheet in the freezer until dough is firm, about 10 minutes. Roll dough into balls and flatten slightly into disks. Press your thumb into the center of each disk, leaving an indentation. Return baking sheet to freezer; freeze until dough is solid, about 20 minutes more.

4 Heat oven to 350°F. Bake until cookies are lightly golden on bottom, puffed, and dry, 16 to 20 minutes per batch. Cool 5 minutes on baking sheet. Transfer cookies to wire racks; cool completely. Place 1 teaspoon jam in the center of each cookie.

CHOCOLATE MACAROONS

PER SERVING Net Carbs: 2 grams; Carbohydrates: 3 grams; Fiber: 1 gram; Protein: 1 gram; Fat: 3.5 grams Calories: 45 Makes 16 (2-cookie) servings; Prep time: 15 minutes; Cook time: 10 minutes

We made these irresistible cookies bite-sized so you can enjoy a taste of chocolate as an accompaniment to another dessert, such as berries.

1½ cups unsweetened shredded coconut

¼ cup unsweetened cocoa powder

3 tablespoons heavy cream

¼ teaspoon vanilla extract

¼ teaspoon coconut extract

2 large egg whites, room temperature

¼ teaspoon cream of tartar

⅔ cup granular sugar substitute

1 Heat oven to 350°F. Line two large baking sheets with parchment or waxed paper; set aside.

2 Combine coconut, cocoa powder, cream, and extracts in a large bowl; mix well.

3 Combine the egg whites and cream of tartar in the medium bowl of an electric mixer. Beat on high speed with the whisk attachment until thick and frothy. Gradually add sugar substitute and continue beating until stiff peaks form. Fold coconut mixture into egg whites in three additions.

4 Drop slightly rounded teaspoonfuls of mixture about ½ inch apart onto prepared baking sheets. Bake, rotating the baking sheets front to back and top to bottom after 5 minutes, until the macaroons are slightly browned at the edges and set, 10 to 12 minutes. Cool cookies on baking sheets 1 minute; transfer to a wire rack cool completely, 15 to 20 minutes. Store in an airtight container.

BÛCHE DE NOËL

PER SERVING **Net Carbs: 5.5 grams;** Carbohydrates: 7.5 grams; Fiber: 2 grams; Protein: 7.5 grams; Fat: 37 grams; Calories: 395

3 4 Makes 18 servings; Prep time: 1 hour, 15 minutes; Cook time: 10 minutes

For holiday revelers who love to bake, this spectacular cake will be the source of great pride and pleasure. And, it tastes even better than it looks! While the cake is not hard or tricky to make, it will take you more than an hour to prepare and assemble, so plan accordingly.

CAKE:

8 whole large eggs, separated

½ cup granulated sugar substitute

¼ cup (½ stick) unsalted butter, at room temperature

3 Atkins Endulge™ Chocolate Candy Bars

¼ cup heavy cream

2 tablespoons strong decaffeinated coffee

½ cup whole-wheat pastry flour

½ cup Atkins Quick Quisine™ Bake Mix

¼ cup unsweetened cocoa powder

1 teaspoon baking powder

FILLING:

2 cups heavy cream

1 tablespoon granular sugar substitute

2 teaspoons grated orange zest

1 teaspoon orange extract

FROSTING:

2 packets Carb Counters™ Instant Chocolate Pudding Mix

2 cups cold water

1 cup cold heavy cream

1 cup (2 sticks) unsalted butter

1 (8-ounce) package cream cheese, at room temperature

1 tablespoon granular sugar substitute

1 Heat oven to 350°F. Butter the bottom and sides of an 11- by 17-inch jelly-roll pan.

2 FOR CAKE: Beat egg yolks and ½ cup of granular sugar substitute with an electric mixer on high speed, until thick ribbons form when beaters are lifted, about 5 minutes. (The ribbon pattern will sink into the batter after a few seconds.) Add butter and continue to beat until smooth.

3 Melt chocolate bars in microwave, stirring in 20-second increments. Whisk in heavy cream until smooth. Stir into egg yolks.

4 Combine pastry flour, bake mix, cocoa powder, and baking powder in a bowl. Add dry ingredients to egg mixture in three additions, beating after each. The mixture will be thick and sticky. Transfer to a large bowl.

5 With clean beaters and bowl, beat the egg whites with an electric mixer on high speed until stiff peaks form. Stir one-third of egg whites into chocolate batter. Fold remaining egg whites into batter until fully incorporated. Spread batter in the prepared pan. Bake until set and a toothpick inserted in the center comes out clean, about 10 minutes. Loosen edges with a butter knife and let cool 5 minutes.

6 Invert cake on a large board covered with plastic wrap. (Don't worry if cake cracks or tears a bit—the filling and frosting will cover it.) Lay another piece of plastic wrap over cake. Starting with a long edge, roll cake to form a log. Let cool, seam-side down, on the board.

7 FOR FILLING: Beat heavy cream, sugar substitute, zest, and extract with an electric mixer on high speed until stiff peaks form. Chill until ready to use.

8 FOR FROSTING: Empty the packets of pudding mix in a large bowl. Add water; whisk until smooth. Whisk in heavy cream until smooth. Chill. Beat butter, cream cheese, and sugar substitute with an electric mixer on high speed until smooth. Pour chilled pudding into butter mixture and beat on low speed until smooth.

9 To assemble, unroll cake, remove plastic wrap, and spread filling over surface, leaving a 1-inch border all the way around. Roll up cake. (Wipe off any excess that squeezes out from edges and ends.) Spread frosting over the surface of the log, setting aside about ½ cup.

Búche de Noël

10 Make a diagonal cut across the cake about 3 inches from one end. Place the cut side of the short piece on the top surface of the log to form the stump. Use the reserved frosting to smooth the edges where the log and stump meet and to frost the sides and top of the stump and the ends of the log.

11 Drag the tines of a fork lengthwise on the log to suggest the grain of the wood. Form concentric circles on the round edge of the stump and on the ends of the log. Chill until ready to serve.

Atkins Tip: Low-carb pudding makes a great short-cut base for frosting. Add cream cheese and butter (or just butter), sugar-free pancake syrup, espresso powder, or flavor extracts to create any frosting. The pudding mix is available at www.atkins.com.

APPLE CRISP

3 | 4 PER SERVING **Net Carbs: 16.5 grams;** Carbohydrates: 21.5 grams; Fiber: 5 grams; Protein: 7 grams; Fat: 7.5 grams; Calories: 168
Makes 10 servings; Prep Time: 20 minutes; Cook time: 45 minutes

Serve this crisp warm and topped with low-carb vanilla ice cream or whipped cream. The crisp can be made in advance and refrigerated or frozen uncooked.

FILLING:

3 pounds Golden Delicious apples, peeled, cored, and cut into ¼-inch thick slices

3 tablespoons granular sugar substitute

1 tablespoon fresh lemon juice

2 teaspoons ground cinnamon

2 teaspoons vanilla extract

¼ teaspoon ground nutmeg

TOPPING:

2 cups Atkins Morning Start™ Crunchy Almond Crisp Cereal, lightly crushed

¼ cup Atkins Quick Quisine™ Bake Mix

2 tablespoons granular sugar substitute

½ teaspoon ground cinnamon

6 tablespoons (¾ stick) unsalted butter, softened and cut into small pieces

1 Heat oven to 375°F. Butter a 6-cup baking dish or an oval gratin.

2 FOR FILLING: Combine apples, sugar substitute, lemon juice, cinnamon, extract, and nutmeg in a large bowl; toss well and pour into prepared baking dish.

3 FOR TOPPING: Combine cereal, bake mix, sugar substitute, and cinnamon in a medium bowl; mix well. Add butter, working it in with your fingers until the mixture forms clumps when pressed together. Sprinkle topping over filling to cover, breaking the larger clumps into smaller ones (there may be a few spots where the apples show through). Bake the crisp until top is golden and apples are tender, about 45 minutes. (If the top begins to brown too quickly, cover it loosely with foil.)

Apple Crisp

APPLE FRITTERS

PER SERVING **Net Carbs: 6 grams;** Carbohydrates: 8 grams; Fiber: 2 grams; Protein: 5 grams; Fat: 10 grams; Calories: 140
Makes 12 (2-piece) servings; Prep time: 15 minutes; Cook time: 20 minutes

Little bits of sweet apple make these fritters irresistible. Be sure to use a deep-fry or candy thermometer to heat the oil to the right temperature—it will help ensure that the fritters come out crisp on the outside and soft inside, and not at all greasy.

¾ cup Atkins Quick Quisine™ Bake Mix

6 tablespoons whole-wheat flour

½ cup granular sugar substitute

1 teaspoon ground cinnamon

½ teaspoon ground allspice

½ teaspoon baking powder

1 cup heavy cream

2 large eggs, lightly beaten

3 cups plus 1 tablespoon canola oil, divided

1 teaspoon vanilla extract

1 Golden Delicious apple, peeled, cored, and cut into
¼-inch dice (1 cup)

1 Combine bake mix, flour, sugar substitute, cinnamon, allspice, and baking powder in a large bowl.

2 Combine heavy cream, eggs, 1 tablespoon oil, and extract in a separate bowl. Stir cream mixture into bake mix mixture until combined. Fold in apple.

3 Heat remaining 3 cups oil in a 3-quart saucepan to 350°F on a deep-fry thermometer. Use an oiled tablespoon to add 5 rounded tablespoonsful of batter, one at a time, to the oil; fry, turning occasionally, until puffed and golden brown, 3½ to 4 minutes. Drain on a baking sheet lined with paper towels. Repeat with remaining batter.

PUMPKIN FLAN

PER SERVING **Net Carbs: 6.5 grams;** Carbohydrates: 7.5 grams; Fiber: 1 gram; Protein: 5.5 grams; Fat: 22.5 grams; Calories: 251
Makes 8 servings; Prep time: 15 minutes; Cook time: 50 minutes, plus 2 hours chilling

The flans may be prepared up to three days ahead and stored in the refrigerator Try them topped with sugar-free praline sauce or pancake syrup.

1¾ cups heavy cream

1¼ cups water

1 cup granular sugar substitute

1 cup canned pumpkin purée

1¾ teaspoons pumpkin pie spice

1 teaspoon vanilla extract

5 large eggs, beaten

Boiling water, for roasting pan

1 Heat oven to 325°F. Combine heavy cream, water, sugar substitute, pumpkin, and spice in a medium saucepan over high heat. Bring to a simmer, remove from heat, and stir in extract. Let stand 5 minutes. Slowly add cream mixture to eggs, whisking constantly until combined. Pour the custard into eight 4-ounce custard cups.

2 Place custard cups in a large roasting pan. Pour enough boiling water into pan to come halfway up the sides of the cups. Bake until custards are set in the center, 40 to 50 minutes. Remove from oven; let cups stand in pan for 15 minutes.

3 Remove cups from pan. Cover each cup with plastic wrap. Refrigerate until chilled, 2 hours.

PUMPKIN PIE WITH PECAN CRUST

PER SERVING **Net Carbs: 8 grams;** Carbohydrates: 10.5 grams; Fiber: 2.5 grams; Protein: 4.5 grams; Fat: 20.5 grams; Calories: 236

Makes 12 servings; Prep time: 15 minutes, plus 15 minutes freezing; Cook time: 55 minutes, plus 1 hour cooling

3 4

Ground pecans, mixed with two kinds of flour (found in natural foods stores),
create a tender and flavorful piecrust.

CRUST:

⅔ cup soy flour

½ cup pecans, finely ground

⅓ cup whole-wheat pastry flour

1 tablespoon granular sugar substitute

¼ teaspoon salt

6 tablespoons (¾ stick) cold butter, cut into 12 pieces

2 tablespoons ice water

FILLING:

1 (15-ounce) can pumpkin purée

7 tablespoons granular sugar substitute

1½ teaspoons ground cinnamon

1 teaspoon ground ginger

½ teaspoon ground cloves

¼ teaspoon salt

2 large eggs

1¼ cups heavy cream

1 Heat oven to 425°F. Whisk soy flour, pecans, pastry flour, pastry flour, sugar substitute, and salt in a large bowl to combine. Cut in butter with a pastry blender or two knives until butter pieces are about the size of peas. Add ice water; stir to combine.

2 Transfer crust mixture to a 9-inch pie plate. Press along bottom and sides of pie plate to form a crust. Place in freezer for 15 minutes.

3 Cover crust with foil. Bake 15 minutes. Remove from oven and take off foil. Reduce oven temperature to 375°F.

4 Whisk pumpkin, sugar substitute, cinnamon, ginger, cloves, and salt in a bowl to combine. Mix in eggs, one at a time. Add heavy cream and mix well.

5 Pour filling into partially baked piecrust. Cover crust edge with foil. Bake until filling is set but still a little jiggly in the middle, 40 minutes. Let cool on a wire rack before serving.

PUMPKIN CHEESECAKE

PER SERVING **Net Carbs: 6 grams;** Carbohydrates: 7.5 grams; Fiber: 1.5 grams; Protein: 8 grams; Fat: 27 grams; Calories: 298

Makes 10 servings; Prep time: 20 minutes; Cook time: 45 minutes, plus 30 minutes cooling and 8 hours chilling

There's no crust in this seasonal cheesecake to interrupt the flavor of its star ingredient,
pumpkin. Add a dollop of cinnamon-flavored whipped cream for holiday flair.

3 (8-ounce) packages cream cheese, softened

1 (15-ounce) can pumpkin purée

⅓ cup granular sugar substitute

1 teaspoon cinnamon

1 teaspoon vanilla extract

¼ teaspoon ground ginger

⅛ teaspoon salt

3 eggs, at room temperature

1 Heat oven to 325°F. Lightly coat a 9-inch springform pan with cooking spray.

2 Beat cream cheese in a large bowl with an electric mixer on medium speed until smooth. Add pumpkin, sugar substitute, cinnamon, extract, ginger, and salt; beat until well blended. Add eggs, one at a time, beating on low speed just until each egg is incorporated.

3 Pour batter into prepared pan. Bake until center of cheesecake barely moves when pan is touched, about 45 minutes. Turn off oven, open oven door, and cool cheesecake in open oven 30 minutes. Remove cheesecake from oven; run a knife around outside edge. Cool to room temperature. Cover and chill at least 8 hours.

HOLIDAY GINGERBREAD

PER SERVING **Net Carbs: 7 grams;** Carbohydrates: 9.5 grams; Fiber: 2.5 grams; Protein: 9.5 grams; Fat: 13.5 grams; Calories: 193

3 4   Makes 10 servings; Prep time: 25 minutes; Cook time: 25 minutes, plus 35 minutes cooling

Fresh ginger gives this cake a kick of flavor. While a microplane zester is the best tool for grating fresh ginger, the finest holes on a box grater will also get the job done.

½ cup whole-wheat pastry flour

½ cup Atkins Quick Quisine™ Bake Mix

3 tablespoons unsweetened cocoa powder

1 teaspoon baking powder

½ teaspoon salt

1 teaspoon ground nutmeg

½ teaspoon ground cinnamon

½ teaspoon ground ginger

¼ teaspoon ground cloves

8 large eggs, separated

9 tablespoons granular sugar substitute

¼ cup (½ stick) unsalted butter, melted and slightly cooled

½ cup heavy cream

1 tablespoon grated fresh ginger

2 tablespoons strong brewed decaffeinated coffee

Whipped cream, flavored with ground ginger and sweetened with granular sugar substitute, for garnish

1 Heat oven to 350°F. Butter a 9-inch round cake pan.

2 Whisk flour, bake mix, cocoa powder, baking powder, salt, nutmeg, cinnamon, ground ginger, and cloves in a bowl to combine.

3 Beat egg yolks and sugar substitute with an electric mixer on high speed until thick ribbons form when the beaters are lifted, 3 to 4 minutes. Beat in butter until smooth. Add heavy cream, fresh ginger, and coffee; beat until thoroughly combined, about 1 minute.

4 With a clean mixing bowl and beaters, beat egg whites until stiff peaks form, about 3 to 4 minutes. Mix one-third of egg whites into batter to lighten. Gently fold remaining egg whites in two additions until just combined. Pour batter into prepared pan. Bake until cake has risen and set, and a toothpick inserted in the center comes out clean, 22 to 25 minutes.

5 Cool cake in pan on a wire rack for 5 minutes. Remove cake from pan and let cool completely on a wire rack. Serve with a dollop of flavored whipped cream.

Holiday Gingerbread

WALNUT BLONDIES

PER SERVING **Net Carbs: 7.5 grams;** Carbohydrates: 10.5 grams; Fiber: 3 grams; Protein: 11 grams; Fat: 19 grams Calories: 242

3 4 Makes 12 servings; Prep time: 20 minutes; Cook time: 14 minutes

These nutty treats make a wonderful alternative to brownies—and a delectable party dessert. Prepare the blondies ahead of time for fuss-free serving.

1 cup (2 sticks) unsalted butter, melted

1 cup granular sugar substitute

3 large eggs, at room temperature

1 teaspoon vanilla extract

1 cup Atkins Quick Quisine™ Bake Mix

½ cup whole-wheat pastry flour

2 tablespoons vital wheat gluten

1½ teaspoons baking powder

½ teaspoon ground cinnamon

1 cup coarsely chopped walnuts, toasted

1 ounce unsweetened chocolate, melted

1 Heat oven to 325°F. Line a 9- by 13-inch baking pan with foil extending 2 inches over both short sides of pan. Butter foil, and set aside.

2 Whisk butter, sugar substitute, eggs, and extract in a large bowl to combine. Whisk bake mix, pastry flour, gluten, baking powder, and cinnamon in another bowl; stir into butter mixture until well combined. Stir in walnuts. Spread batter evenly into prepared pan. Bake until puffed and set (top will not be browned), and a toothpick inserted in center comes out clean, 12 to 14 minutes. Cool completely in pan on a wire rack.

3 Drizzle chocolate in thin lines over entire surface of blondies. Let stand until set, about 1 hour. (The recipe can be prepared up to this point, covered with plastic wrap and stored at room temperature overnight.)

4 Grip the foil firmly on both ends, lift blondies out of pan, and place on work surface. Cut into 12 pieces.

MAPLE PECAN PIE

PER SERVING **Net Carbs: 3.5 grams;** Carbohydrates: 8 grams; Fiber: 4.5 grams; Protein: 9.5 grams; Fat: 41 grams; Calories: 420

Makes 8 servings; Prep time: 30 minutes; Cook time: 37 minutes, plus 20 minutes chilling

Make this traditional holiday pie up to three days in advance and keep it tightly wrapped in the refrigerator.

CRUST:

½ cup almonds, finely ground

¼ cup Atkins Quick Quisine™ Bake Mix

1½ teaspoons granular sugar substitute

4 tablespoons (½ stick) unsalted butter, melted

FILLING:

1 (12-ounce) bottle sugar-free pancake syrup

4 eggs

⅓ cup granular sugar substitute

5 tablespoons unsalted butter, melted and cooled slightly

½ teaspoon salt

1 teaspoon vanilla extract

2 cups pecan pieces, toasted

1 FOR CRUST: Heat oven to 350°F. Whisk almonds, bake mix, and sugar substitute in a large bowl to combine. Stir in butter with a fork. Chill crumb mixture 20 minutes.

2 Use your fingertips to press crumb mixture on bottom and sides of a 9-inch pie plate. Bake until browned and set, 7 minutes. Remove from oven; cool. Increase oven temperature to 375°F.

3 FOR FILLING: Bring syrup to a simmer in a small saucepan. Cook until reduced by half, 10 minutes. Remove from heat; cool to room temperature.

4 Whisk eggs, sugar substitute, butter, salt, and extract in a large bowl to combine. Whisk in syrup. Add pecans and combine well. Pour mixture into prepared crust. Bake until edges are firm (center will be less firm), 20 minutes. Transfer to a wire rack to cool.

MAPLE WALNUT BREAD PUDDING

 PER SERVING **Net Carbs: 9 grams;** Carbohydrates: 16 grams; Fiber: 7 grams; Protein: 19 grams; Fat: 39.5 grams; Calories: 496

Makes 8 servings; Prep Time: 30 minutes; Cook time: 42 minutes

The velvety chocolate crème anglaise on this homey favorite will have guests swooning, and it is a snap to put together. The bread pudding may be served warm or at room temperature.

BREAD PUDDING:

8 large eggs

1¼ cups heavy cream

⅓ cup sugar-free pancake syrup

¼ cup granular sugar substitute

2 teaspoons vanilla extract

¼ teaspoon ground cinnamon

⅛ teaspoon ground nutmeg

10 slices Atkins Bakery™ Ready-to-Eat Sliced White Bread, crusts removed and cut into ½-inch cubes

½ cup chopped walnuts

CRÈME ANGLAISE:

3 egg yolks, lightly beaten

2 Atkins Endulge™ Chocolate Candy Bars, chopped

¾ cup heavy cream

¼ cup granular sugar substitute

½ ounce unsweetened chocolate, chopped

1 teaspoon vanilla extract

1 FOR BREAD PUDDING: Heat the oven to 350°F. Coat a 7- by 11-inch glass baking dish with cooking spray.

2 Combine the eggs, heavy cream, syrup, sugar substitute, extract, cinnamon, and nutmeg in a large bowl. Stir in bread cubes; let stand 15 minutes, tossing occasionally with a wooden spoon. Stir in walnuts.

3 Transfer mixture to prepared baking dish. Bake until top is puffed and golden and eggs are set, 35 minutes. Let cool slightly before cutting.

4 FOR CRÈME ANGLAISE: Combine egg yolks, chocolate, heavy cream, sugar substitute, unsweetened chocolate, and extract in a medium saucepan over medium-low heat. Cook, stirring constantly with a wooden spoon, until the custard thickens, 6 to 7 minutes. (If the chocolate cream begins to separate near the end of cooking, whisk it vigorously off the heat to bring it back together.) Transfer to a bowl and whisk 1 minute.

5 Cut the bread pudding into 8 squares. Place one square on each of 8 dessert plates and spoon 2 tablespoons of chocolate crème anglaise over each. Serve warm or at room temperature.

Maple Walnut Bread Pudding

NUTTY CHOCOLATE SWIRL CHEESECAKE

 PER SERVING **Net Carbs: 7 grams;** Carbohydrates: 10 grams; Fiber: 3 grams; Protein: 12 grams; Fat: 51 grams Calories: 520
Makes 8 servings: ; Prep time: 40 minutes; Cook time: 10 minutes, plus 3 hours chilling

The two-toned filling is a snap to prepare, and it doesn't need baking because it's
set with gelatin.

6 ounces (1½ cups) pecans or walnuts, chopped

½ cup plus 2 tablespoons granular sugar substitute, divided

2 tablespoons butter, softened

1 envelope unflavored gelatin

1 cup cold water, divided

3 (8-ounce) packages cream cheese, softened

1 tablespoon grated orange or lemon zest

1¼ teaspoons vanilla or lemon extract

2 ounces unsweetened chocolate, melted and cooled

Fresh berries and pecans for garnish (optional)

1 Heat oven to 400°F. Butter a 9-inch springform pan.

2 Whisk pecans and 2 tablespoons sugar substitute in a medium bowl to combine. Add butter and mix well.

Use your fingertips to press mixture firmly and evenly onto bottom of prepared pan. Bake 8 to 10 minutes, until crust just begins to brown. Let cool on a wire rack.

3 Place TK water in a small saucepan; sprinkle gelatin over water. Let stand 1 minute. Stir over low heat until dissolved; set aside.

4 Beat cream cheese with an electric mixer on high speed in a large bowl until fluffy. Add remaining ½ cup sugar substitute, zest, and extract and beat until combined. Add dissolved gelatin and remaining cold water and beat on low speed, stopping to scrape down the sides of the bowl, until very smooth. Set aside 1 cup mixture; spread remainder in pecan crust.

5 Return reserved mixture to bowl. Stir in chocolate. Place dollops of chocolate mixture into plain mixture and swirl with knife, being careful not to blend mixtures. Refrigerate 3 hours. Garnish with berries and pecans, if desired.

ESPRESSO PANNA COTTA

 PER SERVING **Net Carbs: 5 grams;** Carbohydrates: 5 grams; Fiber: 0 grams; Protein: 3 grams; Fat: 33 grams; Calories: 323
Makes 6 servings; Prep time: 15 minutes, plus 4 hours to chill

Coffee and cinnamon give this panna cotta ("cooked cream") a sophisticated,
decidedly grown-up flavor—the perfect ending to an elegant dinner party.

2¼ cups heavy cream

½ cup granular sugar substitute

2 cinnamon sticks

2 teaspoons instant decaffeinated coffee

1 teaspoon vanilla extract

1 packet unflavored gelatin

¼ cup water

1 Lightly butter six 4-ounce custard cups. Combine heavy cream, sugar substitute, cinnamon sticks, and coffee in a medium saucepan over high heat; bring to a boil. Remove from heat, stir in extract, and let stand 10 minutes. Remove cinnamon sticks.

2 Meanwhile, sprinkle gelatin over water in a small bowl; let stand 10 minutes. Stir gelatin into coffee mixture.

3 Divide mixture among custard cups. Cover each cup with plastic wrap. Chill until set, 4 hours.

4 To unmold, dip the bottom of each custard cup in hot water to loosen, then invert cup onto dessert plate.

Coconut-Cashew Chocolate Truffles

COCONUT-CASHEW CHOCOLATE TRUFFLES

PER SERVING **Net Carbs: 1.5 grams;** Carbohydrates: 3.5 grams; Fiber: 2 grams; Protein: 1.5 grams; Fat: 11.5 grams; Calories: 122
Makes 32 (1-truffle) servings; Prep time: 40 minutes, plus 1 hour 45 minutes chilling

These rich chocolaty candies are a snap to make. The unsweetened chocolate adds intensity of flavor, making this a very adult confection that's sure to appeal to chocoholics. For subtler chocolate flavor, decrease the amount of unsweetened chocolate.

¾ cup heavy cream

2 tablespoons granular sugar substitute

2 tablespoons (¼ stick) unsalted butter

5 Atkins Endulge™ Chocolate Candy Bars, finely chopped

3 ounces unsweetened chocolate, finely chopped

¾ teaspoon vanilla extract

1 cup unsweetened dried coconut, divided

½ cup very finely chopped unsalted cashews

1 Combine heavy cream, sugar substitute, and butter in a small saucepan. Bring just to a simmer. Place chocolate bars and chopped chocolate in a medium bowl; pour hot cream mixture over chocolate. Let stand 5 minutes.

2 Stir chocolate mixture gently until chocolate is completely melted. Stir in extract and ½ cup of the coconut. Refrigerate until firm, about 1 hour 45 minutes, stirring occasionally. (Truffles will be easier to form if the mixture is not too stiff.)

3 Toast the remaining ½ cup coconut in a dry skillet over medium heat, shaking often, until lightly browned; transfer to a bowl and cool.

4 Roll the chocolate mixture into 32 balls about the size of large marbles. Roll half of the balls in cashews and half in toasted coconut. Place in an airtight container between layers of wax paper. Refrigerate up to one week.

CHOCOLATE-DRIZZLED VANILLA BISCOTTI

2 3 4 PER SERVING **Net Carbs: 1 gram;** Carbohydrates: 3 grams; Fiber: 2 grams; Protein: 5 grams; Fat: 8 grams; Calories: 106
Makes 12 (2-cookie) servings; Prep time: 25 minutes; Cook time: 44 minutes

Enjoy these crisp, aromatic biscotti at breakfast or as a snack on their own. Drizzled with chocolate, they become a festive and elegant dessert.

¾ cup Atkins Quick Quisine™ Bake Mix

⅓ cup granular sugar substitute

6 tablespoons (¾ stick) unsalted butter, softened

1 vanilla bean, split lengthwise and seeds scraped, pod discarded, or 1 teaspoon vanilla extract

2 tablespoons sour cream

2 eggs, lightly beaten

1 Atkins Endulge™ Chocolate Candy Bar, broken into smaller pieces

1 Heat oven to 350°F. Combine bake mix and sugar substitute in a small bowl.

2 Beat butter with an electric mixer on high speed until light and creamy, 3 minutes. Beat in vanilla seeds or extract. Beat in sour cream and eggs, stopping and scraping down the bowl as needed, until combined. Gradually add dry ingredients into butter mixture, beating just until combined. The dough will be very sticky and soft.

3 Form dough into a 2½- by 12-inch log on an ungreased baking sheet (moisten hands with water if necessary to keep dough from sticking).

4 Bake log until almost firm, 25 minutes. Transfer baking sheet to wire rack and cool 10 minutes. Reduce oven temperature to 325°F.

5 Use a serrated knife to carefully cut log crosswise into 24 ½-inch-thick slices. Arrange slices, cut side down, on baking sheet. Bake until firm and crisp, 15 to 17 minutes. Cool completely on baking sheet on wire rack.

6 Place chocolate bars in a small bowl over a pot of gently simmering water, or melt in the microwave. Stir until the chocolate melts, 3 to 4 minutes. Transfer to a small resealable plastic bag. Slice off one corner of the bag and gently drizzle the chocolate over the cookies. Refrigerate until chocolate sets, 15 minutes.

Chocolate-Drizzled Vanilla Biscotti

CHOCOLATE-DIPPED ALMOND COOKIES

PER SERVING **Net Carbs: 4 grams;** Carbohydrates: 8 grams; Fiber: 4 grams; Protein: 6 grams; Fat: 19 grams; Calories: 234
Makes 18 (2-cookie) servings; Prep time: 45 minutes; Cook time: 16 minutes

3 4

These cookies are luscious and extremely satisfying, but remember to store them in the refrigerator or the chocolate will become soft and sticky. If you skip the chocolate, you'll have a lovely cookie for tea that doesn't need refrigeration.

¾ cup (1½ sticks) unsalted butter, softened

½ cup plus 2 tablespoons granular sugar substitute

2 large eggs

½ teaspoon vanilla extract

1¾ cups almond flour, or 1¾ cups blanched almonds, finely ground

½ cup Atkins Quick Quisine™ Bake Mix

½ cup whole-wheat pastry flour

1 teaspoon baking powder

¼ teaspoon salt

⅓ cup sliced almonds

1 large egg, lightly beaten

8 Atkins Endulge™ Chocolate Candy Bars, broken into pieces

1 Heat oven to 400°F. Lightly coat 2 large baking sheets with cooking spray. Cream butter in the bowl of an electric mixer on high speed until smooth. Beat in sugar substitute. Beat in eggs one at a time, scraping down the sides of the bowl after each addition. Beat in extract.

2 Whisk almond flour, bake mix, pastry flour, baking powder, and salt in a medium bowl to combine. Mix dry ingredients into butter on low speed in three batches, scraping down the sides of the bowl as needed.

3 Use your hands to roll dough into walnut-sized balls. Place them 2 inches apart on baking sheets. Flatten each ball slightly; press a few almond slices into the dough, so that the almonds will become partially baked in). Brush the cookies with the lightly beaten egg.

4 Bake until cookies are dry and cracked on top and very lightly browned on the bottom, about 12 minutes. Cool on wire racks.

5 Wash and dry baking sheets and line them with waxed paper. Melt chocolate bars in the top of a double boiler set over barely simmering water, stirring until smooth. Dip a cooled cookie halfway into the chocolate, lift out, and let excess chocolate drip back into bowl. Place cookie on baking sheet; continue until all cookies are coated. Refrigerate until chocolate is set, 20 minutes.

6 Transfer cookies to an airtight container between layers of waxed paper. Store in the refrigerator for up to 3 days.

Atkins Tip: Almond flour is available at most health and specialty food stores—wherever soy flour is sold. It can be substituted with an equal amount of blanched almonds, finely ground in a food processor.

SIMPLE RASPBERRY SAUCE

PER SERVING **Net Carbs: 4 grams;** Carbohydrates: 5 grams; Fiber: 1 gram; Protein: 0 grams; Fat: 0 grams; Calories: 20
Makes 6 servings; Prep time: 15 minutes, plus 4 hours to chill

Serve this sauce warm with your favorite chocolate dessert. Or try it cold over cheesecake or low-carb vanilla ice cream.

1 package (10 ounces) frozen raspberries (not in syrup)

3 tablespoons sugar-free vanilla syrup

Cook frozen berries in a medium saucepan over medium heat 5 minutes, until they begin to release their liquid and defrost. Remove from heat and press through a strainer into a bowl to remove seeds. Stir in vanilla syrup.

FUDGE NUT SWIRL PIE

 PER SERVING **Net Carbs: 5.5 grams;** Carbohydrates: 22 grams; Fiber: 4 grams; Protein: 7.5 grams; Fat: 43.5 grams; Calories: 470
Makes 12 servings; Prep time: 30 minutes; Cook time: 65 minutes, plus 1 hour cooling and 2 hours chilling

This is an over-the-top, luscious, gooey dessert. Guests will devour it—and won't be able to believe you can enjoy this while doing Atkins!

PECAN CRUST

2 cups pecans

1 tablespoon granular sugar substitute

3 tablespoons unsalted butter, melted

FILLING

7 Atkins Endulge™ Chocolate Candy Bars, broken into small pieces

2 ounces unsweetened chocolate, finely chopped

¾ cup heavy cream

2 tablespoons (¼ stick) unsalted butter

2 teaspoons vanilla extract

3 large eggs, at room temperature

SWIRL:

6 ounces cream cheese, softened

½ cup sugar-free praline sauce, plus more for garnish

¼ cup natural peanut butter

2 tablespoons heavy cream

Whipped cream sweetened with granular sugar substitute

1 FOR PECAN CRUST: Heat oven to 350°F. Butter a 9-inch springform pan. Place pecans in the bowl of a food processor; pulse until finely ground but not a paste. Add sugar substitute and pulse to combine. Add the butter and pulse to combine. Scrape the nut mixture into the prepared pan and press to form a crust on the bottom of the pan and about 1 inch up the sides. Bake 10 minutes; remove from oven and cool. Reduce oven temperature to 325°F.

2 FOR FILLING: Combine candy bars and unsweetened chocolate in a large bowl. Combine heavy cream, butter, and extract in a small saucepan over medium-high heat. Bring cream mixture to a boil; remove from the heat and pour over the chocolate mixture. Stir until smooth and melted, 1 to 2 minutes.

3 Beat eggs with an electric mixer on medium-high speed until thick ribbons form when the beater is lifted, 6 to 8 minutes. Stir eggs into chocolate mixture until well combined.

4 FOR SWIRL: Combine cream cheese, praline sauce, and peanut butter in the bowl of an electric mixer and beat on medium-high speed until light and fluffy. Stir in heavy cream with a rubber spatula until well blended.

5 To assemble, pour half of the chocolate filling into the prepared pan, smoothing with a spatula. Spoon half of the swirl mixture onto the filling in evenly spaced mounds. Pull a butter knife through one swirl mound drawing a curved line through chocolate. Repeat several times with each mound. Top with remaining chocolate filling and repeat the swirl procedure to create an attractive marbling.

6 Bake until filling is almost set and a toothpick inserted into the center comes out almost clean, 50 to 55 minutes. Cool in pan on a wire rack 1 hour. Remove from pan. Chill 2 hours before serving. Garnish with whipped cream and additional praline sauce.

Atkins Tip: The swirl technique described in step 5 has other uses. Try it to decorate a dessert plate: put small dots of chocolate or raspberry sauce around the perimeter of the plate and pull a butter knife through the center of each one. Your plate will be ringed with delightful hearts.

Note: You may notice that the carbohydrate and fiber information doesn't add up. The use of sugar alcohols, which sweeten Atkins chocolate candy, do not impact blood sugar and are not counted in the Net Carb count.

Fudge Nut Swirl Pie

LEMON MERINGUE SQUARES

PER SERVING **Net Carbs: 3.5 grams;** Carbohydrates: 5.5 grams; Fiber: 2 grams; Protein: 8.5 grams; Fat: 11 grams; Calories: 149
Makes 9 (1-square) servings; Prep time: 30 minutes; Cook time: 50 minutes, plus 30 minutes chilling

These lemon squares have all the flavor of a classic lemon meringue pie in a convenient package.

CRUST:

⅔ cup Atkins Quick Quisine™ Bake Mix

3 tablespoons unsalted butter, softened and cut into small pieces

2 ounces cream cheese, softened (3 tablespoons)

2 teaspoons sour cream

¼ cup coarsely chopped slivered almonds, toasted

FILLING:

1 large egg

2 large egg yolks

2 tablespoons granular sugar substitute

2 teaspoons freshly grated lemon zest

6 tablespoons fresh lemon juice (2 medium lemons)

1 tablespoon unsalted butter, softened

MERINGUE:

4 large egg whites, at room temperature

½ teaspoon cream of tartar

3 tablespoons granular sugar substitute

1 teaspoon vanilla extract

Lemon Meringue Squares

1 Heat oven to 425°F. Lightly butter an 8-inch-square baking pan. Line pan across bottom and up two opposite sides with parchment paper or foil.

2 FOR CRUST: Combine bake mix, butter, cream cheese, and sour cream in a small mixing bowl. Beat with an electric mixer on low speed just until ingredients are combined. Form dough into a ball; then press into a 4-inch disk. Chill dough 20 minutes. Use your fingers to press dough in an even layer onto bottom of pan. Sprinkle almonds evenly over top and press firmly into dough. Prick dough with a fork in several places. Cover loosely with foil. Bake 10 minutes. Reduce oven temperature to 375°F and bake until crust is browned, about 15 minutes more. Cool on a wire rack. Reduce oven temperature to 325°F.

3 FOR FILLING: Combine egg, egg yolks, and sugar substitute in a 1½-quart saucepan. Whisk in lemon zest and juice. Cook over medium-low heat, whisking constantly, until the mixture thickens, 4 to 6 minutes. Do not overcook, or eggs will scramble. Remove from heat. Add butter; whisk until blended and smooth. Pour into a small bowl, place plastic wrap directly on surface of filling, and refrigerate until chilled, 30 minutes.

4 FOR MERINGUE: Place egg whites in a large mixing bowl. Beat with an electric mixer on medium speed until frothy. Add cream of tartar. Increase speed to medium-high; beat just until egg whites form stiff peaks, about 2 minutes. Beat in sugar substitute, 1 tablespoon at a time, scraping down sides of bowl once or twice. Add extract. Beat until thick, 30 to 45 seconds.

5 Spread lemon filling evenly onto baked crust. Drop mounds of meringue onto lemon filling; spread meringue quickly with the back of a teaspoon to sides of pan, covering lemon filling completely. Bake until meringue is golden brown, 15 to 18 minutes. Cool on wire rack. Run knife along unlined sides of pan. Carefully lift out of pan. Cut into 9 squares. Chill until ready to serve (up to 3 hours).

ALMOND MOUSSE SOUFFLÉ

 PER SERVING **Net Carbs: 6.5 grams;** Carbohydrates: 7.5 grams; Fiber: 1 gram; Protein: 10.5 grams; Fat: 47 grams; Calories: 501
Makes 6 servings; Prep time: 40 minutes; Cook time: 5 minutes, plus 2 hours 30 minutes to chill

Serve the mousse plain, layered with berries in parfait glasses, or in individual custard cups.

2 packages unflavored gelatin

¼ cup cold water

2¾ cups heavy cream, divided

5 large eggs, separated

2 pinches salt

10 tablespoons granular sugar substitute, divided

2½ teaspoons almond extract

1½ teaspoons vanilla extract

1 tablespoon rum (optional)

¼ teaspoon cream of tartar

2 teaspoons grated lemon zest

⅓ cup toasted sliced almonds

1 Place gelatin in a large bowl. Stir in water and set aside.

2 Combine 1½ cups of the heavy cream, egg yolks, salt, and 5 tablespoons of the sugar substitute in a small heavy saucepan. Whisk until smooth. Cook over medium heat, stirring constantly, until custard is just thick enough to coat the back of the spoon, about 5 minutes.

3 Immediately pour custard over gelatin; stir until gelatin melts. Stir in extracts and rum. Cover bowl with plastic wrap; refrigerate until custard cools and begins to thicken, about 20 minutes; stir occasionally.

4 Coat a 1½-quart soufflé dish or serving bowl with cooking spray (or set aside 6 wine or parfait glasses).

5 Whip egg whites and cream of tartar with an electric mixer on high speed until frothy. Reduce speed to medium; gradually add 2 tablespoons sugar substitute. Whip just until the whites hold firm peaks. Stir one-third of the whites into the cooled custard. Fold in the remaining two-thirds.

6 With a clean bowl and beaters, whip remaining ¼ cup heavy cream on medium speed until frothy. Gradually add remaining 3 tablespoons sugar substitute and zest. Fold gently into custard. Transfer into prepared dish or glasses and sprinkle with almonds. Cover with plastic wrap. Refrigerate for at least 2 hours and up to 2 days before serving.

SABAYON WITH BERRIES

 PER SERVING **Net Carbs: 7.5 grams;** Carbohydrates: 10 grams; Fiber: 2.5 grams; Protein: 3 grams; Fat: 4.5 grams; Calories: 105
Makes 6 servings; Prep time: 15 minutes; Cook time: 12 minutes

Use more or less sherry depending on your personal taste—and choose a good quality sherry that you'd find pleasant to drink.

1½ cups stemmed and quartered strawberries

1½ cups raspberries

1 teaspoon grated orange zest

½ teaspoon grated lemon zest

6 large egg yolks

⅔ cup dry sherry

½ cup granular sugar substitute

1 Combine strawberries, raspberries, orange zest, and lemon zest in a bowl; toss well.

2 Bring a large saucepan filled one-third full with water to a simmer over medium heat. Combine egg yolks, sherry, and sugar substitute in a large bowl; whisk well. Set bowl on top of saucepan; whisk constantly (or use a electric mixer) until mixture is thick, foamy, and tripled in volume, and an instant-read thermometer registers 160°F, 10 to 12 minutes. Be sure to whisk continuously so the eggs don't scramble. Remove pan from heat.

3 Divide berries and sabayon evenly among 6 bowls or goblets with ½ cup of the berries topped with ⅓ cup of the sabayon.

COCONUT CAKE WITH LEMON CURD

 PER SERVING **Net Carbs: 7.5 grams;** Carbohydrates: 9 grams; Fiber: 1.5 gram; Protein: 18 grams; Fat: 35 grams; Calories: 409
Makes 12 servings; Prep time: 45 minutes; Cook time: 50 minutes, plus 4 hours chilling

This is a glorious-looking cake, worthy of your most important celebration. Fluffy layers of sweet frosting, topped with shredded toasted coconut, coat two cake layers separated by lemon curd.

COCONUT CAKE:

¾ cup vital wheat gluten

2 teaspoons baking powder

½ teaspoon salt

1 cup unsweetened coconut milk

6 large eggs, separated

¼ cup granular sugar substitute

2 teaspoons coconut extract

1 teaspoon vanilla extract

LEMON CURD:

⅓ cup fresh lemon juice

¼ cup granular sugar substitute

4 large egg yolks

6 tablespoons butter (¾ stick), cut into small pieces

VANILLA FROSTING:

1 packet Carb Counters™ Instant Vanilla Pudding Mix

1 cup water

½ cup heavy cream

½ cup (1 stick) unsalted butter

1 (8-ounce) package cream cheese

2 teaspoons coconut extract

1 cup unsweetened shredded coconut, toasted

1 Heat oven to 350°F. Lightly coat two 8-inch round cake pans with cooking spray. Line bottoms of pans with parchment paper; lightly spray paper.

2 FOR COCONUT CAKE: Whisk wheat gluten, baking powder, and salt in a small bowl to combine. Whisk coconut milk and egg yolks in another bowl. Stir gluten mixture into milk mixture until the two are completely combined.

3 Beat egg whites until soft peaks form with an electric mixer on high speed. Add sugar substitute and extracts; continue beating until firm peaks form (do not overbeat). Gently fold one-third of the egg whites into batter; fold remaining egg whites into batter. Pour evenly into prepared pans. Bake until lightly brown and set, about 35 minutes. Cool 10 minutes in pans on a wire rack. Remove cakes from pans and carefully peel off parchment. Cool completely on wire racks.

4 FOR LEMON CURD: Heat lemon juice, sugar substitute, and egg yolks in a small saucepan over low heat; stir well with a whisk. Cook (do not boil), whisking constantly, until an instant-read thermometer registers 160°F, about 4 minutes. Remove from heat. Add butter, whisking until butter is melted and mixture is smooth. Transfer curd to a small bowl, press plastic wrap onto the surface, and chill until set, about 4 hours.

5 FOR VANILLA FROSTING: Place pudding mix in a bowl. Whisk in water, then heavy cream. Chill until set, 20 minutes. Combine butter and cream cheese in a mixing bowl; beat with an electric mixer on high until smooth. Beat in extract. Reduce mixer speed to medium. Gradually add pudding mixture to butter mixture, beating until frosting is smooth, about 2 minutes.

6 Place one cake layer on a serving plate; spread lemon curd over cake layer, leaving a half-inch border around the edges. Top with remaining cake layer. Spread frosting over top and sides of cake. Sprinkle coconut over top.

Atkins Tip: Be sure to press plastic wrap directly onto the surface of the lemon curd, or it will form a skin.

HANUKKAH JELLY DOUGHNUTS

PER SERVING **Net Carbs: 3 grams;** Carbohydrates: 6 grams; Fiber: 3 grams; Protein: 8 grams; Fat: 8 grams; Calories: 126
Makes 8 (1-doughnut) servings; Prep time: 30 minutes; Cook time: 16 minutes

If you're amazed that you can include our latkes (see page 112) in a controlled-carb
lifestyle, these jelly doughnuts will really knock you out.

1 cup plus 1 tablespoon Atkins Quick Quisine™
  Bake Mix, divided

3 tablespoons granular sugar substitute

1 teaspoon baking powder

1 teaspoon ground cinnamon

½ cup heavy cream

1 large egg, lightly beaten

1 tablespoon canola oil

8 teaspoons no-sugar-added raspberry jam

3 cups canola oil for frying

1 Combine 1 cup of the bake mix, sugar substitute,
baking powder, and cinnamon in a large bowl; stir with
a fork. Combine heavy cream, egg, and oil in a
separate bowl; mix well. Add wet ingredients to the dry
and stir until a stiff dough forms. Turn dough out onto
a surface lightly dusted with 1 tablespoon bake mix.
Knead until smooth, about 1 minute. Divide dough into
8 equal portions.

2 Pat each dough portion into a 3-inch roundp. Place 1
teaspoon of raspberry jam in the center. Fold the
dough over to form a small turnover shape. Pinch the
edges firmly to seal. Repeat for each dough portion.

3 Heat oil in a 3-quart saucepan to 350°F on a deep-fry
thermometer. Add two doughnuts and fry, turning
often, until puffed and golden brown, about 4 minutes.
Drain on a baking sheet lined with paper towels.
Repeat with the remaining doughnuts.

Coconut Cake with Lemon Curd

INDEX

Page numbers in **bold** indicate photographs.

Ale-Infused Onion Soup, 22
Almonds. **See also** Nuts
  Almond Mousse Soufflé, 155
  Chocolate-Dipped Almond
    Cookies, 151
  Green Beans Amandine, **4**,
    112
Anchovies
  Bagna Cauda, 42
Appetizers, 40–61
Apples
  Apple Crisp, 142, **142**
  Apple Fritters, 143
Artichoke, Gratin, Roasted,
  94, **95**
Arugula
  Endive, Arugula, and Radish
    Salad, 33, **33**
  Roast Shallot, Garlic, and
    Zucchini Salad, 37
Asian greens. **See also** Greens
  Sesame-Crusted Tuna over
    Asian Greens, 58, **59**
Asparagus
  Asparagus with Browned
    Butter, 94
  Asparagus and Romaine
    Salad, 32
  Prosciutto-Wrapped
    Asparagus, 55, **55**
  Roasted Asparagus, 95
  Savory Italian Tart, 120, **121**
  Verdemole, 56, **56**
Atkins lifestyle, 12–17
Avocado Salad, Warm Lobster
  and, 39, **39**

Bacon. **See also** Canadian
  bacon; Pancetta
  Bacon-Cheddar Biscuits, 126
  Bacon and Goat Cheese
    Salad, **36**, 37
  Bacon-Wrapped Filet
    Mignon, 66, **66**
  Dubliner Cheese Tart, 124,
    125
  Frisée with Lardons and
    Poached Eggs, 123
  Kale with Bacon and Garlic,
    116
  Scallops Wrapped in Bacon,
    49
  Warm Greens with
    Cornbread Croutons, 34, **35**
Bagna Cauda, 42
Baked Stuffed Mushrooms, 42
Basil
  Citrus and Basil Marinated
    Goat Cheese, 43, **43**
  Green Roasted Shrimp, 87
  Roasted Vegetable Soup
    with Pesto, 24, **24**
  Tomato-Basil Frittata, 131
Beef
  Bacon-Wrapped Filet Mignon,
    66, **66**
  Beef Filet with Pancetta and
    Spinach, 68
  Beef Tenderloin with Dijon
    Herb Crust, 67
  Chipotle Braised Short Ribs,
    68

Classic Brisket, **8**, 67
Prime Rib Roast Beef with
  Red Wine Sauce, 64
Roast Beef with Horseradish
  Cream, 60, **61**
Slavic-Style Hot Borscht, 22,
  23
Standing Rib Roast with
  Onions and Leeks, 64
Walnut Meatballs, 54
Zinfandel Pot-au-Feu, 65, **65**
Beets
  Slavic-Style Hot Borscht, 22,
    23
Bell peppers
  Green Bean, Pepper, and
    Onion Sauté, 113, **113**
  Red Pepper Pancakes with
    Smoked Salmon, 53, **53**
  Roasted Fennel with Red
    Peppers, 115, **115**
  Roasted Pepper and Escarole
    Salad, 34
  Veal with Goat Cheese and
    Roast Peppers, 78
Berries. **See also** specific kinds
  Lemon-Berry Trifle, **132**, 134
  Mixed Berry and Ricotta–
    Stuffed Crêpes, **118**, 121
  Sabayon with Berries, 155
Blackberries. **See** Berries
Blueberries. **See also** Berries
  Blueberry-Pecan Pancakes,
    127, **127**
Bouillabaisse, 86, **86**
Braised Cabbage, 98, **98**
Braised Celery and Leeks, 96
Breads
  recipes using
    Ale-Infused Onion Soup, 22
    Maple Walnut Bread
      Pudding, 147, **147**
    Raspberry Cream Cheese
      Bread Pudding, 128
    Sausage Dressing, 99
    Sausage-Sage Stuffing, 100
    Short-Cut Pigs in a Blanket,
      59
  Southwestern Cornbread,
    93, **93**
  Zucchini Bread, 124
Broccoli
  Broccoli Florets with Lemon
    Butter Sauce, 106
  Verdemole, 56, **56**
  Warm Cauliflower and
    Broccoli Salad, 36
Broccolini with Shallot-Lemon
  Butter, **81**, 106, **107**
Broccoli Rabe, Garlic, and Hot
  Red Pepper, 108
Brunch, 118–31
Brussels sprouts
  Brussels Sprouts with Lemon,
    102
  Sautéed Brussels Sprouts,
    103, **103**
Bûche de Noël, 140–41, **141**
Butter-Braised Turnips, **7**, 99
Butternut Squash Soup,
  Cumin-Lemon, 23

Cabbage, Braised, 98, **98**
Canadian bacon
  Eggs Benedict with
    Béarnaise Sauce, 122, **122**
Candied Ginger Sweet
  Potatoes, **4**, 111
Carrots
  Glazed Carrots, **6**, 102
  Roast Carrots with Cinnamon
    and Cumin, **8**, 102
Cashew Chocolate Truffles,
  Coconut-, 149, **149**
Cauliflower
  Cauliflower-Pea Pancakes,
    104, **104**
  Cauliflower–Sour Cream
    Purée, **4**, 105
  Cream of Cauliflower Soup,
    20
  Crown Roast of Lamb
    Florentine, 76, **77**
  Warm Cauliflower and
    Broccoli Salad, 36
Celery
  Braised Celery and Leeks, 96
  Cream of Celery Soup, 21, **21**
  Jalapeño–Cream Cheese
    Stuffed Celery, **40**, 45
  Seared Scallops with Celery
    and Onion, 38
Celery root
  Cream of Celery Soup, 21, **21**
Cheddar cheese. **See also**
  Cheeses
  Bacon-Cheddar Biscuits, 126
  Cheddar and Scallion Pie
    Squares, 46
  Egg, Cheddar, and Chorizo
    Roulade, 130, **130**
  Smoked Turkey and Cheddar
    Spread, 44
Cheeses. **See also** specific
  kinds
  Cheddar and Scallion Pie
    Squares, 46
  Chorizo Cheese Bake, 44, **45**
  Dubliner Cheese Tart, 124,
    125
  Roasted Artichoke Gratin, 94,
    95
  Savory Italian Tart, 120, **121**
  Tomato-Basil Frittata, 131
Chicken
  Roast Chicken with Wild
    Mushroom Jus, 80
  Tandoori Chicken Wings,
    40, 52
Chicory. **See also** Frisée
  Warm Greens with
    Cornbread Croutons, 34, **35**
Chipotle Braised Short Ribs,
  68
Chive Omelet, Smoked
  Salmon and, 123
Chocolate
  Bûche de Noël, 140–41, **141**
  Chocolate-Dipped Almond
    Cookies, 151
  Chocolate-Drizzled Vanilla
    Biscotti, 150, **150**
  Chocolate Macaroons, 139

Chocolate Mousse Mini
  Cheesecakes, 135, **135**
Coconut-Cashew Chocolate
  Truffles, 149, **149**
Double-Chocolate Brownies,
  10, 137
Fudge Nut Swirl Pie, 152,
  153
Nutty Chocolate Swirl
  Cheesecake, **11**, 148
Chorizo Cheese Bake, **44**, 45
Christmas menus, 6
Cinnamon and Cumin, Roast
  Carrots with, **8**, 102
Citrus and Basil Marinated
  Goat Cheese, 43, **43**
Classic Brisket, **8**, 67
Cocktail franks
  Short-Cut Pigs in a Blanket,
    59
Coconut and coconut milk
  Chocolate Macaroons, 139
  Coconut Cake with Lemon
    Curd, **156**, 157
  Coconut-Cashew Chocolate
    Truffles, 149, **149**
  Coconut Curried Pumpkin
    Soup, **18**, 20
  Pecan-Orange Macaroons,
    138, **138**
Cod
  Bouillabaisse, 86, **86**
Coffee
  Espresso Panna Cotta, 148
Collard Greens with Ham and
  Onions, 105
Cornbread
  Southwestern Cornbread,
    93, **93**
  Turkey with Spinach
    Cornbread Stuffing, **84**, 85
  Warm Greens with
    Cornbread Croutons, 34, **35**
Cornish Game Hens,
  Spice-Roasted, 83, **83**
Crab
  Crab Cocktail, 51
  Oyster and Crab Bisque, 27,
    27
Cranberry-Ginger Pork, 71
Cream of Cauliflower Soup,
  20
Cream of Celery Soup, 21, **21**
Cream cheese
  Chocolate Mousse Mini
    Cheesecakes, 135, **135**
  Chorizo Cheese Bake, **44**, 45
  Fudge Nut Swirl Pie, 152,
    153
  Jalapeño–Cream Cheese
    Stuffed Celery, **40**, 45
  Nutty Chocolate Swirl
    Cheesecake, 148
  Pumpkin Cheesecake, 144
  Raspberry Cream Cheese
    Bread Pudding, 128
Creamed Spinach, **6**, 96
Crown Roast of Lamb
  Florentine, 76, **77**
Cucumber Cups, Smoked
  Trout Mousse in, **40**, 54

Cumin
  Cumin-Lemon Butternut
    Squash Soup, 23
  Roast Carrots with Cinnamon
    and Cumin, **8**, 102
Curry powder
  Coconut Curried Pumpkin
    Soup, **18**, 20
  Cream of Cauliflower Soup,
    20

Delicata Squash, Roasted
  Spiced, 110, **110**
Desserts, 132–57
Double-Chocolate Brownies,
  10, 137
Double Mushroom Soup, 25
Dubliner Cheese Tart, 124,
  125
Duck Breast, Roast, with Syrah
  Sauce, 81, **81**

Eggs
  Egg, Cheddar, and Chorizo
    Roulade, 130, **130**
  Eggs Benedict with
    Béarnaise Sauce, 122, **122**
  Frisée with Lardons and
    Poached Eggs, 123
  Smoked Salmon and Chive
    Omelet, 123
  Tomato-Basil Frittata, 131
Endive, Arugula, and Radish
  Salad, 33, **33**
Entrées, 62–89
Escarole
  Escarole with Pancetta, 97,
    97
  Roasted Pepper and Escarole
    Salad, 34
Espresso Panna Cotta, 148

Fennel (bulb)
  Pork Loin with Fennel and
    Sage, 69, **69**
  Roasted Fennel with Red
    Peppers, 115, **115**
  Roast Salmon with Fennel
    and Herbs, **62**, 87
Fennel seeds
  Lemon-Fennel Biscotti, 57
Field greens. **See also** Greens
  Field Greens, Pears, Pecans,
    and Gouda, 32
Fish and shellfish. **See** specific
  kinds
Fontina cheese. **See also**
  Cheeses
  Shiitake and Fontina–Stuffed
    Veal Breast, **78**, 79
Fried Okra, 101, **101**
Frisée. **See also** Chicory
  Bacon and Goat Cheese
    Salad, **36**, 37
  Frisée with Lardons and
    Poached Eggs, 123
Fudge Nut Swirl Pie, 152,
  153

Garlic
  Broccoli Rabe, Garlic, and
    Hot Red Pepper, 108
  Kale with Bacon and Garlic,
    116
  Roasted Garlic Soup, 25
  Roast Shallot, Garlic, and
    Zucchini Salad, 37

Ginger
  Candied Ginger Sweet
    Potatoes, **4**, 111
  Cranberry-Ginger Pork, 71
  Green Beans with Ginger-
    Pecan Butter, 114
  Holiday Gingerbread, 145,
    145
Glazed Carrots, **6**, 102
Goat cheese
  Bacon and Goat Cheese
    Salad, **36**, 37
  Citrus and Basil Marinated
    Goat Cheese, 43, **43**
  Stuffed Prosciutto Pillows, 58
  Veal with Goat Cheese and
    Roast Peppers, 78
Goose, Tricolor Peppercorn-
  Roasted, **6**, 84
Gouda, Field Greens, Pears,
  Pecans, and, 32
Greek-Style Boneless Leg of
  Lamb, 76
Green beans
  Green Bean, Pepper, and
    Onion Sauté, 113, **113**
  Green Bean Succotash with
    Kielbasa, 114
  Green Beans Amandine, **4**,
    112
  Green Beans with Ginger-
    Pecan Butter, 114
Green Roasted Shrimp, 87
Greens. **See also** Asian
  greens; Field greens;
    Mesclun greens; Spring
    greens; specific kinds
  Warm Greens with
    Cornbread Croutons 34, **35**
Gruyère, and Onion
  Spoonbread, Turkey, 126

Ham
  Collard Greens with Ham
    and Onions, 105
  Maple-Mustard Glazed Baked
    Ham, 70, **70**
  Hanukkah Jelly Doughnuts,
    157
  Hanukkah menus, 9
  Holiday Gingerbread, 145,
    145
Hors d'oeuvres, 40–61
Horseradish Cream, Roast
  Beef with, 60, **61**

Italian Sausage Patties, 120

Jalapeño–Cream Cheese
  Stuffed Celery, **40**, 45

Kale
  Kale with Bacon and Garlic,
    116
  Kale Gratin with Creamy
    Muenster Sauce, 116
  Kale with Pears and Onions,
    117, **117**

Lamb
  Crown Roast of Lamb
    Florentine, 76, **77**
  Greek-Style Boneless Leg of
    Lamb, 76
  Middle Eastern Spice-Crusted
    Lamb, 75, **75**
  Roast Rack of Lamb, 74

Spicy Lamb and Mushroom
  Brochettes, 52
Wine-Braised Lamb Shanks
  with Tomatoes, 74
Latkes, **8**, 112
Lechon Asado (Cuban-Style
  Roast Pork), 71
Leeks
  Braised Celery and Leeks, 96
  Leeks in Vinaigrette, 109,
    109
  Standing Rib Roast with
    Onions and Leeks, 64
Lemons
  Broccoli Florets with Lemon
    Butter Sauce, 106
  Broccolini with Shallot-Lemon
    Butter, **81**, 106, **107**
  Brussels Sprouts with Lemon,
    102
  Coconut Cake with Lemon
    Curd, **156**, 157
  Cumin-Lemon Butternut
    Squash Soup, 23
  Lemon-Berry Trifle, **132**, 134
  Lemon-Fennel Biscotti, 57
  Lemon Meringue Squares,
    154, **154**
  Lemon-Sage Pork Stew, 72
Lettuce. **See also** Greens
  Asparagus and Romaine
    Salad, 32
  Bacon and Goat Cheese
    Salad, 36, **37**
Lobster
  Lobster Bisque, 26
  Lobster Medallions with
    Vanilla Cream, 88
  Warm Lobster and Avocado
    Salad, 39, **39**

Maple-Mustard Glazed Baked
  Ham, 70, **70**
Maple Pecan Pie, 146
Maple Walnut Bread Pudding,
  147, **147**
Marinated Shrimp Salad, 38
Mascarpone cheese
  Mascarpone Parfait, 136,
    136
  Pumpkin-Nut Bake, 92
Menus, 5–10
Mesclun greens. **See also**
  Greens
  Seared Scallops with Celery
    and Onion, 38
  Spring Greens with Basic
    Vinaigrette, 30
Middle Eastern Spice-Crusted
  Lamb, 75, **75**
Mixed Berry and Ricotta–
  Stuffed Crêpes, **118**, 121
Muenster Sauce, Creamy, Kale
  Gratin with, 116
Mushrooms
  Baked Stuffed Mushrooms, 42
  Double Mushroom Soup, 25
  Dubliner Cheese Tart, 124,
    125
  Mushroom Scones, 131
  Roast Chicken with Wild
    Mushroom Jus, 80
  Shiitake and Fontina–Stuffed
    Veal Breast, **78**, 79
  Spicy Lamb and Mushroom
    Brochettes, 52
  Wild Mushroom Stuffing, 100

Mussels
  Bouillabaisse, 86, **86**
Mustard
  Beef Tenderloin with Dijon
    Herb Crust, 67
  Maple-Mustard Glazed Baked
    Ham, 70, **70**

New Year's menus, 10
Nuts. **See also** specific kinds
  Fudge Nut Swirl Pie, 152,
    153
  Nutty Chocolate Swirl
    Cheesecake, **11**, 148
  Pumpkin-Nut Bake, 92
  Sweet and Spicy Nuts, 57

Okra, Fried, 101, **101**
Old-Fashioned Spice
  Doughnuts, 128
Olives
  Roast Snapper Provençal,
    88, **89**
Onions
  Ale-Infused Onion Soup, 22
  Collard Greens with Ham
    and Onions, 105
  Green Bean, Pepper, and
    Onion Sauté, 113, **113**
  Kale with Pears and Onions,
    117, **117**
  Seared Scallops with Celery
    and Onion, 38
  Standing Rib Roast with
    Onions and Leeks, 64
  Turkey, Gruyère, and Onion
    Spoonbread, 126
Oranges and orange extract
  Orange-Herb Pork Roast, 72,
    73
  Pecan-Orange Macaroons,
    138, **138**
Oyster and Crab Bisque, 27,
  27

Pancetta
  Beef Filet with Pancetta and
    Spinach, 68
  Escarole with Pancetta, 97,
    97
Party menus, 10
Peanut butter
  Fudge Nut Swirl Pie, 152,
    153
Pea Pancakes, Cauliflower-,
  104, **104**
Pears
  Field Greens, Pears, Pecans,
    and Gouda, 32
  Kale with Pears and Onions,
    117, **117**
Pecans. **See also** Nuts
  Blueberry-Pecan Pancakes,
    127, **127**
  Field Greens, Pears, Pecans,
    and Gouda, 32
  Green Beans with Ginger-
    Pecan Butter, 114
  Maple Pecan Pie, 146
  Pecan-Orange Macaroons,
    138, **138**
  Pecan Thumbprint Cookies,
    139
  Pumpkin-Nut Bake, 92
  Pumpkin Pie with Pecan
    Crust, 144

Peppercorn-Roasted Goose, Tricolor, **6**, 84
Pepper Jack Quesadillas, 47, **47**
Pesto, Roasted Vegetable Soup with, 24, **24**
Pomegranate Salad, Spinach and, **28**, 30
Pork. **See also** Bacon; Ham; Pancetta; Sausage
Cranberry-Ginger Pork, 71
Italian Sausage Patties, 120
Lechon Asado (Cuban-Style Roast Pork), 71
Lemon-Sage Pork Stew, 72
Orange-Herb Pork Roast, 72, **73**
Pork Loin with Fennel and Sage, 69, **69**
Pork Loin with Green Herb Crust, 70
Sausage-Sage Stuffing, 100
Potatoes (Instant Mashers) Latkes, **8**, 112
Prime Rib Roast Beef with Red Wine Sauce, 64
Prosciutto
Prosciutto-Wrapped Asparagus, 55, **55**
Stuffed Prosciutto Pillows, 58
Pumpkin
Coconut Curried Pumpkin Soup, **18**, 20
Pumpkin Cheesecake, 144
Pumpkin Flan, 143
Pumpkin Mousse, 137
Pumpkin-Nut Bake, 92
Pumpkin Pie with Pecan Crust, 144
Sweet Potato–Pumpkin Purée, 111

Radicchio
Red and Green Holiday Salad, 31, **31**
Radish Salad, Endive, Arugula, and, 33, **33**
Raspberries. **See also** Berries
Simple Raspberry Sauce, 151
Raspberry jams and preserves
Hanukkah Jelly Doughnuts, 157
Raspberry Cream Cheese Bread Pudding, 128
Red and Green Holiday Salad, 31, **31**
Red Pepper Pancakes with Smoked Salmon, 53, **53**
Red snapper. **See** Snapper
Ricotta–Stuffed Crêpes, Mixed Berry and, **118**, 121
Roast Beef with Horseradish Cream, 60, **61**
Roast Carrots with Cinnamon and Cumin, 102
Roast Chicken with Wild Mushroom Jus, 80
Roast Duck Breast with Syrah Sauce, 81, **81**
Roasted Artichoke Gratin, 94, **95**
Roasted Asparagus, 95
Roasted Fennel with Red Peppers, 115, **115**
Roasted Garlic Soup, 25
Roasted Pepper and Escarole Salad, 34

Roasted Spiced Delicata Squash, 110, **110**
Roasted Vegetable Ratatouille, 108
Roasted Vegetable Soup with Pesto, 24, **24**
Roast Rack of Lamb, 74
Roast Salmon with Fennel and Herbs, **62**, 87
Roast Shallot, Garlic, and Zucchini Salad, 37
Roast Snapper Provençal, 88, **89**
Rosemary-Roasted Sweet Potatoes, **90**, 92

Sabayon with Berries, 155
Sage
Lemon-Sage Pork Stew, 72
Pork Loin with Fennel and Sage, 69, **69**
Sausage-Sage Stuffing, 100
Salmon
Roast Salmon with Fennel and Herbs, **62**, 87
smoked salmon
Red Pepper Pancakes with Smoked Salmon, 53, **53**
Smoked Salmon and Chive Omelet, 123
Sausage
Baked Stuffed Mushrooms, 42
Chorizo Cheese Bake, **44**, 45
Egg, Cheddar, and Chorizo Roulade, 130, **130**
Green Bean Succotash with Kielbasa, 54
Italian Sausage Patties, 120
Sausage Dressing, 99
Sausage-Sage Stuffing, 100
Savory Italian Tart, 120, **121**
Sautéed Brussels Sprouts, 103, **103**
Savory Italian Tart, 120, **121**
Scallion Pie Squares, Cheddar and, 46
Scallops
Bouillabaisse, 86, **86**
Scallops Wrapped in Bacon, 49
Seared Scallops with Celery and Onion, 38
Shrimp and Scallop Ceviche, **50**, 51
Seafood. **See** specific kinds
Seared Scallops with Celery and Onion, 38
Sesame seeds and oil
Sesame-Crusted Tuna over Asian Greens, 58, **59**
Sesame-Tofu Dip, 60
Shallots
Broccolini with Shallot-Lemon Butter, **81**, 106, **107**
Roast Shallot, Garlic, and Zucchini Salad, 37
Shiitake and Fontina–Stuffed Veal Breast, **78**, 79
Short-Cut Pigs in a Blanket, 59
Shrimp
Bouillabaisse, 86, **86**
Green Roasted Shrimp, 87
Marinated Shrimp Salad, 38
Shrimp and Scallop Ceviche, **50**, 51
Vietnamese Stir-Fried Shrimp, 48, **49**

Side dishes, 90–117
Simple Raspberry Sauce, 151
Slavic-Style Hot Borscht, 22, **23**
Smoked Salmon and Chive Omelet, 123
Smoked Trout Mousse in Cucumber Cups, **40**, 54
Smoked Turkey and Cheddar Spread, 44
Snapper Provençal, Roast, 88, **89**
Sour Cream Purée, Cauliflower–, **4**, 105
Southwestern Cornbread, 93, **93**
Southwestern Turkey, 82
Spiced Bundt Cake, 129, **129**
Spice-Roasted Cornish Game Hens, 83, **83**
Spicy Lamb and Mushroom Brochettes, 52
Spinach
Beef Filet with Pancetta and Spinach, 68
Creamed Spinach, **6**, 96
Crown Roast of Lamb Florentine, 76, **77**
Spinach and Pomegranate Salad, **28**, 30
Turkey with Spinach Cornbread Stuffing, 84, **85**
Spring greens. **See also** Greens
Spring Greens with Basic Vinaigrette, 30
Squash. **See** specific kinds
Standing Rib Roast with Onions and Leeks, 64
Strawberries. **See** Berries
Stuffed Prosciutto Pillows, 58
Sweet potatoes
Candied Ginger Sweet Potatoes, **4**, 111
Rosemary-Roasted Sweet Potatoes, **90**, 92
Sweet Potato–Pumpkin Purée, 111
Sweet and Spicy Nuts, 57

Tandoori Chicken Wings, **40**, 52
Thanksgiving menus, 5
Tofu Dip, Sesame-, 60
Tomatoes. **See also** Vegetables
Roast Snapper Provençal, 88, **89**
Savory Italian Tart, 120, **121**
Tomato-Basil Frittata, 131
Wine-Braised Lamb Shanks with Tomatoes, 74
Tricolor Peppercorn-Roasted Goose, **6**, 84
Trout Mousse, Smoked, in Cucumber Cups, **40,** 54
Tuna
Sesame-Crusted Tuna over Asian Greens, 58, **59**
Tuna Tartare, 48
Turkey
Smoked Turkey and Cheddar Spread, 44
Southwestern Turkey, 82

Turkey, Gruyère, and Onion Spoonbread, 126
Turkey with Spinach Cornbread Stuffing, 84, 85
Turnips, Butter-Braised, **7**, 99

Vanilla
Chocolate Drizzled Vanilla Biscotti, 150, **150**
Lobster Medallions with Vanilla Cream, 88
Veal
Shiitake and Fontina–Stuffed Veal Breast, **78**, 79
Veal with Goat Cheese and Roast Peppers, 78
Vegetables. **See also** specific kinds
Lemon-Sage Pork Stew, 72
Roasted Vegetable Ratatouille, 108
Roasted Vegetable Soup with Pesto, 24, **24**
Zinfandel Pot au Feu, 65, **65**
Verdemole, 56, **56**
Vietnamese Stir-Fried Shrimp, 48, **49**

Walnuts. **See also** Nuts
Maple Walnut Bread Pudding, 147, **147**
Spiced Bundt Cake, 129, **129**
Walnut Blondies, 146
Walnut Meatballs, 54
Warm Cauliflower and Broccoli Salad, 36
Warm Greens with Cornbread Croutons, 34, **35**
Warm Lobster and Avocado Salad, 39, **39**
Watercress
Red and Green Holiday Salad, 31, **31**
Wild Mushroom Stuffing, 100
Wine
Prime Rib Roast Beef with Red Wine Sauce, 64
Roast Duck Breast with Syrah Sauce, 81, **81**
Sabayon with Berries, 155
Wine-Braised Lamb Shanks with Tomatoes, 74
Zinfandel Pot au Feu, 65, **65**

Zinfandel Pot au Feu, 65, **65**
Zucchini
Roast Shallot, Garlic, and Zucchini Salad, 37
Zucchini Bread, 124

HOLIDAY RECIPE CARB GRAM COUNTER

RECIPE	NET CARBS	PHASES
SOUPS		
Coconut Curried Pumpkin Soup	7 grams	2 to 4
Cream of Cauliflower Soup	4.5 grams	1 to 4
Cream of Celery Soup	8 grams	3 to 4
Ale-Infused Onion Soup	8 grams	2 to 4
Slavic-Style Hot Borscht	8 grams	3 to 4
Cumin-Lemon Butternut Squash Soup	22 grams	3 to 4
Roasted Vegetable Soup with Pesto	8 grams	3 to 4
Roasted Garlic Soup	11 grams	3 to 4
Double Mushroom Soup	6 grams	2 to 4
Lobster Bisque	9 grams	2 to 4
Oyster and Crab Bisque	2 grams	1 to 4
SALADS		
Spinach and Pomegranate Salad	5.5 grams	3 to 4
Spring Greens with Basic Vinaigrette	1 gram	1 to 4
Red and Green Holiday Salad	2 grams	1 to 4
Field Greens, Pears, Pecans, and Gouda	5 grams	2 to 4
Asparagus and Romaine Salad	4 grams	1 to 4
Endive, Arugula, and Radish Salad	4 grams	2 to 4
Warm Greens with Cornbread Croutons	5 grams	2 to 4
Roasted Pepper and Escarole Salad	4 grams	1 to 4
Warm Cauliflower and Broccoli Salad	3 grams	1 to 4
Bacon and Goat Cheese Salad	2.5 grams	1 to 4
Roast Shallot, Garlic, and Zucchini Salad	8.5 grams	2 to 4
Seared Scallops with Celery and Onion	6 grams	2 to 4
Marinated Shrimp Salad	2.5 grams	1 to 4
Warm Lobster and Avocado Salad	3 grams	1 to 4
APPETIZERS & HORS D'OEUVRES		
Bagna Cauda	1 gram	1 to 4
Baked Stuffed Mushrooms	1 gram	1 to 4
Citrus and Basil Marinated Goat Cheese	1 gram	1 to 4
Smoked Turkey and Cheddar Spread	3 grams	2 to 4
Jalapeño–Cream Cheese Stuffed Celery	2.5 grams	1 to 4
Chorizo Cheese Bake	3 grams	1 to 4
Cheddar and Scallion Pie Squares	4 grams	3 to 4
Pepper Jack Quesadillas	5.5 grams	2 to 4
Vietnamese Stir-Fried Shrimp	4.5 grams	2 to 4
Tuna Tartare	1 gram	1 to 4
Scallops Wrapped in Bacon	3.5 grams	1 to 4
Shrimp and Scallop Ceviche	5.5 grams	2 to 4
Crab Cocktail	3.5 grams	1 to 4
Tandoori Chicken Wings	2.5 grams	1 to 4
Spicy Lamb and Mushroom Brochettes	1.5 gram	1 to 4
Red Pepper Pancakes with Smoked Salmon	3 grams	3 to 4
Smoked Trout Mousse in Cucumber Cups	1.5 grams	1 to 4
Walnut Meatballs	1 gram	2 to 4
Prosciutto-Wrapped Asparagus	1 gram	1 to 4
Verdemole	1 gram	1 to 4
Sweet and Spicy Nuts	2 grams	2 to 4
Lemon-Fennel Biscotti	1 gram	1 to 4
Sesame-Crusted Tuna over Asian Greens	1.5 grams	2 to 4
Stuffed Prosciutto Pillows	2 grams	1 to 4
Short-Cut Pigs in a Blanket	4 grams	1 to 4
Roast Beef with Horseradish Cream	2.5 grams	1 to 4
Sesame-Tofu Dip	1 gram	1 to 4
ENTRÉES		
Standing Rib Roast with Carmelized Onion	6 grams	1 to 4
Prime Rib Roast Beef with Red Wine Sauce	2 grams	1 to 4
Zinfandel Pot au Feu	13 grams	3 to 4
Bacon-Wrapped Filet Mignon	3 grams	1 to 4
Beef Filet with Dijon Herb Crust	2 grams	1 to 4
Classic Brisket	6 grams	1 to 4
Beef Tenderloin with Pancetta and Spinach	1 gram	2 to 4
Chipotle Braised Short Ribs	9 grams	2 to 4
Pork Loin with Fennel and Sage	10 grams	2 to 4
Pork Loin with Green Herb Crust	2 grams	1 to 4
Maple-Mustard Glazed Baked Ham	0.5 gram	1 to 4
Lechon Asado (Cuban-Style Roast Pork)	2 grams	1 to 4
Cranberry-Ginger Pork	1 gram	2 to 4
Orange-Herb Pork Roast	1 gram	2 to 4
Lemon-Sage Pork Stew	6.5 grams	3 to 4
Roast Rack of Lamb	2 grams	1 to 4
Wine-Braised Lamb Shanks with Tomatoes	5 grams	1 to 4
Middle Eastern Spice-Crusted Lamb	0 gram	1 to 4
Crown Roast of Lamb Florentine	4 grams	1 to 4
Greek-Style Boneless Leg of Lamb	1 gram	1 to 4
Veal with Goat Cheese and Roast Peppers	3 grams	1 to 4
Shiitake and Fontina–Stuffed Veal Breast	13 grams	3 to 4
Roast Chicken with Wild Mushroom Jus	4 grams	3 to 4
Roasted Duck Breast with Syrah Sauce	3 grams	2 to 4
Southwestern Turkey	2 grams	1 to 4
Spice-Roasted Cornish Game Hens	1 gram	1 to 4
Tricolor Peppercorn-Roasted Goose	3 grams	3 to 4
Turkey with Spinach Cornbread Stuffing	11 grams	2 to 4
Bouillabaisse	10.5 grams	2 to 4
Green Roasted Shrimp	2.5 grams	1 to 4
Roast Salmon with Fennel and Herbs	2.5 grams	1 to 4
Roast Snapper Provençal	5.5 grams	1 to 4
Lobster Medallions with Vanilla Cream	3 grams	2 to 4

RECIPE	NET CARBS	PHASES
VEGETABLES & SIDE DISHES		
Rosemary-Roasted Sweet Potatoes	13 grams	3 to 4
Pumpkin-Nut Bake	4.5 grams	2 to 4
Southwestern Cornbread	9 grams	2 to 4
Roasted Artichoke Gratin	4 grams	1 to 4
Asparagus with Browned Butter	3 grams	1 to 4
Roasted Asparagus	3 grams	1 to 4
Creamed Spinach	4 grams	1 to 4
Braised Celery and Leeks	10 grams	3 to 4
Escarole with Pancetta	3 grams	1 to 4
Braised Cabbage	7 grams	2 to 4
Butter-Braised Turnips	3 grams	1 to 4
Sausage Dressing	8 grams	2 to 4
Sausage-Sage Stuffing	4.5 grams	2 to 4
Wild Mushroom Stuffing	8.5 grams	2 to 4
Fried Okra	3 grams	1 to 4
Roast Carrots with Cinnamon and Cumin	4 grams	3 to 4
Glazed Carrots	7 grams	3 to 4
Brussels Sprouts with Lemon	3 grams	1 to 4
Sautéed Brussels Sprouts	3 grams	1 to 4
Cauliflower-Pea Pancakes	10 grams	3 to 4
Cauliflower–Sour Cream Purée	4 grams	1 to 4
Collard Greens with Ham and Onions	3 grams	1 to 4
Broccolini with Shallot-Lemon Butter	6 grams	2 to 4
Broccoli Florets with Lemon Butter Sauce	2 grams	2 to 4
Broccoli Rabe, Garlic, and Hot Red Pepper	5.5 grams	2 to 4
Roasted Vegetable Ratatouille	17 grams	3 to 4
Leeks in Vinaigrette	12 grams	3 to 4
Roasted Spiced Delicata Squash	9 grams	2 to 4
Sweet Potato–Pumpkin Purée	17.5 grams	3 to 4
Candied Ginger Sweet Potatoes	18 grams	3 to 4
Latkes	5.5 grams	1 to 4
Green Beans Amandine	6 grams	2 to 4
Green Bean, Pepper, and Onion Sauté	9 grams	2 to 4
Green Beans with Ginger-Pecan Butter	3 grams	2 to 4
Green Bean Succotash with Kielbasa	8 grams	3 to 4
Roasted Fennel with Red Peppers	6.5 grams	2 to 4
Kale with Bacon and Garlic	7 grams	2 to 4
Kale Gratin with Creamy Muenster Sauce	4 grams	1 to 4
Kale with Pears and Onions	14 grams	3 to 4
BRUNCH		
Savory Italian Tart	5 grams	2 to 4
Italian Sausage Patties	0.5 grams	1 to 4
Mixed Berry and Ricotta-Stuffed Crêpes	5 grams	3 to 4
Eggs Benedict with Béarnaise Sauce	5 grams	2 to 4
Smoked Salmon and Chive Omelet	2 grams	1 to 4
Frisée with Lardons and Poached Eggs	3 grams	1 to 4
Dubliner Cheese Tart	2 grams	1 to 4
Zucchini Bread	6.5 gram	3 to 4
Turkey, Gruyére, and Onion Spoonbread	10 grams	2 to 4
Bacon-Cheddar Biscuits	3.5 grams	2 to 4
Blueberry-Pecan Pancakes	5.5 grams	2 to 4
Raspberry Cream Cheese Bread Pudding	9 grams	2 to 4
Old-Fashioned Spice Doughnuts	7.5 grams	3 to 4
Spiced Bundt Cake	6 grams	2 to 4
Egg, Cheddar, and Chorizo Roulade	5.5 grams	1 to 4
Mushroom Scones	2.5 grams	1 to 4
Tomato-Basil Frittata	6 grams	1 to 4
DESSERTS & SWEETS		
Lemon-Berry Trifle	9.5 grams	3 to 4
Chocolate Mousse Mini Cheesecakes	5.5 grams	2 to 4
Mascarpone Parfait	3 grams	2 to 4
Double-Chocolate Brownies	5 grams	3 to 4
Pumpkin Mousse	4.5 grams	2 to 4
Pecan-Orange Macaroons	3 grams	2 to 4
Pecan Thumbprint Cookies	5 grams	3 to 4
Chocolate Macaroons	2 grams	1 to 4
Bûche de Noël	5.5 grams	2 to 4
Apple Crisp	16.5 grams	3 to 4
Apple Fritters	6 grams	2 to 4
Pumpkin Flan	6.5 grams	2 to 4
Pumpkin Pie with Pecan Crust	8 grams	2 to 4
Pumpkin Cheesecake	6 grams	2 to 4
Holiday Gingerbread	7 grams	3 to 4
Walnut Blondies	7.5 grams	2 to 4
Maple Pecan Pie	3.5 grams	2 to 4
Maple Walnut Bread Pudding	9 grams	2 to 4
Nutty Chocolate Swirl Cheesecake	7 grams	2 to 4
Espresso Panna Cotta	5 grams	2 to 4
Coconut-Cashew Chocolate Truffles	1.5 grams	2 to 4
Chocolate-Drizzled Vanilla Biscotti	1 gram	1 to 4
Chocolate-Dipped Almond Cookies	4 grams	3 to 4
Simple Raspberry Sauce	4 grams	2 to 4
Fudge Nut Swirl Pie	5.5 grams	2 to 4
Lemon Meringue Tart	3.5 grams	2 to 4
Almond Mousse Soufflé	6.5 grams	2 to 4
Sabayon with Berries	7.5 grams	2 to 4
Coconut Cake with Lemon Curd	7.5 grams	2 to 4
Hanukkah Jelly Doughnuts	3 grams	2 to 4